Strategic Hospitality Human Resources Management

Strategic Hospitality Human Resources Management

Dori Finley Dennison
Melvin R. Weber
School of Hospitality Leadership at East Carolina University

Boston Columbus Indianapolis New York San Francisco Upper Saddle River
Amsterdam Cape Town Dubai London Madrid Milan Munich Paris Montréal Toronto
Delhi Mexico City São Paulo Sydney Hong Kong Seoul Singapore Taipei Tokyo

Acquiring Editor: Vernon Anthony
Program Manager: Alexis Duffy
Editorial Assistant: Lara Dimmick
Director of Marketing: David Gesell
Marketing Manager: Stacey Martinez
Assistant Marketing Manager: Alicia Wozniak
Senior Marketing Assistant: Les Roberts
Team Lead: JoEllen Gohr
Project Manager: Kris Roach
Operations Specialist: Deidra Skahill
Procurement Specialist: Deidra M. Skahill
Senior Art Director: Jayne Conte
Cover Art: Jetta Productions/Blend Images/Getty Images
Cover Designer: Bruce Kenselaar
Media Project Manager: April Cleland
Full-Service Project Management: Saraswathi Muralidhar, PreMediaGlobal
Composition: PreMediaGlobal
Printer/Binder: LSC Communications
Cover Printer: LSC Communications
Text Font: Minion Pro

Microsoft® and Windows® are registered trademarks of the Microsoft Corporation in the U.S.A. and other countries. Screen shots and icons reprinted with permission from the Microsoft Corporation. This book is not sponsored or endorsed by or affiliated with the Microsoft Corporation.

Library of Congress Cataloging-in-Publication Data

Dennison, Doriann Hilton.
 Strategic hospitality human resources management/Doriann Hilton Dennison, Melvin R. Weber.—First edition.
  pages cm
 Includes bibliographical references and index.
 ISBN-13: 978-0-13-508705-3
 ISBN-10: 0-13-508705-8
 1. Hospitality industry—Personnel management. I. Weber, Melvin. II. Title.
 TX911.3.P4D46 2015
 647.94068—dc23

                                                      2013045737

ISBN-10:   0-13-508705-8
ISBN-13: 978-0-13-508705-3

CONTENTS

PREFACE

When we started on the project, we felt that there were no adequate textbooks for our human resource management course. We needed a textbook that covers human resources for the hospitality industry at a level between setting up a human resource department and the opposite of simply supervising employees in an effective manner. The approach for this book is to set the climate for strategic human resources in the hospitality industry, cover the traditional human resource functions from the perspective of this climate, and present the skills needed by hospitality managers to implement an effective human resource program. Each chapter presents the required knowledge applied to hospitality management for the topics followed by exercises to develop the skills and abilities needed to use the knowledge.

The text is divided into three parts: (a) the need for strategic human resource management, (b) traditional human resource management, and (c) skills needed to become a strategic partner. The introductory chapter covers strategic human resource management applied to the hospitality field. This chapter sets the environment for human resource management in our industry. The second section of the text covers the traditional functions of human resource management. Chapters 2 through 8 cover the typical topics in hospitality human resource management courses. The addition of case studies, in-class exercises, and discussion questions makes this section come alive for students. The final section of the text covers the skills needed to be successful in human resource management. There are currently no other hospitality management texts that cover these topics with hospitality applications and exercises that help students develop these skills.

We have enjoyed writing this text and can't wait to use it in our courses. We also hope you and your students will enjoy using the book in your classes.

ONLINE SUPPLEMENTS ACCOMPANYING THE TEXT

An online Instructor's Manual, PowerPoint slides, and MyTest are available to instructors at www.pearsonhighered.com. Instructors can search for a test by author, title, ISBN, or by selecting the appropriate discipline from the pull-down menu at the top of catalog home page. To access supplementary materials online, instructors need to request an instructor access code. Go to www.pearsonhighered.com, click the Instructor Resource Center link, and then click Register Today for an instructor access code. Within 48 hours after registering, you will receive a confirming e-mail including an instructor access code. Once you have received your code, go to the site and log on for full instruction on downloading the materials you wish to use.

ACKNOWLEDGMENTS

We would like to thank the reviewers for their insightful comments and suggestions. They are Bonnie Canziani, University of North Carolina; Catherine Curtis, Oklahoma State University; Ron Evans, Northern Arizona University; Camile Kapoor, University of Houston; Doug Kennedy, University of Wisconsin; Young Hoon Kim, University of North Texas; Marie Kumabe, University of Hawaii; Myron Levy, Roosevelt University; Byron Marlowe, Southern Oregon University; Dennis Reynolds, Washington State University; Rommel Salvador, University of Massachusetts; and LaChelle Wilborn, North Carolina Central University.

The Need for Strategic Human Resource Management

Introduction to Strategic Human Resources in the Hospitality Industry

KEY TERMS

Economy hotels
Full service hotels
Full service restaurants
Hospitality industry
Human capital
Limited service hotels
Limited service restaurants
Lodging industry
Luxury hotels
Outsourcing
Quick service restaurants
Service–profit relationship
Strategic human resource management

OBJECTIVES

- Describe the components of the hospitality industry using the U.S. government and other definitions
- Classify hospitality operations on a service and product continuum
- Identify the components of the service–profit relationship
- Describe the movement from a human capital model to strategic human resource management
- Identify some of the trends and their impacts on human resource management

Consider This

"There's been a change in the way we do business here. If you want to keep things the way they were, you will need to share your expertise elsewhere. If you want to be part of a new and different organization, you are welcome to stay and develop into a strategic partner." Cheryl wasn't sure she understood what the general manager was saying, but it was clear that unless she figured it out, she would quickly lose her assistant manager position in the restaurant. She volunteered to be a part of the first group of management trainees to be trained as strategic partners and the following pages are her notes from each of the training sessions she attended. The trainers began with a new way of looking at the hospitality industry and continued to a discussion of the changes in business models to becoming a strategic thinker.

DESCRIPTION OF THE INDUSTRY

The **hospitality industry** has been defined as including a variety of business categories by a variety of authors. According to the U.S. government, the hospitality industry includes lodging, foodservice, and recreation businesses that serve individuals and groups away from home.[1] A more complex definition includes lodging, foodservice, conventions, leisure, attractions, and travel businesses. Others may include tourism as an umbrella organization covering these industries or may indicate that tourism is a force that impacts hospitality businesses.

There are many types of hospitality operations within any of the major categories and many operations consist of a combination of lodging, food, and recreation components. For example, resorts typically include lodging, foodservice, and a variety of recreation activities, all a part of the same operation. Convention hotels may offer lodging, foodservice, convention and meeting space, and recreation activities. There are many restaurants such as Chuck E. Cheese's and Dave & Buster's that include recreation activities.

A bird's eye view of the hospitality industry shows that the largest numbers of units are small and independently owned—small hotels, restaurants, and other facilities. But the industry is becoming more profitable for large corporations that operate many facilities and many types of facilities within the industry. In addition, every facet of the hospitality industry is labor intensive. Delivering quality products and services requires more labor hours per unit than in any manufacturing operation. While in quick serve restaurants the principles of streamlined production have been implemented and some hotels have quick check-in kiosks, a majority of the products and services that are provided to customers are prepared by and personally delivered by employees to customers. This makes human resources an extremely important component of every manager's job.

TYPES OF HOSPITALITY BUSINESSES

One way of looking at the human resources needed in the hospitality industry is to classify operations based on (a) the complexity of the product and (b) the amount of service that is provided to customers. The product continuum ranges from pre-prepared with minimal preparation for food and beverage operations and basic or limited facilities for lodging operations at one end to extensive preparation of individual items for food and beverage operations and luxury lodging facilities at the other end.

As you can see in Figure 1.1, products in the **lodging industry** range from basic room and bath to complex and upscale facilities with many amenities. In the lodging industry, the initial investment in facilities increases with movement from basic to luxury. The maintenance and upkeep of the facilities is generally highest at the luxury end of the continuum. As demand for

Example of a restaurant combined with recreation.
Credit: Helen Sessions / Alamy.

Restaurant industry

| Reheat menu items | Limited preparation | Complicated preparation |

Lodging industry

| Basic room and bath | Limited amenities | Luxury facilities |

FIGURE 1.1   Hospitality Product Continuum.

luxury increases, the number of employees will increase. In the restaurant industry, food and beverages increase in complexity along the product continuum. At the low end, menu items are purchased in a prepared state, reheated, and served to customers. At the high end, gourmet items requiring complicated preparation are served. Entry-level employees can be trained to reheat items while skilled chefs are required to prepare more complicated gourmet menu items.

The continuum for classifying hotels based on the amount of service provided ranges from economy, to limited service, to full service, and to luxury.[2] At the luxury end of the continuum, everything is upscale. At a minimum, **luxury hotels** have food and beverage outlets, room service, stores or concessions, concierge services, bell staff, and parking services. Many luxury hotels have spas, beauty shops, and exercise facilities. Restaurants at the luxury end of the continuum require an extensive team of wait staff that may include sommeliers and table-side chefs to provide upscale service. Customers expect extensive service and interaction with employees at the luxury end of the continuum. This means that the importance of human resources in luxury properties is increased due to the large numbers and varieties of skills needed to meet customer expectations.

As you move from the luxury end of the service continuum toward the lowest end, **full service hotels** provide many of the same services at a lower level of quality and may involve less guest–employee interaction. At a minimum, full service hotels will have food and beverage outlets, room service, and bell staff. In a **full service restaurant**, an employee will take a customer's order, serve the food to the customer at a table, and handle the check at the end of the meal.[3] Menu items in full service restaurants range from gourmet and complicated to frozen-prepared, which are less complicated.

Example of a luxury restaurant.
Credit: Ollyy / Shutterstock.

Restaurant industry

| Vending | Quick service | Limited service | Full service | Extensive service |

Lodging industry

| Kiosk | Economy | Limited service | Full service | Luxury |

FIGURE 1.2   **Hospitality Service Continuum.**

Limited service hotels cater to the traveler who wants a quality room with few amenities. These hotels have amenities in the rooms and small meeting rooms, and may have business and exercise facilities. Food and beverage operations may be located close by but are typically not a part of the limited service hotel. **Limited service restaurants**, such as cafeterias, involve the customer in the service of the meal. Employees in limited service restaurants may require fewer service skills than in full service restaurants. Cafeteria customers typically select food from a cafeteria line and carry the selected items on a tray to the table. Menu items are prepared in advance and may require less skill in preparation. Figure 1.2 shows the range of service that is found in the hospitality industry.

At the lower end of the service continuum, **economy hotels** provide a quality hotel room with few additional facilities. The types of services provided are basic and include front desk, housekeeping, and security. In economy hotels, there may be little employee–guest interaction outside of the check-in and check-out process.

In **quick service restaurants**, customers place their orders with an employee at a cash register, pay at the cash register, and carry their selected items to a table or take them out to eat. Menu items and preparation techniques are standardized, requiring little skill. The amount of service provided to customers is limited to taking orders and handling transactions.

Hotel check-in kiosks and food-vending operations anchor the lowest end of the service continuum. In these operations, minimal service is provided by a limited number of employees.

Example of an economy hotel.
Credit: Ryan DeBerardinis / Shutterstock.

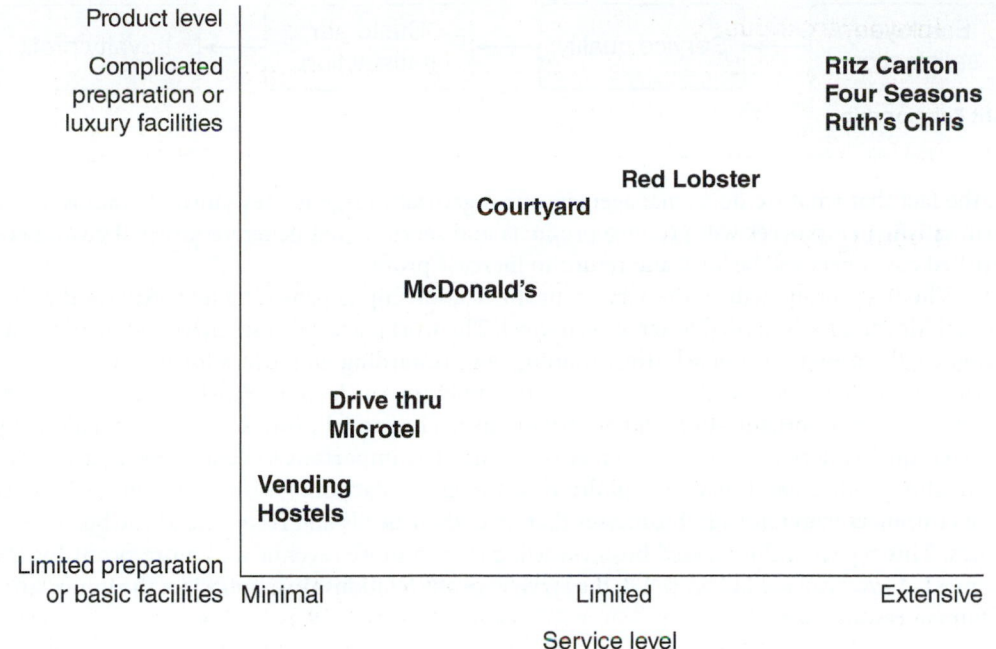

FIGURE 1.3 Hospitality Classifications along a Product and Service Continuum.

There is little to no interaction between the customer and employees, with technology replacing the employee required to provide the service.

The combination of the product continuum and service continuum ranges is presented in Figure 1.3. As you can see, there is a direct relationship between the product and service continuums. As the product increases from limited to complicated, service also increases from minimal to extensive. Most customers expect an increase in service with an increase in product quality.

This classification impacts the number and qualifications of employees required to provide products and services. When the amount of service provided to customers is minimal, the requirement for numbers of employees and their customer service skills are both minimal. When the amount of service provided to customers is extensive, more employees with improved customer service skills will be needed. When the complexity of the product is extensive in food and beverage operations, employees with creativity and sophisticated preparation skills will be needed. In lodging operations that provide luxury amenities to customers, the number of employees and the skills they need will be greater. The type and amount of human resources are directly dependent on the classification of the hospitality operation.

MOVEMENT FROM HUMAN CAPITAL TO STRATEGIC HUMAN RESOURCE MANAGEMENT

Understanding the role of human resources in the hospitality industry has also been affected by changes in the field of human resource management. The importance of employees in the industry has increased with the development of the service–profit relationship, the identification of human capital, and the application of strategic planning to human resources. These changes have impacted the day-to-day operations in the hospitality industry where managers of all levels practice human resource management. In the past, managers focused on producing products and services. The manager of the future will need to develop a different perspective to develop and retain human resources.

Service–Profit Relationship

The basis for all of the changes in human resource management is a concept called the service–profit relationship. Figure 1.4 shows the relationships between organizational effectiveness, employee satisfaction, quality service, customer satisfaction and profitability, which are based on the concept developed by Heskett and colleagues.[4] The service–profit relationship is based

| Organizational effectiveness | → | Employee satisfaction | → | Service quality | → | Customer satisfaction | → | Loyalty profit |

FIGURE 1.4   The Service–Profit Relationship.

on the fact that what we do as managers in our organizations generates satisfied employees. In turn, satisfied employees will produce products and services that generate satisfied customers. Satisfied customers will be loyal and return to increase profit.

The first component of the service–profit relationship is providing a workplace that has the facilities and tools needed to serve customers. The workplace will also include managers who recognize the importance of selecting, training, and rewarding employees for quality customer service. A well-designed workplace will lead to employee satisfaction. Satisfied employees generally stay with an organization and are productive. The model proposes a direct relationship between quality service and customer satisfaction. It is important to remember that providing quality products and services will drive customer satisfaction. Satisfied customers become loyal customers who return to businesses that meet their needs and recommend the business to others. This repeat and increased business will generate more revenue and more profit for the business. As you can see in Figure 1.4, the service–profit relationship emphasizes the importance of human resources.

Human Capital

Historically, the role of human resources in a hospitality management company has been administrative in nature. A national trend in human resources is to move from the administrative role to the incorporation of human resources in strategic planning. This movement was aided by the development of the concept of **human capital** or human assets in an organization. Human capital is defined as the total skills, knowledge, and attributes of people in organizations. Human capital can be measured by identifying the competence of employees, the existence of performance improvement systems, and positive attitudes of employees.

Human capital.   *Credit*: Andresr / Shutterstock.

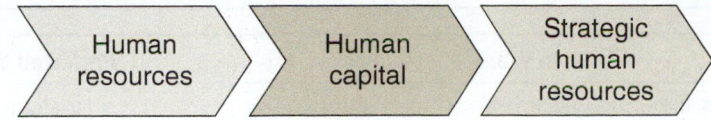

FIGURE 1.5   **Movement of Human Resources to Strategic Human Resources.**

In the hospitality industry, human capital is increased by hiring and developing employees who are service-oriented, empowered, and committed to the goals of the organization. To increase human capital in their organizations, hospitality managers can:

1. hire employees for their customer service orientation and skills,
2. provide training in problem solving and identifying customer needs,
3. practice management by example and develop a service climate, and
4. provide competitive wages and fair work policies.

Strategic Human Resource Management

The movement of human capital into strategic human resource management continued when high-performing employees were viewed as a competitive advantage. Strategic planning requires managers to identify forces driving change in the operation, look at the workforce in terms of needs, and develop employees to serve as a competitive advantage.

The environment outside our organizations is impacted by changes in society, the economy, technological advances, and the political/legal arena. Monitoring demographic shifts, such as the large number of retirement-age employees still in the workforce, is important to the hospitality manager. In the past, when employees reached the age required to receive Social Security, they retired. Now, due to improved health in older age employees and the economic need to work, many traditionalists and Baby Boomers are staying in the workforce. This gives the hospitality manager a source of employees with a strong work ethic and the need for employment income without the benefits that younger employees need.

One challenge that is inherent is that hospitality managers are now working with at least four generations in the workplace. Each of these generations has characteristics that require hospitality managers to acquire or practice different human resource skills (see Figure 1.6). Other changes in society that the hospitality manager will need to monitor include changes in public opinion such as nonsmoking facilities and other health-related concerns, the importance of ecological trends (e.g., green washing), and other fads.

Changes in the economy have a major impact on the hospitality industry. Individual and group spending on travel, leisure activities, and food away from home drive demand for

Different generations in the workplace.   *Credit*: Monkey Business Images / Shutterstock.

Generation	Birth Years	Values	Preferred Workplace
Traditionalists, the Silent Generation	Before 1945	• Privacy • Hard work • Trust • Formality • Authority • Social order • Things	• Loyalty is rewarded • Top-down approach to management • Information on a need-to-know basis
Baby Boomers	1946–1964	• Competition • Change • Workaholics • Success • Teamwork • Antirules and regulations • Inclusion based on performance • Fight for a cause	• Valued for careers, their body of knowledge, and the impact of their contributions
Generation X	1965–1980	• Entrepreneurship • Loyalty to self • Independence • Information access • Feedback • Quality of work–life balance • Communication in the form of sound bites	• Allow flexibility to define work arrangements (such as telecommuting) • Offer child care and elder care benefits • Promote work–life balance • Send e-mail messages
Generation Y, Millennial	1980–1994	• Lots of positive reinforcement • Autonomy • Positive attitudes • Diversity • Spending money • Technology and multitasking • Action and opportunity	• Recognized for their individual contributions within a team • Provide work that is productive and meaningful • Encourage innovation • Provide current technology • Allow flexibility in scheduling, dress/attire, and work arrangements

FIGURE 1.6   **Characteristics of Four Generations in the Workplace.**[5]

the services provided by hospitality businesses. Business and government travel, meetings, and special events also impact the need for hospitality services. The nature of the industry makes it directly dependent on the discretionary money available in the economy. So long as businesses and individuals have money available for entertainment and recreation, the industry will remain in a growing and prosperous mode. When more dollars are required to cover living expenses or income is decreased, discretionary income becomes less, which means there may be less demand for the services provided by the industry. In addition to a change in demand for services, the economy will impact the availability and cost of labor. During economic downturns, the number of unemployed workers increases, which leads to many applicants for job openings. This increase in the number of applicants for hospitality jobs means qualified people can be hired for less money. This means that the competitiveness of salaries and wages will decrease.

Monitor changes in politics and law.   *Credit*: Africa Studio / Shutterstock.

Technology is becoming faster, smaller, and easier to use. Applications for hospitality managers and customers are also increasing. These changes will make hospitality services readily available to customers and streamline the routine functions for managers. Although initially technology is not cost effective, as it becomes developed and accepted in the industry, the impact of technology on the workforce will be increased. Generally, when technology is added to a hospitality organization, the number of employees will be decreased and the role of the manager will change. For example, applications allowing customers to place orders online or through automated ordering systems decrease the number of employees required to take orders. Automated inventory and payroll systems will free up a manager's time from office-oriented work and allow that manager more time to interact with employees and customers.

Hospitality managers must monitor political and legal trends for their impact on the operation. These changes occur at the international, national, state, and local levels. Some examples of these trends at the international level are immigration policies and international conflicts that may have an impact on the hospitality workforce. National-level changes in minimum wage, health care requirements, and other regulations will impact employee expectations for fair wages and competitive benefits. State and local regulations covering unemployment compensation will serve as a basis for policies and procedures relating to terminating employees.

A summary of the trends a manager must monitor is presented in Figure 1.7. In addition to the impact of these trends on the organization and workforce, the manager will need to look at the impacts of these trends on customers, suppliers, and the competition. Strategies or plans to capitalize on the trends are then developed, which determine the needed employee numbers with specified qualifications and the availability of qualified applicants. This gap analysis between employee needs and availability of qualified employees will allow the manager to determine the best way to staff the organization to implement strategies that capitalize on the trends.

As a result, employees are not viewed as a cost to be minimized; instead employees are viewed as an asset that contributes to customer satisfaction, loyalty, and profit. Strategic human resource management involves the consideration of human resources as an important component of strategies adopted by an organization to capitalize on trends in the environment. Due to changes in the world economies, managers have to organize work efficiently, respond to change quickly, and manage employees effectively. The impact of this change is the need to work with employees rather than replacing them. Identifying employees who have the skills needed to meet critical needs, developing the skills of those employees, creating a performance-oriented culture, and providing rewards and recognition have become a priority for hospitality companies in a competitive environment. This means that developing and empowering employees to do their

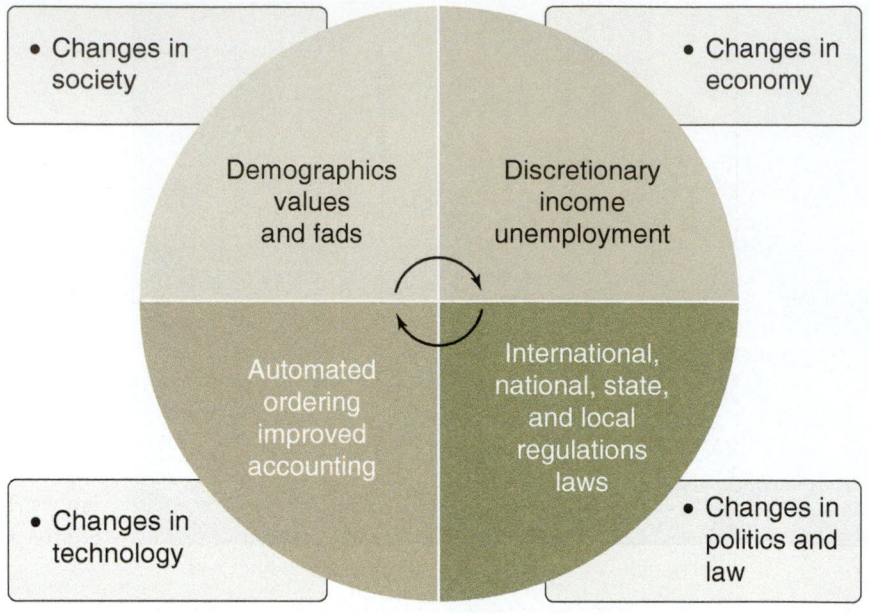

FIGURE 1.7   **Types of Trends to Monitor.**

jobs will give a company a competitive advantage. A summary of the methods managers can use to treat employees as an asset is presented in Figure 1.8.

THE BOTTOM LINE

Cheryl was beginning to see the difference in the way her company was changing. Employees were often seen as a necessary cost to be minimized. In the past, to maintain profit margins, managers were directed to decrease operating costs. Since labor and materials are the top two costs, these were the costs that were targeted. Decreasing the number of employees on the schedule was leading to decreased service to customers, which led to decreased sales and resulted in even more labor cuts. During this time, managers were often forced to lay off their best employees or move employees from full time to part time to reduce costs. The view that employees who had the skills needed to provide quality customer service were valued was a change in the company culture.

In the past, a warm body was hired because there was a critical need for employees, and the company was not able to compete to hire the best employees. In the future, the company will investigate becoming a pay leader to compete for employees with the best skills and provide

View employees as an asset.
Credit: Pincasso / Shutterstock.

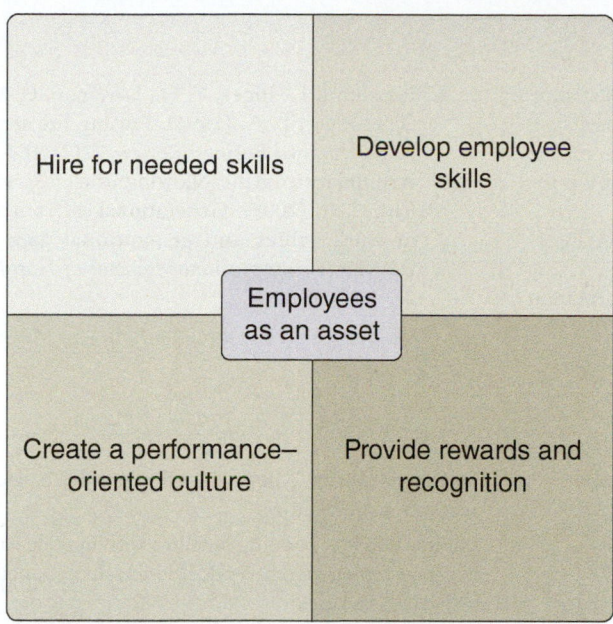

FIGURE 1.8   Focus on Employees as an Asset.

training to improve the skills of their highest performing employees. Cheryl looked forward to working for a company that was competitive with pay, benefits, and a work culture that would help to attract and retain its best employees.

Cheryl also realized that alternative methods to hiring full-time employees might be needed in the future. Some of the methods that were mentioned were hiring more part-time or temporary employees and outsourcing. Outsourcing employees to a contractor was recommended because labor costs were kept constant and predictable, based on the prices negotiated in the contract with the provider. In addition, labor costs are typically lower than staffing with employees, because the cost of turnover, training, and benefits are borne by the contractor.

As a result of the training sessions, Cheryl understood that the hospitality industry is labor intensive because the delivery of products and services is commonly on a one-on-one basis between employees and guests. She also recognized that human resources are extremely important in the industry. These factors increase the need for strategic human resources in the hospitality industry and she was ready to become a strategic partner in the restaurant.

Discussion Questions

1. Give an example of hospitality companies for each of the hospitality industry components included in the U.S. government definition.
2. Using the classifications of hotels based on levels of service, select one hotel chain and identify one brand for each level of service.
3. Give an example of each type of restaurant based on level of service.
4. Add one hotel and one restaurant to the low and high ends of the service continuum and product continuum (use Figures 1.1, 1.2, and 1. 3 as guides).

5. Describe one effect of the economy you have seen in your workplace. Describe its effects on human resources.
6. Give an example of a policy or procedure that would assist a manager in incorporating the four recommendations for developing human capital.
7. Identify resources that will help you monitor trends in the society, economy, technology, and politics.

Application Exercise

1. Interview a manager in the hospitality industry and determine what changes have been made due to the effects of the economy. Ask about changes in numbers, types, and skills of employees. Present your results to the class and compare based on different types of products and services provided.

2. Visit the website of a professional organization, such as the American Hotel & Lodging Association or National Restaurant Association, and determine industry forecasts for the next year. What impacts will these trends have on your workplace? What will the impact be on human resources?

Endnotes

1. This information is available through Bureau of Labor Statistics, U.S. Department of Labor, *Occupational Outlook Handbook*, 2012–13 edition, Hotels and Other Accommodations, on the Internet at http://www.bls.gov/ooh/about/career-guide-to-industries.htm.

2. See the American Hotel & Lodging Association for more information at www.ahla.com.

3. See the National Restaurant Association for more information at www.restaurant.org.

4. Heskett, J. L., Jones, T. O., Loveman, G. W., Sasser, W. E., & Schlesinger, L. A. (1994). Putting the service-profit chain to work. *Harvard Business Review*, 72(2), 164–170.

5. A summary from the following article: Gursoy, D., Maier, T. A., & Chi, C. G. (2008). Generational differences: An examination of work values and generational gaps in the hospitality workforce. *International Journal of Hospitality Management*, 27, 448–458.

Key Terms

Economy hotels   Lodging facilities that provide rooms with few additional facilities.

Full service hotels   Lodging facilities with food and beverage outlets, room service, and bell staff in addition to upgraded rooms.

Full service restaurants   Food and beverage operations that have servers who take care of customers from seating through check settlement.

Hospitality industry   According to the U.S. government, businesses that serve the needs of individuals outside the home by providing lodging, foodservice, and recreation.

Human capital   The collective knowledge, skills, and abilities of an organization's employees.

Limited service hotels   Lodging facilities with quality rooms and few additional facilities (typically catering to business travelers).

Limited service restaurants   Foodservice operations that involve the customer in some part of service, such as cafeterias.

Lodging industry   Businesses that provide a place to sleep and access to bath facilities.

Luxury hotels   Lodging facilities with upscale rooms, food and beverage outlets, room service, concessions, concierge services, bell staff, and valet.

Outsourcing   Contracting with another company to provide staff or services.

Quick service restaurants   Foodservice operations where the customer is responsible for placing an order, paying at a cash register, and taking the meal to a table or to eat out.

Service profit relationship   The positive effect of organizational effectiveness on employee satisfaction that leads to improved service and customer satisfaction, which increase profit and loyalty.

Strategic human resource management   The process of taking a long-term approach to human resource management by identifying the requirements for and contributions of human resources in achieving major long-term business objectives.

PART II

Traditional Hospitality Human Resource Functions

2

Laws Affecting Selection in Hospitality Organizations

OUTLINE

KEY TERMS

Accommodation theory

Affirmative action

Bona fide occupational qualification (BFOQ)

Burden of proof

Business necessity

Complainant

Defendant

Disability

Discrimination

Disparate impact

Disparate treatment

Essential functions

Executive order

Four-fifths rule (80 percent rule)

Impairment

Intent

Major life activities

Minority

Perpetuation theory

Plaintiff

Preponderance of evidence

Prima facie

Protected class

Qualification standards

Reasonable accommodations

Undue hardship

OBJECTIVES

- Describe employer and employee rights
- Define discrimination
- Describe abuses and strategies for preventing discrimination
- Describe the EEOC and distinguish the difference with affirmative action
- Describe the evolution of EEO laws
- List and define specific employment laws

> **Consider This**
>
> Jennifer is 35 and has multiple sclerosis. She has applied for the position of cashier in your food establishment. Your advertisement for the job reads: "able-bodied female to perform cashier responsibilities." The assistant manager explained to Jennifer that the job requires a great deal of stamina, but she insisted on filling out an application. Even though Jennifer was among the first applicants, she was not hired. As the HR director of this operation, you are gravely concerned, and ask what needs to be done to remedy this situation.

INTRODUCTION

Before the 1960s, discrimination in the workplace was widespread. But today, employment law covers all rights and obligations within the employer–employee relationship, between employers and current employees, job applicants, or former employees. Because of the complexity of employment relationships, and because of the wide variety of situations that can arise, employment law involves legal issues as diverse as discrimination, wrongful termination, wages/taxation, and workplace safety. Federal and state laws govern many of these issues. But, where the employment relationship is based on a valid contract entered into by the employer and the employee, state contract law may dictate the rights and duties of the parties.

The basic rights of employees in the public sector include the right to privacy, to fair compensation, and to freedom from discrimination. A job applicant also has certain rights even prior to being hired. These rights include the right to be free from discrimination based on age, gender, race, national origin, or religion during the hiring process (as defined by the Civil Rights Act of 1964). This act is also credited with initiating the Equal Employment Opportunity Commission (as defined by Title VII), which defines today's employment environment.

Employers have an obligation to follow federal and state employment and labor laws—including those pertaining to discrimination, fair pay, employee privacy, and safety in the workplace. The employer's legal obligations do not only pertain to hired employees, but extend to job applicants as well. For example, a prospective employer cannot ask a job applicant certain family-related questions during the hiring process.

DEFINING DISCRIMINATION

Discrimination is defined as the treatment or consideration of making a distinction in favor of (or against) a person based on a group, class, or category to which that person belongs. Human resource management is the practice of legal discrimination. Legal discrimination means that

Defining *discrimination*.
Credit: El Greco / Shutterstock.

criteria used to make employment decisions are following those included in the laws. Technically, we have all been discriminated against, by not being selected for a job, by receiving substandard training, or by receiving a rather harsh job evaluation. Discrimination that follows the guidelines, laws, and regulations of the Equal Employment Opportunity Commission (EEOC) is legal. It is illegal to discriminate in any aspect of employment, including the following:

1. Hiring and firing
2. Compensation, assignment, or classification of employees
3. Transfer, promotion, layoff, or recall
4. Job advertisement
5. Recruitment
6. Testing
7. Use of company facilities
8. Training, development, or apprenticeship programs
9. Fringe benefits
10. Pay, retirement plans, and disability leave
11. Other terms of employment

Discriminatory practices under these laws also include the following:

- Retaliation against an individual for filing a charge of discrimination, participating in an investigation, or opposing discriminatory practices;
- Employment decisions based on stereotypes or assumptions about the abilities, traits, or performance of individuals of a certain sex, race, age, religion, ethnic group, or individuals with disabilities;
- Denying employment opportunities to a person because of marriage to, or association with, an individual of a particular race, religion, or national origin, or an individual with a disability. Title VII also prohibits discrimination because of participation in schools or places of worship associated with a particular racial, ethnic, or religious group.

THEORIES AND DEFENSES OF DISCRIMINATION

It is unlawful to retaliate against an individual for opposing employment practices that discriminate based on sex, or to harass an individual in any way for filing a discrimination charge or for testifying or for participating in an investigation, proceeding, or litigation under Title VII. The impacts of the four theories on hospitality managers are presented in Figure 2.1.

In the process of defining discrimination and harassment, there are four theories of discrimination viewed by the courts. Prior to discussing the theories, it is important to be familiar with the terms and processes involved:

1. Complainant — the person filing the complaint with an agency (say the EEOC)
2. Plaintiff — is the complainant after the case goes to the federal district court (FDC)

Discrimination Theory	Hospitality Impact
Disparate Treatment	Managers must make sure they do not intentionally treat employees or make hiring decisions based on protected status (race, color, gender, or age).
Disparate Impact	Managers will need to review their hiring practices and treatment of employees to determine if there is an unintentional effect on members of minority groups.
Accommodation Theory	Managers will need to make reasonable accommodation for an employee, based on the employee's protected class or status.
Perpetuation Theory	Managers should be concerned with righting the wrongs of the past.

FIGURE 2.1 **Theories of Discrimination and Impact on Hospitality Managers.**

Minority and protected class.
Credit: Rob Marmion /
Shutterstock.

3. **Defendant**   the party against which a civil claim is filed
4. **Burden of proof**   the duty of the party (plaintiff or defendant) to provide evidence of legal standing
5. **Preponderance of evidence**   the balance of evidence in which a court decision is made on the slightest weight in one direction (beyond a reasonable doubt is the rule of evidence for criminal cases)
6. **Minority**   a label attributed to individuals who fall into a protected class as defined by civil rights statutes
7. **Protected class**   those who fall within the jurisdiction of legal protection

Disparate Treatment

The first theory of discrimination is disparate treatment. Disparate treatment is that in which a protected class (or individual) is intentionally treated in an adverse manner that results in harm. In this case, the complainant or plaintiff has the burden of proof to show the intent to discriminate through some form of unfavorable treatment. There are three elements to a disparate treatment claim: (a) the complainant must have incurred harm, resulting from a decision of the employer; (b) the complainant must show that the employer intended to discriminate; and (c) if the respondent articulates a nondiscriminatory reason for the employment action, the complainant must show that the reason was a pretext to discrimination. In reality, the burden of proof is very shallow for the complainant, because this person only needs to make the allegation. This is called **prima facie**, or "first face" evidence, or the evidence at first glance. The real burden of proof rests with the employer, because the employer must demonstrate proof of nondiscrimination.

Disparate Impact

This second theory is similar to disparate treatment, but here the complainant does incur hardship due to the decisions of the employer. The difference is the plaintiff does not discriminate intentionally, but rather unintentionally. The key difference is **intent**, or the willful action of illegal discrimination. Claims of disparate impact usually come about due to the statistical representation of a protected individual/class within an organization. This is why human resource professionals collect applicant data, and maintain statistical counts of employees. This theory deals with the four-fifths rule, which will be discussed in the next section.

Accommodation Theory

This third theory requires the employer to accommodate an employee, based on protected class status at a level the courts deem to be within reason, thus the term **reasonable accommodation**. The burden of responsibility is placed on the employer who must determine the legal level of accommodation (usually in dollar amounts). This can include reasonable accommodation in scheduling for religious practices, or in payment for overtime to another party to cover shifts.

Perpetuation Theory

This fourth theory is concerned with righting the wrongs of discriminatory practices that existed in the past, and is the basis of affirmative action (discussed in the next section). An example of this would be an organization that has a policy of promoting individuals based on seniority and individuals from a protected class do not have seniority required for promotion due to prior discriminatory hiring practices.

Defenses for Employers

While the courts assumed the responsibility of defining the actions that constitute discrimination, the courts also defined two defenses for employers to justify apparent discriminatory practices. The first defense is known as a business necessity. A **business necessity** is a job-related reason to discriminate on the safe and efficient operation of an organization. The courts have adopted a narrow interpretation of this statement. Usually safety is a better argument than efficiency. For instance, a pregnant x-ray technician may be precluded from working for safety reasons. But note, it would be the responsibility of the employer to find a reasonable accommodation for this employee.

A second defense for an employer is called a **bona fide occupational qualification (BFOQ)**. This is the scenario in which an employer must discriminate, based on a characteristic associated with the nature of the job. For instance, an attendant in a female's bathroom could require that the position be filled by a female, thus gender discrimination. But note, race and color can never be an acceptable BFOQ or business necessity, as there is no good reason for a job to require a specific race or color. Other examples could include a male model for a men's clothing line, a native Hawaiian performer for a Hawaiian luau, or a Roman Catholic employee to care for the sanctuary of the church.

THE EVOLUTION OF EQUAL EMPLOYMENT OPPORTUNITY LEGISLATION

The first set of equal employment opportunity (EEO) laws emphasized personnel policies. The second set of laws targeted unequal treatment, while the third set focused on the effects of past discrimination. To date, the fourth set has been emphasizing adverse impact on protected groups. Adverse impact relates to those laws designed to reverse the effect of past employment practices, or in other words, **affirmative action**. EEO laws and affirmative action are not the same. EEO laws and regulations protect the rights of identified groups or classes. Affirmative action

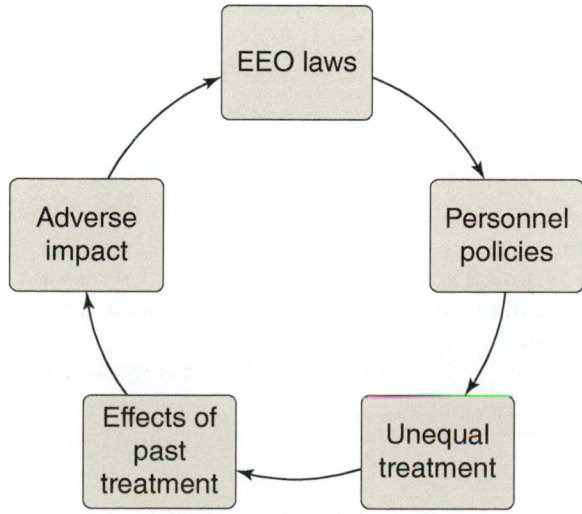

FIGURE 2.2   Evolution of EEO Laws.

represents an obligation placed on employers to hire members of protected groups in order to overcome past discriminatory practices. All employers must abide by EEO laws. However, only employers holding large federal contracts (sometimes state contracts) are required to have affirmative action programs.

Executive Order 11246

In contrast to a federal law passed by Congress, the president of the United States issues an executive order. Executive Order 11246, issued by President Lyndon Johnson in 1965, went beyond Title VII of the Civil Rights Act of 1964. It ordered all employers with U.S. government contracts of $10,000 or more annually to engage in affirmative action, and it required those organizations with 50 or more employees and $50,000 in contracts to develop affirmative action plans. These plans had to set specific, measurable, and realistic goals to address past discrimination against protected groups.[1]

Affirmative action programs are acceptable only when they consider applicants on an individual basis and do not set rigid quotas that prevent people who are not in protected groups from competing equally. In 1999, the Supreme Court of the United States presented a split decision on affirmative action. In two lawsuits challenging the University of Michigan's admission policies, the court ruled 5–4 in favor of the law school to use an affirmative action program, but by a vote of 6–3 reversed the university's undergraduate policy (in part) not to use an affirmative action policy.

One such affirmative action program is called the "four-fifths rule." The **four-fifths rule** was established by the Uniform Guidelines on Employee Selection Procedures in 1978. Under this rule, also known as the **80 percent rule**, the selection of any racial, ethnic, or gender group at a rate less than 80 percent of the group with the highest selection rate is regarded as strong evidence of adverse impact. To illustrate, suppose a new hotel opens and hires 100 out of 200 Caucasian applicants, and only 30 out of 90 African American applicants. The Caucasian selection rate is 50 percent, and the African American selection rate is 33.3 percent. The African American hire rate is 66.6 percent (33.3/50) of the Caucasian hire rate. Because this number falls short of the 80 percent, this may indicate the hotel's hiring practices may have adverse impact on African American applicants. The hotel would need to hire 36 out of 90 African Americans to reach the desired four-fifths rule (i.e., 36/90 = 40%; and 40/50 = 80%).

Affirmative action selection procedures can be categorized according to the following:

- Selection among equally qualified candidates—female or minority candidates are chosen from a poll of equally qualified applicants
- Selection among comparable candidates—female or minority candidates are roughly comparable to other candidates
- Selection among unequal candidates—qualified female or minority candidates are chosen over candidates with a substantially better record
- Selection among qualified and unqualified candidates—unqualified female or minority members are chosen over those who are qualified[2]

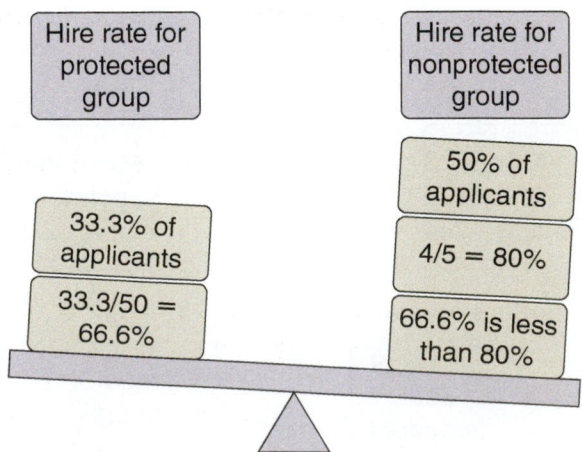

FIGURE 2.3   Four-Fifths Rule Example.

Applicant testing is a common area of selection discrimination. In *Griggs v. Duke Power Company* (1971), the U.S. Supreme Court ruled that by requiring a high school education (or equivalent) as a condition of employment, the employer unlawfully discriminated against African Americans. Since this ruling, educational and testing practices have been scrutinized by the EEOC. In *Albemarle Paper Company (United Papermakers) v. Moody* (1975), the Court found that tests used by the company were not sufficiently job related to be valid under Title VII and held that the trial court should have enjoined the use of the tests and awarded back pay. In deciding the issue of back pay awards, the Court ruled that such awards should follow closely upon a finding of discrimination and that ordering back pay was an appropriate incentive to employers to comply with Title VII. It concluded that the certainty of the remedy would best effectuate the statute. In all essential aspects, this holding continues to provide a major form of relief under Title VII. In *Weber v. Kaiser Aluminum (Steelworkers)* (1979), the Supreme Court ruled that companies and unions could establish quotas to eliminate racial imbalances in the workplace (later modified by *Firefighters Union No. 1784 v. Stotts*). In 1989, in the case of *Wards Cove Packing Co. v. Atonio*, the Supreme Court held that the comparison between the racial compositions of the high- and low-paying jobs was flawed because the data failed to take into account the pool of qualified job applicants.

The Court ruled again on applicant testing in *Ricci v. DeStefano* in 2009 (5–4 vote). The city of New Haven, Connecticut, went to great lengths to devise a written examination that would fairly test members of the New Haven firefighters for promotion to captain and lieutenant. But ultimately, the results on this test, like the results of so many other qualification tests, generated a sharp disparate impact. African American and Hispanic applicants did far worse than the white candidates, such that none of them would have been eligible for consideration in the first wave of promotions. Black and Hispanic applicants threatened to sue the city to invalidate the test because of that disparate impact. The city decided, in effect, to settle that case without litigation by abandoning its tests and refusing to certify any successful candidates for promotion. The disappointed white firefighters then went to court themselves, claiming that the city had no reason to set aside the test, which had been fairly vetted and properly administered. The Supreme Court upheld the validity of the test, thus determining the actions of the city to be discriminatory.[3]

FEDERAL LAWS ENFORCED BY EEOC

Beginning in the early 60s and continuing today, the U.S. Congress has passed a series of laws that have impacted all employers in the country. These laws create an opportunity for all qualified applicants and employees to have equal access to job, promotion, and salary. Equal opportunity laws differ from affirmative action in that they have been established to protect the rights of groups or classes. Affirmative action was established through an executive order and was established to overcome past practices.

Equal Pay Act of 1963

This act was the true beginning of the EEO movement in the United States. This act was an amendment to the Fair Labor Standards Act of 1938, and required that men and women working for the same organization be paid the same rate of pay for substantially equal work.

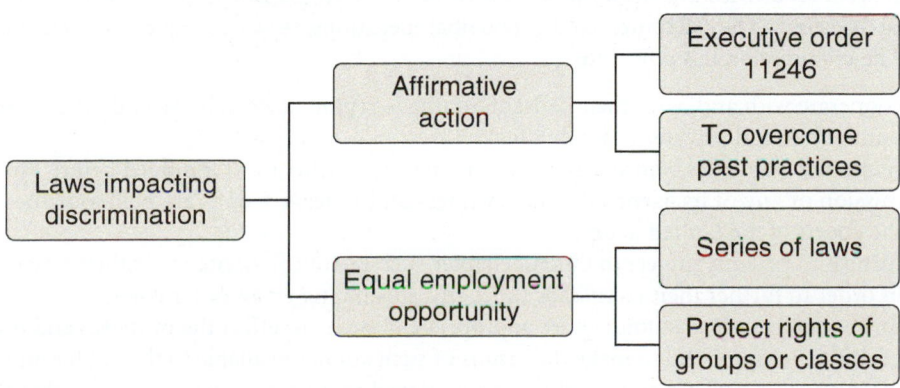

FIGURE 2.4   Laws Impacting Discrimination.

Pay issues prior to the Equal Pay Act of 1963.   *Credit*: iofoto / Shutterstock.

Title VII of the Civil Rights Act of 1964

Title VII of the Civil Rights Act of 1964 applies to employers with 15 or more employees and prohibits unfair employment discrimination based on race, color, sex, religion, and national origin. Employers with 14 or fewer employees may still be subject to state antidiscrimination laws that are similar to the federal act. This act also applies to employment agencies, labor organizations, or training programs. This act created the EEOC, which is composed of five members, not more than three of whom shall be members of the same political party. Members of the commission shall be appointed by the president by and with the advice and consent of the Senate for a term of five years. Any individual chosen to fill a vacancy shall be appointed only for the unexpired term of the member whom he or she shall succeed. All members of the commission shall continue to serve until their successors are appointed and qualified. But, no such member of the commission shall continue to serve (a) for more than 60 days when the Congress is in session unless a nomination to fill such vacancy shall have been submitted to the Senate, or (b) after the adjournment *sine die* of the session of the Senate in which such nomination was submitted. The president shall designate one member to serve as chairman of the commission, and one member to serve as vice chairman.

The commission has three principal roles. First, it oversees the administration of existing EEO laws and regulations, and refers charges of violation to state or local EEO agencies. The second responsibility is to issue guidelines for Title VII compliance. While these guidelines are not technically laws, they have been viewed by the Supreme Court to be important for the effective administration of the EEOC. And finally, the EEOC is to gather information. Each organization in the United States with 100 or more employees must file an annual report to a regional EEO office. This report outlines the number of women and minorities employed in nine different categories. Also, in accordance with this third role, in September of 2004, the EEOC established a centralized national call center. The call center handles potential allegations, as well as requests for information.

The commission has power to:

1. cooperate with and, with their consent, to utilize regional, state, local, and other agencies, both public and private, and individuals;
2. reimburse witnesses whose depositions are taken, or who are summoned before the commission or any of its agents, the same witness and mileage fees as are paid to witnesses in the courts of the United States;
3. furnish to persons subject to this subchapter such technical assistance as they may request in order to further their compliance with this subchapter or an order issued;
4. make such technical studies as are appropriate in order to effect the purposes and policies of this subchapter and to make the results of such studies available to the public; and
5. intervene in a civil action brought by an aggrieved party against a respondent other than a government, governmental agency, or political subdivision.

Title of Law	Workplace Impact
Equal Pay Act of 1963	Men and women working for the same organization doing the equal work must receive equal pay
Title VII of the Civil Rights Act of 1964	Applies to employers with 15 or more employees - Prohibits discrimination based on race, color, sex, religion, and national origin - Established the EEOC
Age Discrimination in Employment Act of 1967	Applies to employers with 20 or more employees - Prohibits discrimination based on age of those 40 and older
Pregnancy Discrimination Act of 1978	Requires employers to treat pregnancy as any other medical condition - Prohibits discrimination during the hiring process
Retirement Equity Act of 1984	Requires companies to consider all years of service since the age of 18 and earnings since the age of 21 when determining vested retirement benefits
Americans with Disabilities Act of 1990, amended in 2008	Prohibits discrimination against persons with disabilities - Defines disability and requirements for reasonable accommodation
Civil Rights Act of 1991	Increases the employer's burden of proof in disparate impact and disparate treatment cases - Sets limits for compensatory and punitive damages

FIGURE 2.5   Laws Enforced by the EEOC.

A charge shall be filed within 180 days after the alleged unlawful employment practice occurred and notice of the charge (including the date, place, and circumstances of the alleged unlawful employment practice) shall be served upon the person against whom such charge is made. The commission also requires all employers to post employee rights' posters, so that all employees know their rights in the workplace.[4]

Age Discrimination in Employment Act of 1967

The Age Discrimination in Employment Act of 1967 (ADEA) prohibits employment discrimination on the basis of age against people 40 years of age or older. The EEOC views employees of this age to be a protected group. All employment actions (recruiting, advertising, selection, evaluation, promotions, etc.) are subject to scrutiny under ADEA. One different provision of the act is that all private employers with 20 or more employees or all unions with 25 or more members must comply with this act. As the hospitality industry's workforce becomes older, this act will have an impact on the organizations.[5]

Pregnancy Discrimination Act of 1978

The Pregnancy Discrimination Act of 1978 (PDA) stipulates that pregnancy must be treated the same as any other medical condition in the workplace. Before this act, the employer had the right to set the date and time for the employee to take a leave of absence. Today, the employer cannot do this; rather the employer must work in conjunction with the employee. This act also prohibits employers from discriminating against pregnant applicants in the hiring process. Also, this act does not force employers to provide health insurance if none had been provided in the past. This act prohibits any organization from discriminating on the basis of image, and at the same time, employers cannot force a pregnant employee to perform duties other than those she normally does.

According to the U.S. Department of Labor, women currently comprise 47 percent of the workforce, and women are expected to account for more than half of the total growth in the workforce from 2002 to 2012. Thus, this act does affect the hospitality industry due to its large number of female employees. According to the Centers for Disease Control and Prevention, in 1970, the average age of a woman having a first baby was 21.4 years; today the average age is 25 years,[6] showing another potential impact on the hospitality industry.

Retirement Equity Act of 1984

This act requires companies to count all years of service since the age of 18 in determining vesting in retirement benefits, plus all earnings since age 21, even if there are breaks in service up to five years. This law also states that pension benefits may be considered a joint asset in divorce settlements. Employers must provide survivor benefits to spouses of fully vested employees who pass away before reaching the minimum retirement age. This law applies to both sexes, but affects more women. With the recent Supreme Court case of *Hulteen v. AT&T*, the Court ruled in favor of AT&T (7–2 vote). The case hinged on AT&T's classification of "leave time" prior to the PDA. The Court ruled that AT&T was not liable to treat pregnancy leave (pre PDA) to the new standards established by the PDA. The ruling impacted the vested pension benefits of numerous employees.[7]

Americans with Disabilities Act of 1990

The Americans with Disabilities Act of 1990 (ADA) is probably the most comprehensive piece of civil rights legislation since Title VII of the Civil Rights Act of 1964. This law was amended in 2008, with changes taking effect on January 1, 2009. This law forbids discrimination against people with disabilities, and it has five titles (or parts). They are:

Title I	Employment
Title II	Public Services
Title III	Public Accommodations and Services Operated by Private Entities
Title IV	Miscellaneous Provisions
Title V	Telecommunications (Title 47—Telegraphs, Telephones, and Radiotelegraphs; and Chapter 5—Wire or Radio Communication)

This textbook will focus mainly on Title I. According to the ADA Amendments Act of 2008*, the purposes of this act are to:

1. carry out ADA's objectives of providing "a clear and comprehensive national mandate for the elimination of discrimination" and "clear, strong, consistent, enforceable standards addressing discrimination" by reinstating a broad scope of protection to be available under the ADA;
2. reject the requirement enunciated by the Supreme Court in *Sutton v. United Air Lines, Inc.* (1999), and its companion cases as to whether an impairment substantially limits a major life activity is to be determined with reference to the ameliorative effects of mitigating measures;
3. reject the Supreme Court's reasoning in *Sutton v. United Air Lines, Inc.* (1999), with regard to coverage under the third prong of the definition of disability and to reinstate the reasoning of the Supreme Court in *School Board of Nassau County v. Arline* (1987), which set forth a broad view of the third prong of the definition of handicap under the Rehabilitation Act of 1973;
4. reject the standards enunciated by the Supreme Court in *Toyota Motor Manufacturing, Kentucky, Inc. v. Williams* (2002), that the terms substantially and major in the definition of disability under the ADA "need to be interpreted strictly to create a demanding standard for qualifying as disabled," and that to be substantially limited in performing a major life activity under the ADA "an individual must have an impairment that prevents or severely restricts the individual from doing activities that are of central importance to most people's daily lives";
5. convey congressional intent that the standard created by the Supreme Court in the case of *Toyota Motor Manufacturing, Kentucky, Inc. v. Williams* (2002), for "substantially limits," and applied by lower courts in numerous decisions, has created an inappropriately high level of limitation necessary to obtain coverage under the ADA, and to convey that it is the intent of Congress that the primary object of attention in cases brought under the ADA should be whether entities covered under the ADA have complied with their obligations, and to convey that the question of whether an individual's impairment is a disability under the ADA should not demand extensive analysis; and
6. express Congress's expectation that the EEOC will revise that portion of its current regulations that defines the term substantially limits as "significantly restricted" to be consistent with this act, including the amendments made by this act.[8]

---

*From THE AMERICANS WITH DISABILITIES ACT 2008. September 25, 2008. Washington, DC: United States Department of Justice, Civil Rights Division.

The term **disability** with respect to an individual is defined as: (a) a physical or mental impairment that substantially limits one or more **major life activities** of such individual, (b) a record of such an **impairment**, or (c) being regarded as having such an impairment. Major life activities include caring for oneself, performing manual tasks, seeing, hearing, eating, sleeping, walking, standing, lifting, bending, speaking, breathing, learning, reading, concentrating, thinking, communicating, and working. Major bodily functions includes the operation of a major bodily function, including but not limited to, functions of the immune system, normal cell growth, digestive, bowel, bladder, neurological, brain, respiratory, circulatory, endocrine, and reproductive functions. An impairment (that is episodic or in remission) is a disability if it would substantially limit a major life activity when active. The determination of whether an impairment substantially limits a major life activity shall be made without regard to the ameliorative effects of mitigating measures, such as: (a) medication, medical supplies, equipment, or appliances, low-vision devices (which do not include ordinary eyeglasses or contact lenses), prosthetics (including limbs and devices), hearing aids and cochlear implants or other implantable hearing devices, mobility devices, or oxygen therapy equipment and supplies; (b) use of assistive technology; (c) reasonable accommodations or auxiliary aids or services; or (d) learned behavioral or adaptive neurological modifications.

Under the ADA, people with disabilities are considered qualified if they can perform the **essential functions** of the job with or without **reasonable accommodations**. Essential functions are job tasks that are fundamental. Cooking skills are essential for a cook position, but hearing orders called to them by a server may not be considered fundamental, since there are other delivery methods. Hence, a reasonable accommodation should be made. The term reasonable accommodation may include:

1. making existing facilities used by employees readily accessible to and usable by individuals with disabilities; and
2. job restructuring, part-time or modified work schedules, reassignment to a vacant position, acquisition or modification of equipment or devices, appropriate adjustment or modifications of examinations, training materials or policies, the provision of qualified readers or interpreters, and other similar accommodations for individuals with disabilities. The term **undue hardship** means an action requiring significant difficulty or expense, when considered in light of these factors: (a) the nature and cost of the accommodation needed, (b) the overall financial resources of the facility or facilities involved in the provision of

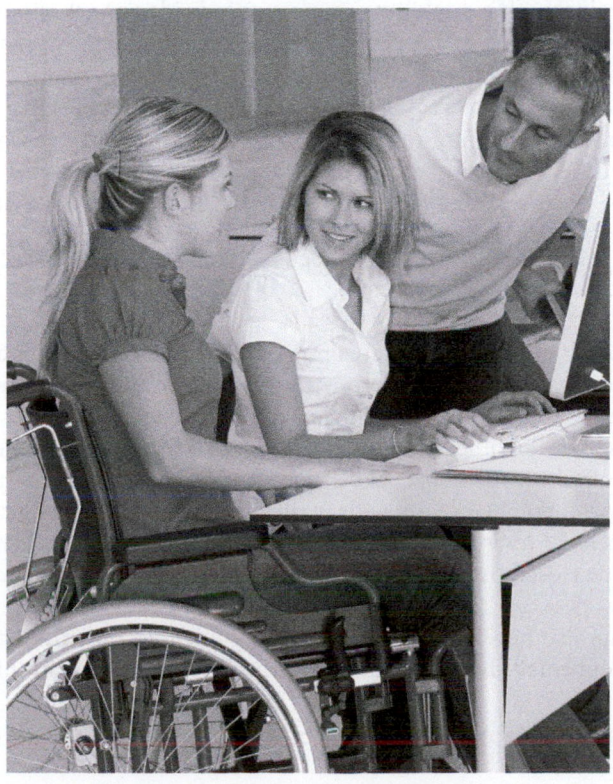

Working with disabilities.
Credit: Goodluz / Shutterstock.

the reasonable accommodation, (c) the number of persons employed at such facility, (d) the effect on expenses and resources, or (e) the impact otherwise of such accommodation upon the operation of the facility; and

3. the type of operation or operations of the covered entity, including the composition, structure, and functions of the workforce of such entity; the geographic separateness, administrative, or fiscal relationship of the facility or facilities in question to the covered entity.

The ADA defined discrimination against a qualified individual on the basis of disability* as:

1. limiting, segregating, or classifying a job applicant or employee in a way that adversely affects the opportunities or status of such applicant or employee because of the disability of such applicant or employee;
2. participating in a contractual or other arrangement or relationship that has the effect of subjecting a covered entity's qualified applicant or employee with a disability to the prohibited discrimination (such relationship includes a relationship with an employment or referral agency, labor union, an organization providing fringe benefits to an employee of the covered entity, or an organization providing training and apprenticeship programs);
3. utilizing standards, criteria, or methods of administration that have the (a) effect of discrimination on the basis of disability or (b) that perpetuate the discrimination of others who are subject to common administrative control;
4. excluding or otherwise denying equal jobs or benefits to a qualified individual because of the known disability of an individual with whom the qualified individual is known to have a relationship or association;
5. taking no action, for example (a) not making reasonable accommodations to the known physical or mental limitations of an otherwise qualified individual with a disability who is an applicant or employee, unless such covered entity can demonstrate that the accommodation would impose an undue hardship on the operation of the business of such covered entity; or (b) denying employment opportunities to a job applicant or employee who is an otherwise qualified individual with a disability, if such denial is based on the need of such covered entity to make reasonable accommodation to the physical or mental impairments of the employee or applicant;
6. using **qualification standards**—the term qualification standards may include a requirement that an individual shall not pose a direct threat to the health or safety of other individuals in the workplace, employment tests or other selection criteria that screen out or tend to screen out an individual with a disability or a class of individuals with disabilities unless the standard, test, or other selection criteria, as used by the covered entity, is shown to be job related for the position in question and is consistent with business necessity; and
7. failing to select and administer tests concerning employment in the most effective manner to ensure that, when such test is administered to a job applicant or employee who has a disability that impairs sensory, manual, or speaking skills, such test results accurately reflect the skills, aptitude, or whatever other factor of such applicant or employee that such test purports to measure, rather than reflecting the impaired sensory, manual, or speaking skills of such employee or applicant (except where such skills are the factors that the test purports to measure).

Organizations spend thousands of dollars annually on reasonable accommodation activities. Examples are 32-inch wide doorways (with the door open at a 90-degree angle, thus the door width will actually need to be greater than 32 inches, or the common width is 36 inches), ADA hotel rooms that are dispersed among the other hotel rooms have roll-in showers, wheelchair-accessible sinks, wheelchair-accessible toilets, visual strobe alarms, visual alarms on phones, or some signage (black on white, or white on black, and with Braille). Also, many hospitality companies may have to exchange faucets, lamps, drapery controls, heating/air-conditioning controls. These companies need to apply the closed fist test. If the device can be controlled with a closed fist, then it is ADA acceptable.

Food service establishments also have to be aware of ADA guidelines regarding contagious diseases. The EEOC has confirmed that, in some cases, employees with communicable

---

* From THE AMERICANS WITH DISABILITIES ACT 2008. September 25, 2008. Washington, DC: United States Department of Justice, Civil Rights Division.

diseases must be afforded disability status because it affects their ability to work. The guidelines include the potential to transmit a disease through food handling. The Department of Health and Human Services, through the Centers for Disease Control and Prevention, has listed several of these diseases. Pathogens that can cause diseases after an infected person handles food are the following:

1. Noroviruses
2. Hepatitis A virus
3. *Salmonella Typhi* (Kauffmann-White scheme for designation of Salmonella serotypes)
4. *Shigella* species
5. *Staphylococcus aureus*
6. *Streptococcus pyogenes*[9]

Finally, while some workers take advantage of the law through frivolous claims and requests, employers have mostly been the beneficiary of ADA. The statutes provide opportunities for highly productive workers who make significant contributions to their organizations.

Civil Rights Act of 1991

The Civil Rights Act of 1991 (CRA) was enacted to amend the Civil Rights Act of 1964. The purposes of this act are to:

1. provide appropriate remedies for intentional discrimination and unlawful harassment in the workplace;
2. codify the concepts of "business necessity" and "job related" enunciated by the Supreme Court in *Griggs v. Duke Power Co.* (1971), and in the other Supreme Court decisions prior to *Wards Cove Packing Co. v. Atonio* (1989);
3. confirm statutory authority and provide statutory guidelines for the adjudication of disparate impact suits under title VII of the Civil Rights Act of 1964; and
4. respond to recent decisions of the Supreme Court by expanding the scope of relevant civil rights statutes in order to provide adequate protection to victims of discrimination.[10]

In other words, the law has increased the employer's burden of proof in disparate impact cases. It has also increased the employer's burden of proof in disparate treatment cases (especially relative to the discriminatory intent provision). Finally, this act has added compensatory and punitive damages to be awarded to prevailing plaintiffs to a limit of $300,000 (no monetary damages were allowed under the 1964 act). This act is a clear case of the legislative branch of the U.S. government, creating a new law in response to the disagreement with the interpretations of the Supreme Court in regard to the 1964 act.

Applications to Hospitality Management

A large portion of time is spent by managers dealing with their employees. An organization can make managing much easier by adhering to EEO laws. Organizations adhering to EEO laws need to complete a job analysis on every position to determine BFOQs for every position. Organizations can also assist with effective management of employees by training managers to eliminate discrimination in the workplace. Managers need to be aware of potential discrimination in regard to gender, age, disability, national origin, race, religion, and pregnancy.

Besides knowing the BFOQs for each job, workplace selection laws are going to impact the hiring decisions and promotion decisions within the hospitality industry. The HR managers will need to be well versed in the laws that apply to the selection process in order to avoid any potential discriminatory practices. Likewise, the HR managers will want to be consistent when promoting individuals within their organizations. By adhering to the laws, the HR managers will create an environment free of discrimination.

THE BOTTOM LINE

It is important to note that the body of law presented in this chapter contains only some of the major federal laws affecting the selection process. There are numerous other statutes and matters of tort or common law that fall within the domain of human resource management. One requirement for HR management is a thorough knowledge of statutes and laws that have anything to do with the terms, conditions, rights, or privileges of employment. HR managers must always be prepared to learn new laws, or amended laws. In fact, it would be irresponsible if they were not constantly updating their knowledge of the pertinent laws. HR managers can (and often do) retain legal counsel with expertise in this area, but it should be noted that legal professionals are not usually trained in the techniques of management. As we will discover in the remaining chapters of this text, the responsibility of HR managers is to provide employees with a workplace that is professionally managed.

Discussion Questions

1. Why is the defense for disparate treatment different or more important than disparate impact?
2. What is the difference between a business necessity and a BFOQ?
3. How is affirmative action different from equal employment opportunities?
4. Why will the 80 percent rule play a major role within hospitality organizations?
5. How has the U.S. Supreme Court influenced employment standards?
6. What are the principal roles of the EEOC?
7. Why should hospitality companies be concerned with the Pregnancy Discrimination Act?
8. Why did the legislature amend the ADA in 2008?
9. Why is the ADA concerned with contagious diseases?
10. How is the Civil Rights Act of 1991 different from the act of 1964?

Application Exercise

Consider the case of Jennifer discussed at the beginning of the chapter. You are the HR manager for this hotel and Jennifer has written a letter to the general manager, claiming discrimination and infractions against ADA. You have to respond to this situation. Write a one-page business memo to the general manager and state three specific actions steps that will be taken by your organization.

Endnotes

1. From http://www.dol.gov/ofccp/regs/compliance/ca_11246.htm
2. From http://www.eeoc.gov/types/sexual_harassment.html
3. From http://supremecourtus.gov/opinions/08pdf/07-1428.pdf
4. From http://www.eeoc.gov/policy/vii.html
5. From http://www.eeoc.gov/policy/adea.html
6. From https://healthlibrary.epnet.com/print.aspx?token=c5987b1e-add7-403a-b817-b3efe6109265&chunkiid=100913
7. From http://www.equalrights.org/media/Hulteen_Press_Release.pdf
8. From http://www.ada.gov/pubs/adastatute08mark.htm
9. Taken from *Federal Register*: November 17, 2008 (Volume 73, Number 222, Page 67871–67872) via http://cryptome.info/0001/cdc111708.htm
10. Taken from Civil Rights Act of 1991 (Pub. L. 102-166), as enacted on November 21, 1991, from http://www.eeoc.gov/policy/cra91.html

Key Terms

Accommodation theory   A theory of discrimination that requires employers to reasonably accommodate the practice of specified protected class members under certain circumstances.

Affirmative action   Any program, policy, or procedure an employer implements in order to correct past discrimination and prevent current and future discrimination within the workplace.

Bona fide occupational qualification (BFOQ)   A very narrowly interpreted exception to EEO laws that allows employers to base employment decisions for a particular job on such factors as sex, religion, or national origin, if they are able to demonstrate that such factors are an essential qualification for performing a particular job.

Burden of proof   The burden placed on an employer, as a result of a claim of discriminatory treatment, to provide a verifiable, legitimate, and nondiscriminatory reason for any employment action taken, which may have resulted in adverse treatment of a member(s) of a protected group.

Business necessity   Discrimination allowed by Title VII of the Civil Rights Act of 1964 as a legal reason for choosing one employer over another. To date, most of the acceptable cases have involved job-related safety issues such as special training or experience.

Complainant   Designation of an individual who has filed a claim of discrimination with an agency.

Defendant   The party against which a civil claim is filed in a court of law.

Disability   Defined as a physical or mental impairment that substantially limits one or more of an individual's major life activities (walking, talking, standing, sitting, etc.).

Discrimination   The treatment or consideration of making a distinction in favor of (or against) a person or thing based on a group, class, or category to which that person belongs.

Disparate impact   Under Equal Employment Opportunity (EEO) law, a less favorable effect for one group than for another group.

A disparate impact results when rules applied to all employees have a different and more inhibiting effect on women and minority groups than on the majority.

Disparate treatment Such treatment results when rules or policies are applied inconsistently to one group of people over another. Discrimination may result when rules and policies are applied differently to members of protected classes.

Essential functions The primary job functions or tasks that an individual must be able to perform with or without a reasonable accommodation.

Executive order An official presidential directive that has the same force as a law.

Four-Fifths rule (also known as the 80 percent rule)—Rule established by the Uniform Guidelines on Employee Selection Procedures in 1978 that states selection or promotion of any racial, ethnic, or sex group must occur at a rate of at least 80 percent (four-fifths) of the rate of the group with the highest selection rate.

Impairment A physical or mental condition resulting from injury or illness, which diminishes an individual's faculties such as ability to hear, see, walk, or talk.

Intent A knowing and willful action of illegal discrimination.

Major life activities Include caring for oneself, performing manual tasks, seeing, hearing, eating, sleeping, walking, standing, lifting, bending, speaking, breathing, learning, reading, concentrating, thinking, communicating, and working.

Minority A label attributed to individuals who fall into a protected class as defined by civil rights statutes.

Perpetuation theory A theory of discrimination that precludes employers from perpetuating past discriminatory practices that may have existed prior to the enactment of a statute.

Plaintiff The filing party in a legal dispute.

Preponderance of evidence The balance of evidence in which a court decision is made on the slightest weight in one direction (beyond a reasonable doubt is the rule of evidence for criminal cases).

Prima facie Latin for "at first view" or "at first appearance," a prima facie case is a lawsuit that requires an employer to articulate a reason that sufficiently proves that any decision or action taken was made based on legitimate and nondiscriminatory factors.

Protected class A group of workers with a characteristic specifically identified by an employment-related law or ordinance as protected.

Qualification standards This term may include a requirement that an individual shall not pose a direct threat to the health or safety of other individuals in the workplace, employment tests or other selection criteria that screen out or tend to screen out an individual with a disability or a class of individuals with disabilities unless the standard, test or other selection criteria, as used by the covered entity, is shown to be job related for the position in question and is consistent with business necessity.

Reasonable accommodations Modifying or adjusting a job process or a work environment to better enable a qualified individual with a disability to be considered for or perform the essential functions of a job.

Undue hardship An ADA action requiring significant difficulty or expense, when considered in light of these factors.

3

Laws Affecting Hospitality Workplaces

OUTLINE

Defining Harassment

Federal Laws—Enforced by the Department of Labor

    Fair Labor Standards Act of 1938

    Occupational Safety and Health Act of 1970

    Family and Medical Leave Act (FMLA) of 1993

Federal Laws—Enforced by Other Federal Agencies

    Uniformed Services Employment and Reemployment Rights Act of 1994

Employee Polygraph Protection Act of 1998

Immigration Reform and Control Act of 1986 (amended in 1990 and 1996)

The Wagner Act of 1935

Taft Hartley Act of 1947

Civil Service Reform Act of 1978

Worker Adjustment and Retraining Notification Act of 1991

State Laws

    Applications to Hospitality Management

The Bottom Line

KEY TERMS

Arbitration

Bargaining in good faith

Closed shop

Collective bargaining

Emergency standard

Employee assistance programs (EAPs)

Featherbedding

Harassment

HazComm

Interim standard

Jurisdictional strikes

Material safety data sheet (MSDS)

Mediation

Permanent standard

Polygraph

Right-to-work laws

Secondary boycotts

Serious health condition

Sexual harassment

Wildcat strikes

OBJECTIVES

- Define harassment
- Define sexual harassment
- Understand the impact that workplace laws have on hospitality operations
- Define and describe employee assistance programs
- Define serious health conditions
- Describe collective bargaining
- Describe the impact of unions on the work environment
- Determine the difference between mediation and arbitration

> **Consider This**
>
> You are a server at the local pancake house (corporately operated). You notice a crack in the glass door of the microwave oven. You are concerned with the safety of all employed. You tell the manager, and two weeks later, it is still not repaired. You ask the manager, and she says it is fine, and not to worry about it. The following week you start to get headaches, and wonder why. You tell the manager about your headaches at work, and she says to take some aspirin. You think it is the microwave oven, and contemplate what to do about it. Should you call the district manager? Should you call the corporate office? Should you call OSHA's office?

INTRODUCTION

Working environments and conditions are not always perfect, and sometimes there can be hazards in the workplace. In the early 1900s, little emphasis was placed on health and safety in the business world; rather emphasis was placed on profitability. Beginning in the early 1930s, emphasis was beginning to be placed on the pay and working conditions of the people in the employ of businesses in the United States. Important employee rights include the following:

- Right to privacy (may be limited where e-mail and Internet use is concerned)
- Right to be free from discrimination and harassment of all types
- Right to a safe workplace free of dangerous conditions, toxic substances, and other potential safety hazards
- Right to be free from retaliation for filing a claim or complaint against an employer (these are sometimes called "whistleblower" rights)
- Right to fair wages for work performed

Employers have a moral duty to follow federal, state, and local laws that concern the work environment. The employers' legal obligations pertain to their employees, as well as to their customers.

DEFINING HARASSMENT

Harassment is unwelcome conduct that is based on race, color, sex, religion, national origin, disability, and/or age. Harassment becomes unlawful where: (a) enduring the offensive conduct becomes a condition of continued employment, or (b) the conduct is severe or pervasive enough to create a work environment that a reasonable person would consider intimidating, hostile, or abusive. Antidiscrimination laws also prohibit harassment against individuals in retaliation for filing a discrimination claim, for testifying, or for participating in any way in an investigation, proceeding, or lawsuit under these laws, or by opposing employment practices that they reasonably believe discriminate against individuals, in violation of these laws. Petty slights, annoyances, and isolated incidents (unless extremely serious) will not rise to the level of illegality. To be unlawful, the conduct must create a work environment that would be intimidating, hostile, or offensive to reasonable people.

Offensive conduct may include, but is not limited to, offensive jokes, slurs, epithets or name calling, physical assaults or threats, intimidation, ridicule or mockery, insults or putdowns, offensive objects or pictures, and interference with work performance. Harassment can occur in a variety of circumstances, including, but not limited to, the following:

- The harasser can be the victim's supervisor, a supervisor in another area, an agent of the employer, a coworker, or a nonemployee (i.e., a customer).
- The victim does not have to be the person harassed, but can be anyone affected by the offensive conduct.
- Unlawful harassment may occur without economic injury to, or discharge of, the victim.

Prevention is the best tool to eliminate harassment in the workplace. Employers are encouraged to take appropriate steps to prevent and correct unlawful harassment. They should clearly communicate to employees that unwelcome harassing conduct will not be tolerated. They can do this by: (a) establishing an effective complaint or grievance process, (b) providing antiharassment training to their managers and employees, and (c) taking immediate and appropriate

Communicate harassment will not be tolerated in a clear policy		
Establish a complaint or grievance process	Provide antiharassment training	Take immediate action in response to complaints

FIGURE 3.1 Tools for Preventing Harassment in Your Workplace.

action when an employee complains. Employers should strive to create an environment in which employees feel free to raise concerns and feel confident that those concerns will be addressed. Employees should be encouraged to inform the harasser directly that the conduct is unwelcome and must stop. Employees should also be encouraged to report the harassment to management at an early stage in order to prevent its escalation. See Figure 3.1.

The employer is automatically liable for harassment by a supervisor or manager that results in a negative employment action such as termination, failure to promote or hire, and loss of wages. If the supervisor's harassment results in a hostile work environment, the employer can avoid liability only if he or she can prove that: (a) a reasonable effort was made to prevent and promptly correct the harassing behavior, and (b) the employee unreasonably failed to take advantage of any preventive or corrective opportunities provided by the employer.

The employer will also be liable for harassment by nonsupervisory employees or nonemployees over whom it has control (e.g., independent contractors, vendors, or customers on the premises), if it knew, or should have known about the harassment and failed to take prompt and appropriate corrective action.

When investigating allegations of harassment, the Equal Employment Opportunity Commission (EEOC) looks at the entire record, including the nature of the conduct and the context in which the alleged incident occurred. A determination of whether harassment is severe or pervasive enough to be illegal is made on a case-by-case basis.

Sexual harassment is unwelcome sexual advances, requests for sexual favors, and other verbal or physical conduct of a sexual nature. When this conduct explicitly or implicitly affects

Sexual harassment. *Credit*: Lisa S. / Shutterstock.

an individual's employment, unreasonably interferes with an individual's work performance, or creates an intimidating, hostile, or offensive work environment, then this constitutes sexual harassment.

Sexual harassment can occur in a variety of circumstances including, but not limited to, the following:

- The victim as well as the harasser may be a woman or a man. The victim does not have to be of the opposite sex.
- The harasser can be the victim's supervisor, an agent of the employer, a supervisor in another area, a coworker, or a nonemployee.
- The victim does not have to be the person harassed but could be anyone affected by the offensive conduct.
- Unlawful sexual harassment may occur without economic injury to or discharge of the victim.
- The harasser's conduct must be unwelcome.

The victim should inform the harasser directly that the conduct is unwelcome and must stop. The victim should also use any employer complaint mechanism or grievance system available.

Prevention is the best method to eliminate sexual harassment in the workplace. Employers are encouraged to take necessary steps in order to prevent sexual harassment from occurring. They should clearly communicate to employees that sexual harassment will not be tolerated. They can do so by having policies on sexual harassment in place and by establishing an effective complaint or grievance process. Immediate and appropriate action must be taken when an employee makes a complaint.

In fiscal year 2008, EEOC received 13,867 charges of sexual harassment; males filed 15.9 percent of those charges. EEOC resolved 11,731 sexual harassment charges in FY 2008 and recovered $47.4 million in monetary benefits for charging parties and other aggrieved individuals (not including monetary benefits obtained through litigation).[1]

FEDERAL LAWS—ENFORCED BY THE DEPARTMENT OF LABOR

Fair Labor Standards Act of 1938

The Fair Labor Standards Act of 1938 (FLSA), which prescribes standards for the basic minimum wage and overtime pay, affects most private and public employment. It requires employers to pay covered employees, who are not otherwise exempt; at least the federal minimum wage and overtime pay equal to one and one-half times the regular rate of pay. For nonagricultural operations, it restricts the hours that children under age 16 can work and forbids the employment of children under age 18 in certain jobs that are deemed too dangerous. For agricultural operations, it prohibits the employment of children under age 16 during school hours and in certain other jobs deemed too dangerous. The act is administered by the Wage and Hour Division within the U.S. Department of Labor (DOL). Managers will need to review 17 different areas in regard to FLSA. See Figure 3.2 for an overview.

Occupational Safety and Health Act of 1970

The purpose of Occupational Safety and Health Act of 1970 (OSHA) was to centralize the regulation of workforce safety and to expand workplace safety. This act has been deemed one of the most controversial since World War II. OSHA was created to legitimize and standardize workplace safety rules and regulations. This act created three new government agencies: (a) Occupational Safety and Health Administration—responsible for enforcing regulations for job safety, issuing citations, and deciding on penalties; (b) Occupational Safety and Health Review Commission—an appeal board of three members chosen by the president of the United States whose job is to settle any disputes between OSHA and organizations; and (c) National Institute of Occupational Safety and health (NIOSH)—an agency responsible for research into work safety.

In the late 1970s, the U.S. Supreme Court ruled against OSHA, stating its "no risk" policy was too strict, and employers could not follow the regulations. OSHA changed the requirement to a "sufficiently risk-free workplace." The term sufficiently risk-free work place emphasizes the protection of employees from foreseeable health and safety issues. Organizations engaged in any form of

FLSA Component	Caution
1. Exempt versus nonexempt employees	Exempt employees are generally executive, administrative, or professional employees. Job description, wage (salary) rates, methods of payment, and functions performed by the employee should be consistent with exempt or nonexempt status.
2. Time period	Nonexempt employees are entitled to overtime pay, which is calculated for all hours worked over 40 hours in a consecutive seven-day period.
3. Hours worked	Time sheets, time cards, or computerized records should include the time employees signing into work and signing out of work during training programs.
4. Compensable time	Break times when employees are at work but not compensated need to be documented. Restrictions should be in place covering "on-call" employees. These employees, while not at the place of work, are considered to be ready to come to work if needed.
5. Calculation of overtime rates	The regular rate of pay and the hourly rate of pay may differ for some employees. An example may be a pizza delivery person who is paid $7.25 per hour and $1 per delivery. The regular rate of pay is the total of $7.25 and $1 for each delivery within the hour.
6. Exemptions from the regular rate	Commissions or service charges for employees must be documented in addition to other types of compensation (flat or hourly rate).
7. Employees working on more than one job	Employees who perform two jobs with differing job descriptions and rates of pay should receive a weighted average of the two rates for overtime hours.
8. Gratuity versus service charge	Hospitality companies are required to keep accurate records of compensation paid in service charges (i.e., banquet service or room service).
9. Tip credit	Employers must create and maintain a record of all employees who receive tips and amount received as tips. Documentation needs to be kept to assure that employees are actually being covered by the tip credit.
10. Tip pooling	Employers should document and maintain a list of employees included in any tip pooling, percentages for tip-pooling distribution, employer's tracking methods for tip pooling, and management participation in the process.
11. Discrimination	Employers should be prepared to defend their pay discrepancies between men and women in similar jobs.
12. Policies and handbooks	Handbooks and policy manuals have been interpreted as implied contracts between employee and employer. Any actions taken by management must be consistent with these documents.
13. Recordkeeping	Employee records are to be kept for specific time periods. Hard copies or digital records must be kept.
14. Independent contractors	When working with independent contractors, written records or contracts must document that an individual is not an employee, but a contractor.
15. Training time	Hospitality employees must be paid a training wage equal to or greater than the minimum wage.
16. Payment procedures upon termination	A terminated employee is usually paid at the time of termination. The final check should include vacation pay and all other benefits.
17. I-9 documentation	The I-9 form and all supporting documents must be accurate and correct.

FIGURE 3.2 Cautions for Components of FLSA.

Federal laws.   *Credit*: alejandro dans neergaard / Shutterstock.

commerce are subject to OSHA's three types of standards: (a) interim—standards established immediately after the act, and used for a two-year period, (b) permanent—based on NIOSH research, or research by employers, unions, industries, and (c) emergency—issued by the U.S. secretary of labor when immediate action is needed. Citations can be issued in eight different categories:

1. Imminent danger—generally results in a restraining order to stop the work conditions or practice that caused the violation
2. Willful or repeated violations
3. Serious danger
4. Nonserious danger
5. Failure to correct a violation
6. Willful violation that causes an employee's death
7. Posting requirement
8. Minimal violation (or de minimis)

OSHA requirements.   *Credit*: Kathie Nichols / Shutterstock.

Component of OSHA	Impact on Hospitality Managers
Employee rights	Hospitality managers should ensure that employees are provided a safe place to work and should not punish employees who report a violation to OSHA.
HazComm—Employees have the right to know about all hazardous materials in the workplace	Hospitality managers must provide MSDSs for all hazardous materials and make these available to employees in the workplace. Training in the safe use of these materials and a signed statement confirming the training should also be included.
EAPs	Hospitality managers should assess the needs of employees and establish programs to enhance the health of employees.

FIGURE 3.3 Impacts of OSHA on the Workplace.

Under OSHA regulations, employees have certain rights. Employees cannot be punished for refusing to work in an unsafe environment, they cannot be punished for reporting a violation, and they have the right to know about all hazardous material in the workplace. This last right is known as **HazComm**. HazComm states that all chemicals in the workplace must have a **material safety data sheet (MSDS)**. The MSDS states all properties of the chemical, safety concerns, and what to do in case the chemical is spilled or consumed by an employee. The MSDS must be stored in an area where all employees have access while working (not locked in the manager's office). Most hospitality operations now have a policy verifying that each employee has been trained on chemical usage within the workplace.

Employee assistance programs (EAPs)—OSHA is also concerned with the well-being of employees in the workplace. One way employers can help their employees is by establishing EAPs. They are employer-sponsored counseling programs designed to help employees deal with personal problems related to drug or alcohol abuse, stress, family tension, finances, career goals, or other situations that affect their work. EAPs generally involve internal or external counseling services.

EAPs can help companies thrive by promoting healthy practices and lifestyles among employees. Good health leads to happier and more efficient employees. Total annual health care costs reached $2.6 trillion in 2010 and are projected to reach $3.5 trillion in 2015 There appears to be no end in sight to this trend. To reduce health care costs and increase value, a growing number of organizations are empowering their employees to take charge of their health through wellness programs. In 2008, 77 percent of employers offered health and wellness programs, and more than half of those currently without programs plan to add them, many within the next 6 to 12 months. The following practices help build, expand, and continuously evolve a successful wellness program: (a) assess your population, (b) secure visible leadership commitment, support, and participation, (c) build a program that focuses on behavior changes across the health care continuum, (d) leverage data to proactively identify health risks and personalize programs, (e) develop compelling communications and incentives, and (f) create a culture of health.[2] Companies report that they receive a 3-to-1 return for every dollar invested in an EAP.[3]

Family and Medical Leave Act (FMLA) of 1993

The Family and Medical Leave Act of 1993 (FMLA) was established to force employers to grant an eligible employee up to a total of 12 workweeks of unpaid leave during any 12-month period for one or more of the following reasons:

- birth and care of the newborn child of the employee,
- placement for adoption or foster care of a child with the employee,
- care for an immediate family member (spouse, child, or parent) with a serious health condition, or
- care of the employee's own serious health condition.

Serious health condition. *Credit*: Cecilia Lim H M / Shutterstock.

This act requires employers with 50 or more employees who work within a 75-mile radius to adhere to the guidelines. The right to leave applies equally to male and females. Employers who employ both husband and wife can limit their total to 12 weeks annually. Employers must continue health care coverage to employees while on leave. Finally, penalties are severe; employers can be penalized for 100 percent of lost wages and benefits, plus attorney/court cost fees.[4]

Serious health condition means an illness, injury, impairment, or physical or mental condition that involves either:

- inpatient care (i.e., an overnight stay) in a hospital, hospice, or residential medical care facility, including any period of incapacity (i.e., inability to work, attend school, or perform other regular daily activities) or subsequent treatment in connection with such inpatient care; or
- continuing treatment by a health care provider, which includes:
  1. A period of incapacity lasting more than 3 consecutive (a possible revision of up to 10 days is being considered) full calendar days, and any subsequent treatment or period of incapacity relating to the same condition that also includes: (a) treatment two or more times by or under the supervision of a health care provider (i.e., in-person visits, the first within 7 days and both within 30 days of the first day of incapacity), or (b) one treatment by a health care provider (i.e., an in-person visit within 7 days of the first day of incapacity) with a continuing regimen of treatment (e.g., prescription medication, physical therapy);
  2. Any period of incapacity related to pregnancy or for prenatal care. A visit to the health care provider is not necessary for each absence;
  3. Any period of incapacity or treatment for a chronic serious health condition that continues over an extended period of time, requires periodic visits (at least twice a year) to a health care provider, and may involve occasional episodes of incapacity. A visit to a health care provider is not necessary for each absence;
  4. A period of incapacity that is permanent or long-term due to a condition for which treatment may not be effective. Only supervision by a health care provider is required, rather than active treatment; and
  5. Any absences to receive multiple treatments for restorative surgery or for a condition that would likely result in a period of incapacity of more than three days if not treated.[5]

In response to several Supreme Court cases, the FMLA was amended in 2008 by the National Defense Authorization Act for Fiscal Year 2008. It implemented two important new military family leave entitlements for eligible specified family members:

- up to 12 weeks of leave for certain qualifying exigencies arising out of a covered military member's active duty status, or notification of an impending call or order to active duty status, in support of a contingency operation; and

- up to 26 weeks of leave in a single 12-month period to care for a covered service member recovering from a serious injury or illness incurred in the line of duty on active duty. Eligible employees are entitled to a combined total of up to 26 weeks of all types of FMLA leave during the single 12-month period.[6]

FEDERAL LAWS—ENFORCED BY OTHER FEDERAL AGENCIES

Uniformed Services Employment and Reemployment Rights Act of 1994

The Uniformed Services Employment and Reemployment Rights Act of 1994 (USERRA) protects service members' reemployment rights when returning from a period of service in the uniformed services, including those called up from the reserves or National Guard, and prohibits employer discrimination based on military service or obligation. The DOL's Veterans' Employment and Training Service administers USERRA. The act was amended in 1996, 1998, and 2000 to clarify certain points.

The preservice employer must reemploy service members returning from a period of service in the uniformed services if those service members meet five criteria:

- The person must have held a civilian job;
- The person must have given notice to the employer that he or she was leaving the job for service in the uniformed services, unless giving notice was precluded by military necessity or otherwise impossible or unreasonable;
- The cumulative period of service must not have exceeded five years;
- The person must not have been released from service under dishonorable or other punitive conditions; and
- The person must have reported back to the civilian job in a timely manner or have submitted a timely application for reemployment.[7]

Employee Polygraph Protection Act of 1998*

The Employee Polygraph Protection Act of 1988 (EPPA) generally prevents employers from using lie detector tests, either for preemployment screening or during the course of employment, with certain exemptions. Employers generally may not require or request any employee or job applicant to take a lie detector test, or discharge, discipline, or discriminate against an employee or job applicant for refusing to take a test or for exercising other rights under the act. In addition, employers are required to display the EPPA poster in the workplace for their employees. The Employment Standards Administration's Wage and Hour Division enforces the EPPA.

The act defined the following:

- A lie detector includes a polygraph, deceptograph, voice stress analyzer, psychological stress evaluator, or similar device (whether mechanical or electrical) used to render a diagnostic opinion as to the honesty or dishonesty of an individual.
- A polygraph means an instrument that records continuously, visually, permanently, and simultaneously records changes in cardiovascular, respiratory, and electrodermal patterns as minimum instrumentation standards, and is used to render a diagnostic opinion as to the honesty or dishonesty of an individual.

Federal, state, and local governments are excluded. In addition, lie detector tests administered by the federal government to employees of federal contractors engaged in national security intelligence or counterintelligence functions are exempt. The act also includes limited exemptions where polygraph tests (but no other lie detector tests) may be administered in the private sector, subject to certain restrictions:

- to employees who are reasonably suspected of involvement in a workplace incident that results in economic loss to the employer and who had access to the property that is the subject of an investigation,
- to prospective employees of armored car, security alarm, and security guard firms who protect facilities, materials, or operations affecting health or safety, national security, or currency and other like instruments, and

---

* From "FACT SHEET #36: EMPLOYEE POLYGRAPH PROTECTION ACT OF 1988. Revised July 2008. Washington, DC: Wage and Hour Division, U.S. Department of Labor.

- to prospective employees of pharmaceutical and other firms authorized to manufacture, distribute, or dispense controlled substances who will have direct access to such controlled substances, as well as current employees who had access to persons or property that are the subject of an ongoing investigation.[8]

Immigration Reform and Control Act of 1986 (amended in 1990 and 1996)

The Immigration Reform and Control Act of 1986 is designed to mandate employers to document that prospective employees possess the right to work in the United States. Employers with four or more employees are prohibited from discriminating against applicants based on nationality or citizenship. This act is administered by the Department of Justice, and requires employers to distinguish undocumented aliens in the workplace. Aliens hired before 1986 are not affected by the act. Employers are required to have all employees provide authorized documentation for the I-9 form, or documents that prove their right to work within the United States. These documents include: (a) U.S. passport, (b) certificate of nationalization, (c) birth certificate, (d) Social Security card, or (e) other forms listed on the I-9. This act also requires employers to provide a working environment free of ethnic slurs, and verbal or physical abuse related to an individual's national origin. The current I-9 form and other documents are available at the e-verify website.

The Wagner Act of 1935

Also known as the National Labor Relations Act (NLRA), this act's aim was to protect the rights of employees and employers, to encourage collective bargaining, and to curtail certain private sector labor and management practices, which can harm the general welfare of workers, businesses, and the U.S. economy. **Collective bargaining** is defined as the mutual obligation of the employer and the representative of the employees to meet at reasonable times and confer in good faith with respect to wages, hours, and other terms and conditions of employment. **Bargaining in good faith** defines the willingness of each side (management and union) to: (a) attempt to reach an agreement, (b) provide relevant information, and (c) be willing to compromise. Unfair labor practices were defined as:

- interfering with, restraining, or coercing employees
- dominating or interfering with the formation or administration of any labor organization or contributing financial or other support to it
- discriminating in regard to the hire or tenure of employment, or any term or condition of employment, to encourage or discourage membership in any labor organization
- discharging or otherwise discriminating against an employee because he has filed charges or given testimony under this act
- refusing to bargain collectively with the representatives of his employees.[9]

This act also established the five-member (amended in 1947 from the previous count of three members) National Labor Relations Board (NLRB). The board primarily acts as a quasi-judicial body in deciding cases on the basis of formal records in administrative proceedings.[10]

Taft Hartley Act of 1947

The Taft Hartley Act of 1947 amended the Wagner Act, and was renamed the Labor-Management Relations Act. This act qualified or amended much of the NLRA, the federal law regulating labor relations of enterprises engaged in interstate commerce, and it nullified parts of the Federal Anti-Injunction (Norris-LaGuardia) Act of 1932. The act established control of labor disputes on a new basis by enlarging the NLRB and providing that the union or the employer must, before terminating a collective-bargaining agreement, serve notice on the other party and on a government mediation service. The government was empowered to obtain an 80-day injunction against any strike that it deemed a peril to national health or safety. The act also:

- prohibited **jurisdictional strikes** (dispute between two unions over which should act as the bargaining agent for the employees),

Unfair Management Practices	Unfair Union Practices
Interfering with union organizing attempts	Jurisdictional strikes
Discriminating against employees who are union members	Secondary boycotts
Discharge or discrimination against employees who have filed charges	Closed shop, union shop only with majority vote of employees
Refusing to bargain with a union that is certified to represent employees	Featherbedding

FIGURE 3.4   **Management and Union Unfair Practices.**

- prohibited secondary boycotts (boycott against an already organized company doing business with another company that a union is trying to organize),
- declared that it did not extend protection to workers on wildcat strikes,
- prohibited closed shop, **which is where union membership is required before hiring,**
- permitted the union shop only on a vote of a majority of the employees,
- prohibited featherbedding, **which is when a union requires an employer to pay for services that were not performed,**
- established the rights of states to enact right-to-work laws,
- retained collective bargaining provisions, with the extra provision that, before using the facilities of the NLRB, a union must file with the DOL financial reports and affidavits that union officers are not Communists, and
- forbade unions to contribute to political campaigns.[11]

Civil Service Reform Act of 1978

The Civil Service Reform Act of 1978 abolishes the U.S. Civil Service Commission and distributes its functions primarily among three agencies: (a) the newly established Office of Personnel Management, (b) the Merit Systems Protection Board, and (c) EEOC. EEOC assumes responsibility for enforcing antidiscrimination laws applicable to the civilian federal workforce as well as for coordinating all federal equal employment opportunity programs.[12] This act:

- established the Federal Labor Relations Authority (this independent agency included the Office of General Council),
- restricted the issues in collective bargaining between union and management,
- established binding arbitration to resolve disputes (Note: There are three types of intervention: (a) mediation—nonbinding agreement, (b) arbitration—binding agreement, and (c) **mediation/arbitration**—mediation is used first to bring the two sides closer, and then arbitration is used to bind the agreement.)
- prohibited strikes by government employees.

Worker Adjustment and Retraining Notification Act of 1991

The Worker Adjustment and Retraining Notification Act of 1991 (WARN) offers protection to workers, their families, and communities by requiring employers to provide notice 60 days in advance of covered plant closings, covered mass layoffs, or the sale of a business. This notice must be provided to: (a) either affected workers or their representatives (e.g., a labor union), (b) the state dislocated worker unit, and (c) the appropriate unit of local government. In general, employers are covered by WARN if they have 100 or more employees, not counting employees who have worked less than 6 months in the last 12 months, and not counting employees who work an average of less than 20 hours a week.[13] The U.S. Supreme Court has ruled that employers failing to abide by this act will be held responsible, and can be sued by employees or by unions.

STATE LAWS

In addition to the many federal laws, there exist state and local laws that replicate the existing federal laws. In the case of the state and local laws, they add to the provisions of the federal laws. One simple example of this is minimum wage laws. Many states have enacted laws that provide more compensation for hourly workers than the federal law. Also, many states have employment laws that broaden the scope of who must adhere to the federal law by making all employers accountable to the federal standard.

Many states and municipalities have enacted laws that add more protected groups to the federal law list of protected groups. Some of these include: (a) physical appearance, (b) political affiliation, (c) contagious diseases, and (d) sexual preference.

Applications to Hospitality Management

Hospitality employers, managers, and employees, need to be made aware of the potential for harassment, and avoid it at all costs. If a grievance is filed, an employer should not retaliate against the individual, rather the employer should see it as an opportunity to improve the communication process.

Managers must know their responsibility when it comes to I-9 forms, and the length of time documents must be kept on file. I-9 forms are kept in each employee's personnel file, and these files usually are kept on hand for three years.

Employers cannot interfere with union organizing campaigns, and should not coerce or restrain employees from participating. Organizations who don't want unions formed within their structures should be proactive, rather than reactive. These organizations need to be proactive in regard to communication, and understand their employees' wants and desires. Organizations need to be proactive in establishing fair pay policies, safe working conditions, and fair grievance procedures. Reactive measures could include hiring an expert consultant on union organizations, or hiring an expert to explain how the employee–management relations change when a union is formed.

Managers need to be aware of changes in the minimum wage laws, be aware of overtime laws, know child labor standards, and know how to establish pay scales. Again, not only organizations need to train managers to be aware of DOL laws, but also organizations need to train managers on how to keep their workplace safe and their employees healthy. Managers need to be aware of all posting regulations, and organizations can make this easier by provide checklists for managers to follow. Organizations need to set concise policies and procedures in regard to FMLA and USERRA. Finally, hospitality organizations need to outlaw the use of lie detectors.

THE BOTTOM LINE

It is important to note that the body of law presented in this chapter contains only some of the major federal laws affecting the work environment. There are numerous other statutes and matters of tort or common law that fall within the domain of HR management. One requirement for HR management is a thorough knowledge of statutes and laws that have anything to do with the terms, conditions, rights, or privileges of employment. HR managers must always be prepared to learn new laws, or amended laws. In fact, it would be irresponsible if they were not constantly updating their knowledge of the pertinent laws. HR managers can (and often do) retain legal counsel with expertise in this area. It should be noted that legal professionals are not usually trained in the techniques of management. As we will discover in the remaining chapters of this text, the responsibility of HR managers is to provide employees with a workplace that is safe, healthy, and professionally managed.

Discussion Questions

1. How does harassment differ from discrimination?
2. How do companies manage the aspects of FLSA?
3. In the next few years, what are the emerging issues for OSHA?
4. How can OSHA help with employee health?
5. How do EAPs impact the work environment?
6. What impact will FMLA have on hospitality companies?
7. How is a serious health condition different than a reasonable accommodation?

8. What is the difference between a lie detector and a polygraph?

9. How has the Wagner Act and Taft-Hartley Act been an influence on hospitality employees?

10. Hospitality companies want employees who come in contact with customers to look good.
    Can they do this? Why or why not?

11. What is the difference between arbitration and mediation?

Application Exercise

1. At the beginning of this chapter, you were presented with a situation where you noticed a crack in a microwave oven door, your manager has told you that it is safe to work around the microwave, and you begin to have headaches. You decide to call OSHA, and report the microwave oven. The next time you go to work, an OSHA representative is present, and is inspecting the entire restaurant. The inspector cites the cracked glass on the microwave, and gives the manager immediate notice to fix it. The manager has two cooks remove the microwave to the dumpster, which makes the inspector very happy.

2. Two weeks later, you are asked to the general manager's office, and she terminates you for your tardiness (even though this was the first time you have ever been tardy). You begin to wonder if she terminated you for reporting the microwave to OSHA.

3. Place yourself into the position of the general manager of the pancake house, and prepare a memo to the district manager on how you will address this issue in the future. Please have a minimum of three action steps to take.

Endnotes

1. From http://www.eeoc.gov/types/sexual_harassment.html
2. Rosen, M., & Spaulding, T. (2009). Best practices for wellness programs. *Occupational Health & Safety*, 78(7), 55.
3. SAP Services: A natural extension of EAPs. *Journal of Employee Assistance*, July 2005.
4. From http://www.dol.gov/esa/whd/fmla/
5. From http://www.dol.gov/esa/whd/regs/compliance/whdfs28.pdf
6. From http://www.dol.gov/esa/whd/fmla/finalrule.htm
7. From http://www.dol.gov/compliance/laws/comp-userra.htm
8. From http://www.dol.gov/esa/whd/regs/compliance/whdfs36.htm
9. From http://www.nlrb.gov/about_us/overview/national_labor_relations_act.aspx
10. From http://www.nlrb.gov/about_us/overview/national_labor_relations_act.aspx
11. From http://www.infoplease.com/ce6/bus/A0847620.html
12. From http://www.reference.com/browse/Civil%20Service%20Reform%20Act%20of%201978
13. From http://www.doleta.gov/programs/factsht/warn.htm

Key Terms

Arbitration   An alternative dispute resolution method that uses a neutral third party (i.e., arbitrator) to resolve individual, group, or labor management conflicts and issue a binding decision.

Closed shop   Organizations that require union membership prior to hiring.

Collective bargaining   An agreement or a contract, which discloses the terms and conditions that, shall apply to the union–management relationship within a particular operation.

Emergency standard   Issued by the U.S. secretary of labor when immediate action is needed to correct a workplace safety issue.

Employee assistance programs (EAPs)   A work-based intervention program designed to identify and assist employees in resolving personal problems (i.e., marital, financial, or emotional problems; family issues; substance/alcohol abuse) that may be adversely affecting the employee's performance.

Featherbedding   An unfair labor practice occurring when a union requires an employer to pay an employee for services he or she did not perform.

Good faith bargaining   Principles applied to conducting negotiations where two parties meet and confer at reasonable times with open minds and the intention of reaching an agreement.

Harassment   Conduct or actions—based on race, religion, sex, national origin, age, disability, military membership, or veteran status—severe or pervasive enough to create a hostile, abusive, or intimidating work environment for a reasonable person. State laws may further define *harassment* to include additional protections, such as sexual orientation, marital status, transsexualism or cross-dressing, political affiliation, criminal record, prior psychiatric treatment, occupation, citizenship status, personal appearance, matriculation, tobacco use outside work, Appalachian origin, receipt of public assistance, or dishonorable discharge from the military.

HazComm   The employee's right to know about all hazardous material in the workplace.

Interim standard   A guideline established by OSHA immediately after the act, and used for a two-year period.

Jurisdictional strikes   Disputes between two unions over which should act as the bargaining agent for the employees.

Mediation   A private negotiation and decision-making process in which a mediator assists individuals or groups in finding a resolution to a particular issue or conflict.

Material safety data sheets (MSDSs)   Required by OSHA, an MSDS is a detailed description of each hazardous chemical located in the workplace, which includes information regarding potential health risks, symptoms, and treatment measures to be taken if exposure occurs.

Permanent standard   Guidelines established by OSHA and based on NIOSH research, or research by employers, unions, industries.

Polygraph test   An instrument that records continuously, visually, permanently, and simultaneously records changes in cardiovascular, respiratory, and electrodermal patterns as minimum instrumentation standards, and is used to render a diagnostic opinion as to the honesty or dishonesty of an individual.

Right-to-work laws   A state law preventing labor–management agreements requiring an individual to join a union as a condition of employment.

Secondary boycotts   A boycott against an already organized company doing business with another company that a union is trying to organize.

Serious health condition   An illness, injury, impairment, or physical or mental condition that involves inpatient care in a hospital, hospice, or residential medical care facility or continuing treatment by a health care provider.

Sexual harassment   Unwelcome sexual advances, requests for sexual favors, and other verbal or physical conduct of a sexual nature constitute sexual harassment when this conduct explicitly or implicitly affects an individual's employment, unreasonably interferes with an individual's work performance, or creates an intimidating, hostile, or offensive work environment.

Wildcat strikes   Strikes not recognized by union leadership. In most wildcat strikes, one group of employees strikes over issues that relate only to their work unit. Employers can replace workers in wildcat strikes and can sue the union for damages.

Planning for Staffing

KEY TERMS

Alternative employees

Autonomy

Career ladders

Career lattices

Dictionary of Occupational Titles

Feedback from job

Fixed labor expense

Hawthorne Effect

Heisenberg Effect

Highly structured questionnaire (PAQ)

Job analysis

Job compatibility index (JCI)

Job description

Job design

Job enlargement

Job enrichment

Job rotation

Job simplification

Job specification

Labor forecasting

Outsourced employees

Part-time employees

Performance standards

Permanent employees

Productivity

Productivity standards

Seasonality

Task characteristics

Task identity

Task significance

Task variety

Team building

Temporary employees

Variable labor expense

OBJECTIVES

■ Explain the importance and functions of job design, and then use this information to help managers apply the techniques of job design

■ Explain the six steps in job design

- Define knowledge, skills, and abilities
- Define career ladders and lattices
- Explain methods of forecasting
- Demonstrate, and then apply forecasting and trend analysis

Consider This

You are the HR director for a large restaurant company. You are accompanying the CEO of the company on a tour of a restaurant. You witness an extremely busy dinner shift, but notice that employees seemed to be very stressed about their jobs. You overhear the general manager talking to his assistant manager about staffing, and their need to have more employees. Do they really need more employees? Or do you need to analyze the jobs in your company, to better match the current work environment?

INTRODUCTION

The success of every organization is dependent upon the performance of its employees. Ideally, all of the jobs in an organization should interrelate so that the achievement of the organization's vision, mission, goals, and objectives is optimized. The stakeholders' return on investment of this synergistic effect will be influenced to a large extent by how well each employee understands his or her role in the organization. The outstanding performance of employees in well-structured jobs has the potential to impact every major core competency area of HR, for better or for worse, depending on the adequacy of the underlying job analysis practices in place within the organization.[1] Many times companies will discuss the knowledge, skills, and abilities of their applicants as they seek the "best fit" for their company. Most of the companies will assess the knowledge of their applicants by testing and determining the intelligence of the applicant. Every company strives for a succinct and efficient staffing system.

JOB ANALYSIS AND JOB DESIGN

In order to properly match jobs and workers, the public employment service system requires that a uniform occupational language be used in all of its local job service offices. Occupational analysts collect data provided to job interviewers and then systematically compare and match the specifications of employer job openings with the qualifications of applicants who are seeking

Job analysis.   *Credit*: Minerva Studio / Shutterstock

jobs through its facilities. Through this work, these analysts have compiled the Dictionary of Occupational Titles (DOT). The DOT was developed in response to the demand for standardized occupational information to support an expanding public employment service. The U.S. Employment Service established a federal–state employment service system, and initiated an occupational research program, utilizing analysts located in numerous field offices throughout the country, in order to collect the information required. The use of this information has expanded from matching job applications to various uses for employment counseling, occupational and career guidance, and labor market information services.[2]

The DOT can be very useful in job analysis and design. Job design is often used simultaneously with job analysis. Job design makes the work interesting and meaningful; it allows for ability and skill development, or explains how the job will be done. Job design involves defining the combination of tasks and responsibilities associated with the job. Job analysis is the systematic study of jobs to determine what activities and responsibilities they include, their relative importance in comparison with other jobs, the personal qualifications necessary for performance of the jobs, and the conditions under which the work is performed.

An important concept in job analysis is that an evaluation is conducted of the job, not the person doing the job (even though some job analysis data may be collected from incumbents).[3]

Providing this kind of work means taking a close look at how jobs are designed. For example, by organizing work into teams, or making better use of job rotation, job enlargement, job simplification, and cross-training strategies, employers can better meet the expectations of all parties involved (employees, stakeholders, and management). One way that employers can meet these aspirations is through more flexible forms of work organization that may provide more opportunities for workers to use their skills, do a variety of tasks, and have more influence over their work. An example of this is when a server in a restaurant has the knowledge, skills, and abilities to become a greeter, a cook, or even a bartender. While job design and job analysis are similar, we recognize six steps that are important to both processes.

Determining Knowledge, Skills, and Abilities: Methods of Data Collection

It is not easy to determine what employees actually do on the job. Direct observation is influenced by the perceptions of the observer. The most effective technique, if feasible, is to collect information directly from the most qualified job incumbent(s). One of the best ways to understand a job is to have the job analyst do the job. This allows the analyst to perform the job functions, and hopefully get a better understanding of the job. Usually, it is preferable to use two methods, if possible—for example, direct observation and a set of questionnaires from job incumbents for the analysis, or interviews and open-ended questionnaires from the job incumbents. Figure 4.1 provides a comparison of methods.

The simplest and least expensive way to collect the information is direct observation, but note that this is not free of problems. The Hawthorne Effect can have an impact on employee performance. The name came from a study conducted at the Western Electric Company's Hawthorne Works in the Chicago area. Researchers observed employees at work in this plant to gauge productivity. They hypothesized that if the lighting level were increased, productivity would increase. One floor of the plant was left alone (the control group), and on the other floor, the lighting level was increased. Researchers found that productivity levels did increase. The next hypothesis was to decrease lighting levels, and checking for a decrease in productivity (again using a control group). Researchers found that productivity increased rather than decrease. The researchers surmised that if employees knew they were being observed, they would perform at higher levels, thus the Hawthorne Effect.

The second phenomenon in collecting data dealt with interviews. When most people are interviewed, the interviewees are susceptible to the Heisenberg Effect. This effect describes the tendency of people to subconsciously give answers they think the interviewer wants to hear. The interviewer has to be aware of this phenomenon, and must account for it in data collection. Another way around this effect is to interview multiple employees.

The next area of concern is with questionnaires. The highly structured questionnaires (or sometimes referred to as the position analysis questionnaire, the PAQ) asks employees to rate their work on a predetermined scale. These scales are often designed to evaluate the difficulty, frequency, and importance of the job. While the PAQ provides a useful method of quantifying

Job Analysis Method	Description	Benefits
Open-ended questionnaire	Questionnaires filled out by employees and managers asking about the knowledge, skills, and abilities necessary to perform the job. Answers are combined to form a list of job requirements	Produces reliable job requirements with input from both employees and managers
Highly structured questionnaire	Questionnaires that allow specific responses to determine the frequency, importance, and the skills required for tasks	Objective approach that enables analysis using computer models
Interview	Face-to-face interview with the employee about knowledge, skills, and abilities needed to perform the job	Consistent format with new questions added based on the response of the employee
Observation	Direct observation of employees performing the tasks of a job. Observations are analyzed to determine required knowledge, skills, and abilities	Provides a realistic view of the daily tasks and activities performed in a job
Work diary or log	Diary or anecdotal record maintained by the employee. Frequency and timing of tasks are recorded over an extended period of time. Logs are analyzed to determine duties and responsibilities	Provides an enormous amount of data that may be difficult to interpret
Critical incidents	Observation and recording of actual events	Provide examples for how services should be provided
Performance evaluations	Periodic reviews and evaluation of an individual's job performance	Provide multiple perspectives if the process is two-sided

FIGURE 4.1 **Methods of Data Collection for Jobs.**[4]

information about the job, it is dependent on the employee to provide honest answers to all questions. Other types of questionnaire are the management position description questionnaire (MPDQ) and the Minnesota job description questionnaire (MJDQ). The MPDQ collects information about management work in 13 different areas, while the MJDQ is a more popular generic instrument. Research has shown that the MJDQ is not effective because jobs are as unique as the people doing the jobs. Each company will need to analyze and design its jobs appropriately in order to fit the company's needs.[5]

The Heisenberg Effect.
Credit: StockLite / Shutterstock

Combine Similar Tasks

The following information is generally helpful in making distinctions between jobs: (a) knowledge, skills, and abilities needed, (b) work activities and behaviors, (c) interactions with others (internal and external), (d) performance standards, (e) financial budgeting and impact, (f) machines and equipment used, (g) working conditions, and (h) supervision given and received.

While this information provides the job analyst with an overview of the organizational context in which a job interacts with others, it is also helpful in understanding how jobs are grouped within organizations. One unique approach in combining similar tasks is from Carroll and Sturman.[6] Their **job compatibility index (JCI)** provides a method for comparing jobs based on their component skills. The index compiles the compatibility score and importance rating of each of 35 skills for the job in question. To arrive at a single index score, the compatibility of each skill is weighted by its importance. By adding up the resulting scores, one can see how a seemingly unrelated job is in fact a potential source for hospitality employees. Caroll and Sturman use an example of a hotel front-desk clerk. Their index identifies nine jobs that involve most of the same skills, only three of them in the hospitality industry, expanding the reach of the potential labor pool by tenfold. Some nonhospitality jobs that require skills similar to the front-desk job include personal and home-care aides, nursery workers, and lifeguards; they can be a potential source of applicants for employers. Thus, the JCI identifies opportunities for both employers and workers.[7]

Determine Responsibilities and Outcomes

The HR department and line management must work closely together to ensure that the job analysis process works efficiently and effectively. A typical division of responsibilities between human resources and line management is outlined in Figure 4.2.

Determine Equipment Needs

Current employment law requires job descriptions to describe the physical requirements needed to perform the primary duties of the job. These include the ability to meet minimum strength demands, agility demands, sensory demands, and mobility standards to effectively and safely satisfy the job requirements. The law also requires the inclusion of environmental conditions. This could include conditions of extreme temperatures, high elevations, enclosed spaces, high noise levels, extended periods of standing/sitting, or any other extraordinary condition. Many times, the other conditions are influenced by machinery. An example could be a hotel maintenance person who needs to use a floor buffer. This individual would need to have knowledge about the machine, the ability to control the machine, and the skill to operate the machine; and the job requires usage of ear plugs to block possible noise pollution.

Motivational Work Characteristics

Numerous categories of job characteristics are significant in terms of motivation and performance. First, **task characteristics** have been the most commonly investigated motivational work

Human Resources	Line Management
• Coordinates job analysis process	• Completes or designates staff members to complete job analysis information
• Drafts job descriptions and specifications for review by management	• Reviews and maintains accuracy of job descriptions and specifications
• Periodically reviews job descriptions and specifications	• Requests revisions to analysis as jobs change
• Reviews managerial input to ensure accuracy	• Identifies performance standards based on job analysis information
• May seek advice from outside sources for difficult or unusual analyses	• May serve as subject matter expert/panel member
• May serve as job analyst or panel facilitator	

FIGURE 4.2   Typical Division of Responsibilities: Job Analysis.

Determine equipment needs.
Credit: Christian Delbert /
Shutterstock

design characteristics. Task characteristics are primarily concerned with how the work itself is accomplished and the range and nature of tasks associated with a particular job.

AUTONOMY   Perhaps the most widely studied work characteristic is that of autonomy, which has assumed a central place in motivational work design approaches. It was initially viewed as the amount of freedom and independence an individual has in terms of carrying out his or her work assignment; however, recent research has expanded this conceptualization to suggest that autonomy reflects the extent to which a job allows freedom, independence, and discretion to schedule work, and also to make decisions to choose the methods used to perform tasks. Thus, autonomy includes three interrelated aspects centered on freedom in (a) work scheduling, (b) decision making, and (c) work methods.

TASK VARIETY   Task variety refers to the degree to which a job requires employees to perform a wide range of tasks on the job. As such, it is similar to notions of task enlargement discussed in the literature. Jobs that involve the performance of a number of different work activities are likely to be more interesting and enjoyable to perform.

TASK SIGNIFICANCE   Task significance reflects the degree to which a job influences the lives or work of others, whether inside or outside the organization. People in jobs that have a significant effect on the physical or psychological well-being of others are likely to experience greater meaningfulness in their work.

TASK IDENTITY   Task identity reflects the degree to which a job involves a whole piece of work, the results of which can be easily identified. Jobs that involve an intact task, such as providing a complete unit of service or putting together an entire product, are invariably more interesting to perform than jobs that involve only small parts of the task.

FEEDBACK FROM JOB   Feedback from the job reflects the degree to which the job provides direct and clear information about the effectiveness of task performance. The focus is on feedback directly from the job itself or knowledge of one's own work activities, as opposed to feedback from others. This focus is thought to enhance knowledge of the results of the job.[8]

Other techniques that can help motivate employees are job simplification, job enlargement, job enrichment, job rotation, team building, and career ladders. **Job simplification** is breaking down a job into its smallest tasks and evaluating the work in each of these smaller components. **Job enlargement** is just the opposite of simplification; here tasks are added. Typically, the tasks involve similar skills and abilities. This is sometimes referred to as horizontal job expansion because the job is developed with more tasks, or the employee is being stretched to do more. This acts to help motivate employees because of the added responsibilities.

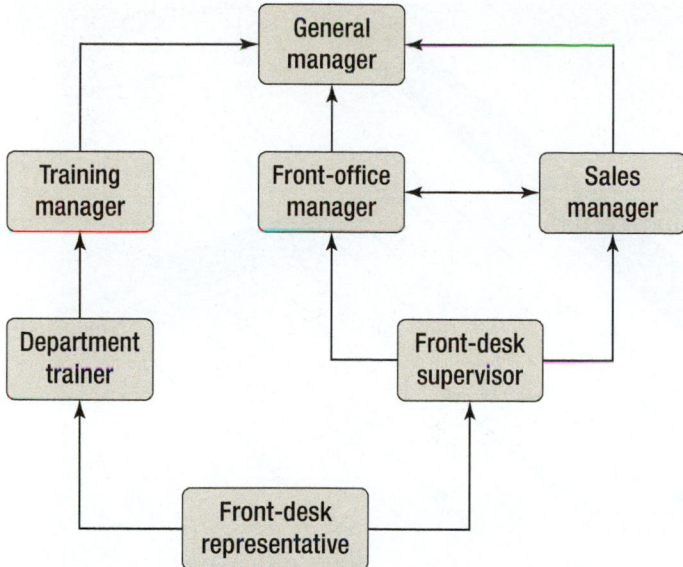

FIGURE 4.3   Sample Career Ladder.

Job enrichment, also called vertical job expansion, is when responsibilities are added to the jobs that are not similar to other tasks/responsibilities. Because the tasks are not similar, the motivating factor is to enhance the job with more responsibilities, thus expanding the job with more management responsibilities. An example could be a cook is given the additional tasks of rotating stock, completing product-ordering procedures, inventorying products at the end of the business period, and then possibly calculating a food cost percentage. **Job rotation** is used to alleviate some of the boredom that is inherent in jobs. Here, an employee is rotated among different jobs; an example may be from a pizza order taker, to assembly of the pizzas, to cutting and boxing the finished product, to delivering the product. This system requires employees to be cross-trained. **Team building** views employees as members of work groups rather than individuals. The goal is to promote productivity within the team, and to get the team motivated. This technique will take several training sessions, and can also be counterproductive as it can lead to competition within the group.

Career ladders and **lattices** consist of a group of related jobs that comprise a career. They often include a pictorial representation of job progression in a career as well as detailed descriptions of the jobs and include the experiences that facilitate movement between jobs. Career ladders/lattices are not necessarily organization-specific; they frequently span multiple organizations because movement within one organization may not be possible. Career ladders display only vertical movement between jobs. In contrast, career lattices contain both vertical and lateral movement between jobs and may reflect more closely the career paths of today's work environment.[9] A sample career ladder is included in Figure 4.3.

DEVELOP JOB DESCRIPTIONS AND JOB SPECIFICATIONS

The output from the job design/analysis process is used to develop a job description and its job specifications. **Job descriptions** summarize the tasks, responsibilities, and duties of the job, while **job specifications** summarize the knowledge, skills, and abilities (KSAs) of the job. Together, they represent a summary of the job analysis information in an organized format and provide a basis for job-related actions on the part of the company. As a general rule, job descriptions and job specifications are combined into one document but compartmentalized into separate sections, which can be updated independently as job changes occur. These sections are outlined next.

IDENTIFICATION   The first part of the job description is the identification section, in which the title, reporting relationships, department, location, and the date of the analysis may be provided.

Job description. *Credit*: Pixsooz / Shutterstock

It is customary to note other information that is useful in tracking positions and employees through the human resource information system. Additional items commonly noted in this section are the following:

- Job code
- Pay grade
- Exempt/nonexempt status under the Fair Labor Standards Act of 1938 (FLSA)
- EEOC (Equal Employment Opportunity Commission) Classification (from EEO-1 form)

JOB SUMMARY   The second part, a descriptive summary, is a concise statement of the general duties and responsibilities that make the job unique.

DUTIES AND RESPONSIBILITIES   The third part of the job description lists the essential duties and responsibilities of the position. It should contain clear, declarative statements in order of priority of the major tasks, duties, and responsibilities of the job incumbent.

JOB SPECIFICATIONS   The fourth section identifies the essential skills and experience plus the nonessential skills and experience (i.e., preferred qualifications) to perform the job. It should provide all information necessary to determine what accommodations might or might not be possible under Americans with Disabilities Act of 1990 (ADA) regulations. Job specifications are typically designated as KSAs, education and experience, physical demands, and work environment, depending on the nature and scope of the job.

DISCLAIMER AND APPROVAL SECTION   It is recommended that the final section of the job description includes a formal legal disclaimer and approval section. The purpose of the disclaimer is to notify the employee that the job description is not a "contract" between the employee and the employer, that the job description duties may be changed at the discretion of the employer, and/or that the employer may request the employee to perform duties that are not listed on the job description. The approval component should include a section for the signature and the date approved by the supervisor and the HR department. The job description should also be acknowledged and dated by the job incumbent.[10]

Job descriptions and career ladders can be used to develop a pipeline of employees who are trained and ready to move up in the organization. This succession plan identifies at least one potential employee with the ability and performance needed for each position in the organization. Once the employee is identified, a plan for training and development is prepared and executed. Figure 4.4 presents an example of a job description and a job specification.

Title: Wait Staff.

Reports to shift manager
Hourly, tipped position, 20 to 40 hours per week

Job Summary: Take customer's orders, serve food and beverages, prepare itemized checks, and accept payments

Duties and Responsibilities:
Serve food and beverages to guests at 4 to 6 tables as determined by the management
Prepare itemized checks, accept payments, and handle transactions using point of sale system
Must know menu items, prices, and methods of preparation
Interact with guests to meet their needs
Use ServsSafe Alcohol principles when serving alcoholic beverages to guests
Maintain sanitation standards and complete side work
Dress in appropriate uniform and meet required appearance standards
Perform additional duties as escorting guests to tables, setting up tables, and clearing tables

Job Specification:

Essential skills:
Should be professional and polite, have good interpersonal skills, and be reliable
Should be able to sell menu items to guests while meeting their needs
Must learn about menu items and describe food proficiently
Have basic reading, writing, and math skills
Must transport food and beverage items between dining room and kitchen
Must be of legal age to serve alcoholic beverages

Preferred skills and experience:
Experience working in a full service restaurant is preferred

Working conditions:
High temperatures and humidity and slick floors and surfaces
Lifting up to 30 pounds
Standing on feet for full shift
Continuously reach, bend, lift, carry, stoop, and wipe

FIGURE 4.4   Sample Job Description and Job Specification.

DETERMINING FULL-TIME AND PART-TIME NEEDS

Once an organization's jobs have been legally analyzed and designed with job descriptions and job specifications, the organization then needs to hire the necessary people to perform the tasks. The organization needs to determine the type (or classification) of employees needed. The organization will need to consider the size, image, culture, and current status of the job market. Next, the organization will need to determine the status of the employees, either permanent employees or alternative employees. **Permanent employees** are the main staff in the organization and usually work 30 to 40 hours per week and receive some type of benefit package. **Alternative employees** often do not work regularly scheduled shifts, and are predominant in hospitality companies. There are usually three types of alternative employees: temporary, part time, and outsourced. **Temporary employees**, or temps, are not employed by the organization; rather, they are obtained from an employment agency. Besides paying the employment agency the wages for their employees, there is also a fee paid to the agency. **Part-time employees** generally work 20 hours or less, and many times may work only one to three shifts per week. They are extremely valuable for covering the busy shifts of many hospitality companies. Part-time employees are rarely provided a benefits package. **Outsourced employees** are contracted by a third party to perform a specific task or function for a significant period of time. The task or function may be performed on-site or off-site. An example of outsourcing is when housekeeping functions are contracted to an outside cleaning agency.

To determine staffing patterns, managers must be aware of several terms:

- **Productivity** is the amount of work output by an individual employee during a given time period.
- **Productivity standards** are the defined and acceptable criteria of work output units (quantity).
- **Performance standards** are the quality criteria established for each task of the job.
- **Labor forecasting** is any method used to determine minimum number of positions and relationships with various factors of the organization (i.e., numbers of servers to customers, numbers of servers per meal period, and number of front-desk agents to rooms sold).
- **Fixed labor expense** is the costs associated with the minimum number of employees needed to operate the business.
- **Variable labor expense** is the costs that vary with the volume of the business. Managers usually have more control over variable labor expenses.

Determining Minimum Number of Positions

If productivity standards have not been set, the organization can establish these by reviewing historical data over a determined period. Productivity standards need to be set so that they are specific, measurable, attainable, and realistic, and should have a time frame. When productivity standards are set too high (or too low), then they can serve to de-motivate employees. This is because the standards are not achievable. Many times productivity standards are based on the required labor hours, but organizations can choose numerous possibilities (number of employees, number of meals, number of rooms available, number of rooms sold). Once the productivity standards are set, the business will need to monitor the standards with actual results (by comparing actual results to budgeted results). The ratio of employees to guests is a productivity standard that assists a manager when preparing schedules for employees. The manager will then only need the other component, that is, anticipating guest volume (or sales volume).

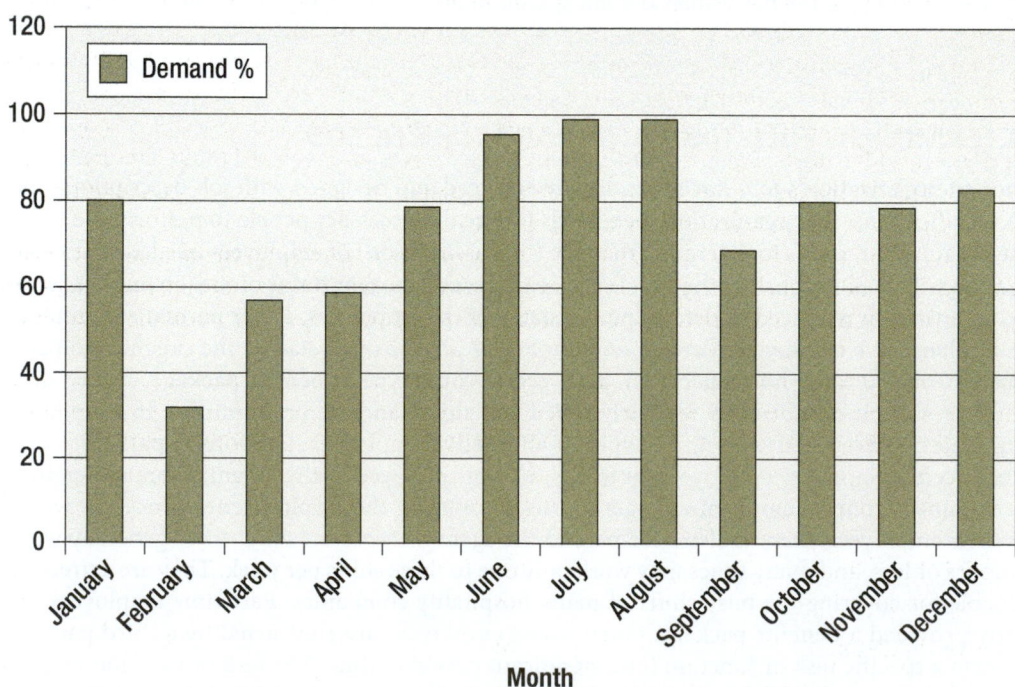

FIGURE 4.5   **Example of Seasonality of Demand.**   (*Credit*: Doriann Hilton Dennison)

Sales	Weight	Projection
Last week = $5,325	25%	$1,331,25
Prior week = $6,775	75%	$5,081.25
Forecast	100%	$6,412.50 or $6, 412

FIGURE 4.6 Sales Forecast Calculations.

Determining Relationships with Number of Customers Served

Accuracy in forecasting is essential for any organization, and this is especially true for the hospitality industry. The best source of information is accumulated from previous periods. Some organizations will forecast by using last year's data, some by using last month's data, and some by using last week's data. Whatever source is used, the business seeks accuracy. Most hospitality organizations will start with sales information (meals or rooms) to determine the number of guests that will visit the business.

There are numerous methods of forecasting. A more complicated model of forecasting such as regression analysis is beyond the scope of this book. Whatever method of forecasting a business chooses to use, the business must consider seasonality. Seasonality is a variation in business volume due to a particular season. An example of seasonality is a restaurant that is located within a popular shopping mall, and it is the week before Christmas. The business will need to forecast the history of this event compared to other seasons of the year. It will more than likely see an increase in sales due to the season, and will thus adjust its forecast based on seasonality.

The simplest method is to calculate an average. Again, this will be done with the data from a specific time period. A manager may use a weighted average, putting more emphasis on a certain period of information. An example of a weighted average is to use a two-week period because many companies pay their employees every two weeks. Let's say a pizza company wants to project sales for a busy Friday night. This Friday is a payday, so it could use last Friday's sales and weight it at 25 percent, and then use the prior Friday's sales at a weight of 75 percent because it would also coincide with a payday. With this information, the manager can calculate the projected number of guests. This is accomplished by dividing the sales amount by guest check average (GCA). If a restaurant's GCA = $16.03, then according to the calculation explained, 400 guests are expected ($6,412/$16.03). These calculations are presented in Figure 4.6.

Once the manager has forecasted sales, the manager can then use the productivity standard to determine the number of employees needed. Continuing with the previous example, if the productivity standard for servers is ten customers per hour, and the restaurant is open for 5 hours on Friday night (5 p.m. to 10 p.m.), then eight servers are required (400/5 hours/10 customers). But the manager must know to expect fluctuations in the business volume (within the hours), and must schedule accordingly (see Figure 4.7).

To maximize profits, and because the business volume is not steady, the manager will need to stagger schedules. The manager must schedule someone before 5 p.m. to set up, and will probably keep more than one person on the schedule after 9 p.m. to help facilitate the cleanup of

Hours of Operation	Anticipated Customers	Labor Requirement
5 p.m. to 6 p.m.	60	6
6 p.m. to 7 p.m.	150	15
7 p.m. to 8 p.m.	150	15
8 p.m. to 9 p.m.	30	3
9 p.m. to 10 p.m.	10	1

FIGURE 4.7 Staffing Schedule Example.

the restaurant. If the manager schedules all servers to come in and leave at the same time, the manager will not maximize profits.

To help maximize profits, the manager will need to determine total labor hours. Again, the manager will depend on productivity standards and history. Once the manager has this information, the manager will be able to stagger the schedule to maximize profits. Once the manager has determined total labor hours, the manager will be able to calculate a budget for labor dollars. The easiest way to do this is by taking the total labor hours multiplied by the average wage paid to the position. (In our example, total labor hours times the average wage of servers.) Or the manager could complete the schedule, and use each server's wage rate to compile the budgeted labor expense. After the time period is over, the manager can calculate an actual labor expense and compare it to the budgeted labor expense. Most companies use a number of software programs to make these calculations for them.

THE BOTTOM LINE

A job is the building block of an organization. Jobs help the organization form a basis for work groups, teams, departments, or larger units. Jobs help the organization achieve its' mission and vision. Because we live in a dynamic world, jobs are constantly changing; thus the organization will constantly study its jobs to ensure efficiency in the work setting. This is accomplished with job analysis and job design. There are numerous ways to collect information about the job; the organization must know that it is not always an easy task. While collecting the data, the job analyst must also consider the mental and physical needs of the job, and relate this to the employee.

The organization must also plan for its labor needs. It must establish productivity standards and performance standards for its employees. And the organization must establish service requirements, as dictated by its customers. Once these standards and requirements are established, the company will have to determine its forecasts—whether it is sales, customers, or employees—and many times a combination of all of these forecasts is needed to create efficiency within the company.

Discussion Questions

1. How does job analysis differ from job design?
2. What are the advantages and disadvantages of job analysis?
3. How do the Hawthorne Effect and the Heisenberg Effect influence the productivity within a company?
4. How is job enlargement different from job enrichment?
5. What is the difference between job descriptions and job specifications?
6. What are some of the legal issues hospitality managers must consider when designing a job?
7. How can a career ladder be used to develop employees?
8. How can productivity be defined in the workplace?
9. How will a hotel manager determine forecast for a holiday?
10. How will seasonality impact a hotel's forecast?

Application Exercise

Complete a job analysis for a lodging manager position using the description at the Bureau of Labor Statistics website. Answer the following questions.

1. What is the job title?
2. How does the job fit into the rest of the organization? What jobs are comparable in the organization?
3. What is the chain of command? Is this person responsible for monitoring the work of others?
4. Describe the internal and external contacts of this position.
5. What duties and tasks are performed by the person holding this job? What are the physical requirements of the job?
6. What tools and equipment are needed for this job?
7. Describe the baseline KSAs needed to perform this job.

Endnotes

1. Weatherley, L. (2004). *SHRM Learning System: Workforce planning and employment: Module two.* Alexandria, VA: Society for Human Resource Management.
2. From http://wwwm.info.org/onet/
3. Weatherley, *SHRM Learning System.*
4. Weatherley, *SHRM Learning System.*
5. Edwards, J., Scully, J., & Brtek, M. (1999). The measurement of work: Hierarchical representation of the multi-method job design questionnaire. *Psychology*, 52(2), 305–335.
6. Carroll, W., & Sturman, M. (2009). A new approach to defining the hospitality job market. *Cornell Hospitality Report*, 9(1), 1–13.

7. Ibid.
8. Morgeson, F., & Humphrey, S. (2006). The work design questionnaire (WDQ): Developing and validating a comprehensive measure for assessing job design and the nature of work. *Journal of Applied Psychology*, 91(6), 1321–1339.
9. www.onetcenter.org
10. Weatherley, *SHRM Learning System*.

Key Terms

Alternative employees   People who often do not work regularly schedule shifts.

Autonomy   Viewed as the amount of freedom and independence an individual has in terms of carrying out his or her work assignment.

Career ladders   A progression of increasingly more responsible positions within an organization or an industry.

Career lattices   Contain both vertical and lateral movements between jobs and may reflect more closely the career paths of today's work environment.

Dictionary of Occupation Titles   A listing developed by U.S. Employment Services containing over 2,100 new occupational definitions.

Feedback from job   Reflects the degree to which the job provides direct and clear information about the effectiveness of task performance.

Fixed labor expense   Costs associated with minimum number of employees needed to operate the business.

Hawthorne Effect   The Hawthorne Effect is a psychological phenomenon that produces an improvement in human behavior or performance as a result of increased attention from superiors, clients, or colleagues.

Heisenberg Effect   Named after German Nobel-laureate physicist Werner Karl Heisenberg (1901–1976), it is reflected in the interviewing process where the interviewees tend to give answers they think the interviewer wants to hear.

Highly structure questionnaire (PAQ)   Sometimes referred to as the position analysis questionnaire (the PAQ), the survey asks employees to rate their work on a predetermined scale.

Job analysis   The systematic process of gathering, examining, and interpreting data, regarding the specific tasks comprising a job.

Job compatibility index (JCI)   A method for comparing jobs based on their component skills. This index compiles the compatibility score and importance rating of each of 35 skills for the job in question. To arrive at a single index score, the compatibility of each skill is weighted by its importance.

Job description   A written description of a job, which includes information regarding the general nature of the work to be performed, specific responsibilities and duties, and the employee characteristics required to perform the job.

Job design   The process of structuring a job by adding, changing, or eliminating certain tasks or functions in order to make the job more satisfying or challenging.

Job enlargement   A method used to keep workers motivated, this process involves adding new tasks that are of the same level of skill and responsibility to a job.

Job enrichment   The practice of adding tasks to a job as a means of increasing the amount of employee control or responsibility.

Job rotation   The practice of transferring employees for temporary periods of time between varying jobs within an organization. Often used as a training and development method.

Job simplification   The practice of breaking down a job into its smallest tasks and evaluating the work in each of these smaller components.

Job specification   A form that details the personal characteristics such as education level, training, work experience, and abilities required in an applicant in order to be successful in a specific job or position.

Labor forecasting   A business analysis conducted in order to assess what future trends are likely to happen, especially in connection with a particular situation, function, practice, or process that is likely to affect the organization's business operations.

Outsourced employees   Employees who are provided by a third party to perform a specific function through a contract arrangement.

Part-time employee   A person who is employed by a company and works a minimal amount of time, usually less than 20 hours per week.

Performance standards   The tasks, functions, or behavioral requirements established by the employer as goals to be accomplished by an employee.

Permanent employees   The main staff in the organization who usually work 30 to 40 hours per week and receive some type of benefit package.

Productivity   The amount of work output by an individual employee during a given time period.

Productivity standards   The defined and acceptable criteria of work output units (quantity).

Seasonality   A variation in business volume due to a particular season.

Task characteristics   How work is accomplished is defined by autonomy, task variety, task significance, task identity, and feedback.

Task identity   An observable work activity reflecting the degree to which a job involves a whole piece of work, the results of which can be easily identified.

Task significance   An observable work activity reflecting the degree to which a job influences the lives or work of others, whether inside or outside the organization.

Task variety   An observable work activity referring to the degree to which a job requires employees to perform a wide range of tasks on the job.

Team building   A training program designed to assist a group of people to work together as a team while they are learning.

Temporary employees   An individual who works on either short-term or long-term assignments with an employer without being treated as a permanent employee and who lacks the benefits of permanent employees. They are normally utilized by employers to meet seasonal or other demands that they do not have the internal resources to meet.

Variable labor expense   Labor costs that vary with the volume of the business.

5

Selecting Employees

KEY TERMS

Behavioral interview	Nondirect approach
Concurrent validity	Nonverbal communication
Construct validity	Overweighing negative information
Content validity	People plan
Contrast errors	Predictive validity
Criterion-related validity	Race, sex, and age biases
Data-gathering interview	Reliability
Desired qualification	Required qualification
Devil's horn	Screening interview
Direct approach	Semi-structured interview
Dominate the interview	Similarity errors
Faulty listening and memory	Situational interview
First impression error	Skills inventory
Halo effect	Stress interview
Inter-rater reliability	Structured interview
Labor force population	Succession planning program
Labor market	Unstructured interview
MAU model	Validity

OBJECTIVES

- Identify the advantages and disadvantages of internal and external recruiting
- Describe the importance of the selection process
- Describe how managers use application forms and preemployment testing
- Identify different types of interviewing techniques
- Identify the types of selection errors and biases managers must overcome
- Define the dos and don'ts of the interviewing process, including the reference check

> **Consider This**
>
> Tom is in the middle of an interview for a manager position that he really wants. The interview has gone well so far when he is asked to describe a situation where he identified a problem at work and the methods he used to solve the problem. He is caught off guard and can't come up with a situation that answers this question. What should have happened?

INTRODUCTION

During 2012, managers in the hospitality industry hired 7,465,000 people into new jobs.[1] The number of hires peaked in 2007 at 9,457,000 and decreased annually until a low of 6,506,080 jobs was reached in 2010. The number of hires has been slowly increasing in 2011 and 2012. The average annual turnover rate for the services industry is one of the highest in the country at 35 percent. With the average cost per hire of $1,062, this means that companies spend billions of dollars on the expenses of hiring and training new employees.[2] The strategic HR manager recognizes the importance of minimizing these expenses, which begins with matching the right individual to the organization in order to ensure retention.

RECRUITING EMPLOYEES

When a company has completed its forecasting, it is then ready to start recruiting. The process of recruiting involves generating a pool of qualified applicants for all positions within the organization, with more emphasis on open positions. Today's war for talent is driven by increasing mobility, an aging employee base, and shortage of highly skilled workers. In the past three decades, the nation's economy has doubled while the birth rate has dropped by 24 percent. According to the U.S. Bureau of Labor Statistics, the U.S. gross domestic product should grow 3 percent per year

Recruiting employees.   *Credit*: Elena Elisseeva / Shutterstock.

on average through 2020. Yet the annual growth rate of the U.S. labor force is projected to be 0.7 percent annually between 2010 and 2020. In the United States, the labor force in the "prime age" group aged 25 to 54 is projected to drop to 63.7 percent by the year 2020. By 2020, the number of workers aged 16 to 24 is expected to be 11.2 percent of the U.S. labor force. By 2020, the Baby Boom generation will all be over 55 and will make up 25.2 percent of the workforce. That percentage will have increased from 19 percent in 2010.[3]

A business has to know the labor market. The labor market consists of the individuals in possession of knowledge, skills, and abilities (KSAs). The business also needs to understand the labor force population, or the number of individuals in a targeted population. The labor force population could tell the HR manager that there is an abundance of potential employees, or if potential employees may be scarce. If there is an abundance of potential employees, the HR manager can be very selective in his or her recruiting/hiring process. However, when resources are scarce, whether it is the supply of commodities or human resources, businesses need to rely on planning to maintain the competitive edge. Human capital needs must be an integral part of every strategic plan for the foreseeable future. In order to meet the demands of growth and changing technology, it is critical that companies develop a people plan that includes both ways to increase retention and to improve recruitment efforts. A business needs to continuously develop new ways of improving the human capital return on investment (ROI). Such changes require a plan and a system that will develop, implement, monitor, and control the cost of maintaining adequate human capital inventories. To be successful, the business proposition for human capital must be analyvzed and a plan developed for both internal and external recruiting.

Internal Recruiting

Filling positions with internal candidates can be an efficient and effective way of staffing positions and of sending a positive message to the workforce about the possibility for upward mobility. The benefits of "hiring from within" are as follows:

- Improves the morale of the promoted employee and current staff
- Provides an opportunity to assess promotion potential of the current staff
- Lowers costs for recruiting and training

There are also disadvantages to internal recruiting, which include the following:

- Limits infusion of new people in the company
- Causes morale problems for those employees not promoted
- May cause political problems due to promotions based on friendships or relationships between employee and manager
- Can create gaps in one department when employees are promoted to another department within the organization

It is important for a company considering an internal job posting system to establish a formal process for using the system and to communicate that process to all employees. Most commonly, when there is a job opening, all employees are notified of the position and given specific information on the job title, salary, department, supervisor's name and title, responsibilities of the job, qualifications, and skills required. The posting remains displayed in a prominent place for a specified number of days. The supervisor or manager doing the hiring reviews internal applications before looking at outside talent. Generally, employees are required to notify their current supervisor or manager when applying for an internal position.

However, even if there is an internal process for posting available jobs, there may be times when it is better not to follow this process. For instance, a position may need to be changed to accommodate the needs of a particular employee. In this case the job may not be included in the internal posting process. The most important consideration when using a job posting system is to be fair and consistent. Morale will be reduced dramatically if employees begin to feel that the system is administered in a biased or inconsistent manner.[4]

Another method for internal candidates to express interest in promotions or transfers is a succession planning program. Succession planning programs help identify internal candidates

Do	Don't
Clearly communicate the system and apply this system consistently	Be cavalier about the hiring process
Generate a high awareness of the positions and the KSAs needed for the position	Overlook employees in other departments
Provide training and development for employees to prepare them for the transition to the promotion	Overlook your management staff, make sure they are committed to the recruiting plan
Offer general training for all employees so they have a chance to develop their KSAs	Forget to offer prompt feedback to the internal candidate
Offer internal candidates an interview whenever feasible	
Make sure your hiring policies are above reproach	

FIGURE 5.1 Dos and Don'ts of Internal Recruiting.[5]

for the next step in the career ladder. These plans usually quantify KSAs of the candidates. Many times a **skills inventory** (or management inventory) is completed to document a current employee's KSAs. To be effective, (a) skill inventories must be regularly updated, and (b) both manager and employee must agree on the information. Management inventories emphasize critical-thinking skills, problem-solving skills, and the ability to prioritize tasks. Other guidelines for internal recruiting are presented in Figure 5.1.

External Recruiting

External recruiting, or hiring from outside sources, is usually easier at the entry-level position, and becomes more complex as the HR professional recruits for executive-level positions. The current status of the labor market is the largest influence on external recruiting. With the national unemployment rate currently above 7 percent, recruiters are seeing an abundance of applicants, thus increasing the size of their recruiting pool of applicants.

Social media. *Credit*: Vasya Kobelev/Shutterstock.

Professional	Community	Business
Employment agencies—state and private	Churches, synagogues, and mosques	Tele-recruiting
Job fairs—both high school and college	Youth groups (i.e., Boys and Girls clubs)	Point-of-sale messages
Guest-speaking engagements—again, both high school and college	Apartment complexes (includes the possibility of a newsletter)	Box toppers
Chamber of Commerce meetings	Local sports teams	Direct mailers
Government agencies (i.e., veterans' agency)	Women's and men's groups	Database recruiting
Social organizations (i.e., PTA or YMCA)	Child care centers	Sign-on bonuses
Volunteer groups	Senior citizen groups	Banners
Welcome Wagon groups	Craft centers	Window paintings
Military agencies	Exercise centers	Billboard announcements
Restaurant associations—national, state, or local	Student organizations (FMLA or FFA)	
American Hotel & Lodging Association—national, state, or local	Community events	
Local or state assistance programs (i.e., food bank)		

FIGURE 5.2 **Sources of External Applicants.**

Although external recruiting is costlier than internal recruiting, it has some advantages, which include the following:

- Brings new ideas into the company
- Gives recruiters the opportunity to interview candidates from their competitors
- May be cheaper to hire skilled employees than train current employees
- Minimizes the appearance of political promotions from within

Just as with internal recruiting, there are also disadvantages to external recruiting. The disadvantages are as follows:

- During the recruiting process, it may be difficult to assess the "fit" of the candidate with the company's culture and philosophy.
- Morale problems can develop when internal candidates are passed over for a promotion.
- Job orientation can take longer because the external candidate does not know the culture and philosophy of the company.

Depending on the local community, there are a number of possible sources for external candidates. Examples of sources for external candidates are included in Figure 5.2.

In addition to local sources for external candidates, a manager may locate potential employees in other countries. J-1 interns and H2B workers are generally used to meet short-term temporary needs for employees. International recruiters and international labor brokers typically assist with the location of both types of employees.

One of the uses of social media by businesses has been to recruit external candidates. The three most commonly used sites are LinkedIn, Facebook, and Twitter. These sites are used for developing connections and building brand image. It is recommended that companies develop links between their Facebook sites to their application web page to facilitate the ease of applying for open positions. While this may be useful for management-level jobs now, using social media to recruit for entry-level positions may be more common in the future.

SELECTING APPLICANTS

Reviewing and Screening Applicants

Many people consider the recruiting and selection process to be one and the same, or a single process. Recruiting is generating a pool of applicants, and selection is choosing the most qualified applicant who "fits" the job. To comply with employment law, the applicant must complete an application. This application must be nondiscriminatory, and must be structured so that it will generate the most information. The format of the application is vital. By leaving too little room, the organization will not get enough information; by having too much room, the applicant may be intimidated. Some of the pertinent areas on the application are: (a) personal information (name, address, contact information), (b) education and training, (c) previous employment information (employer's name, dates of employment, contact information, ending title, pay rate, and description of duties), (d) military services, and (e) security data (felony conviction). If the application starts the process, the process must be tied with the job specification. By using the job specification, the HR professional can determine the need for any preemployment testing. These tests can be used to assess knowledge (e.g., an aptitude test), ability (e.g., keyboard test for administrative assistants), and skills (e.g., reading a map to enable a driver to find the most efficient route). There are also numerous other possibilities for preemployment testing, which could include personality tests, honesty tests, assessment centers, psychological batteries, or drug tests. See Figure 5.3.

One important aspect for HR professionals is that they must ensure the recruitment process to be reliable and valid. Reliability refers to the statistical process where the selection process consistently produces the same result. A selection strategy is reliable if it consistently leads the employer to the same employment decision, regardless of who is making the selection. Validity

Cognitive Ability Tests	Tests that measure intelligence - Types of cognitive tests include general mental ability, verbal ability, math ability, spatial perception, inductive reasoning, and deductive reasoning. Psychomotor tests (i.e., reaction time and response time) also fall under the heading of cognitive ability tests
Physical Ability Tests	Physical ability tests measure individual abilities such as strength, endurance, and muscular movement
Aptitude Tests	Aptitude tests measure the ability of an individual to learn or acquire a new skill
Personality Tests	Personality tests are a psychological measure of an individual's basic characteristics, such as attitudes, emotional adjustment, interests, interpersonal relations, and motivation
Honesty/Integrity Tests	Tests designed to measure propensity toward undesirable behaviors such as lying, stealing, and abusing drugs or alcohol - These tests are criticized for invasion of privacy and self-incrimination, and potential for candidates to provide "politically correct" answers - *Overt integrity tests* ask questions about honesty, attitudes, and behavior regarding theft - *Personality-oriented integrity tests* ask questions about dependability, respect for authority and others
Polygraph Tests	A polygraph test provides a diagnostic opinion about a person's honesty. The Employee Polygraph Protection Act of 1988 prohibits employers from requiring or requesting preemployment polygraphs under most circumstances
Substance abuse tests	Substance abuse testing is intended to ensure a drug-free workplace. Concern about workplace safety issues, alcohol use, and illegal and unsafe drug use in the workplace has prompted many employers to require employees/applicants to submit to substance abuse testing

FIGURE 5.3 Types of Selection Tools and Test Methods.[6]

is the statistical process used to demonstrate that the selection process measures or predicts what was intended to be measured or predicted. The key is to develop measures that will increase the success of the chosen applicant for the job. There are three primary forms of validity approved by the EEOC (Equal Employment Opportunity Commission):

- **Content validity** represents job-function testing (e.g., typing, mathematics, and examinations for certified public accountants). Content validity is an appropriate strategy when a job specialty is defined through job analysis by identifying the important required behaviors, tasks, or knowledge, and the assessment or test is a representative sample of the behaviors, actual tasks, or knowledge drawn from that specialty. The Uniform Guidelines on Employee Selection Procedures state that, in order to demonstrate the content validity of a selection procedure, a user should show that the behaviors demonstrated in the selection procedure are a representative sample of the behaviors of the job in question and/or that the selection procedure provides a representative sample of the work product of the job in question. This is the least sophisticated type of validity to assess, provided the HR practitioner, or consultant, is a competent job analyst.
- **Criterion-related validity** is measured by a procedure that uses a test as a predictor to determine how well a person will perform on the job. The desired KSAs and measures for job performance are the criterion variables. Job analysis determines which KSAs and behaviors are needed for each task in the job. Tests (predictors) are then devised and used to measure different job dimensions of the criterion-related variables. Examples of tests are: (a) having a college degree, (b) scoring a required number of words per minute on a typing test, or (c) having five years of medical transcription experience. These predictors are then validated against the criteria used to measure job performance, such as performance appraisals, attendance, and proficiency in relation to quality and quality of work performed. Two different approaches to criterion-related validity are concurrent and predictive.
  - *Concurrent validity* Concurrent means "at the same time." When an employer measures concurrent validity, a test is given to current employees and the scores are correlated (compared) with their performance ratings (by such measures as supervisory performance appraisals, accident rates, and absenteeism records). The reason it is called concurrent is because job performance measures and the test score(s) are available at the same time (concurrently), as opposed to being subject to a time lag as in the criterion (predictive) validity approach.[7]
  - *Predictive validity* Predictive means "before the fact." To measure predictive validity, test results of applicants are compared with their subsequent job performance. For example, an employer has established a one-year preferred experience requirement for a certain position, and success on the job will be measured by such factors as quality and quantity of work, performance appraisals, absenteeism, and accident rates. After one year on the job, if those employees who had one year of work experience at the time of hire demonstrate better performance on the job than those hired without such experience, then the experience requirement can be considered a valid predictor of performance and may be used in future hiring decisions. This is with the provision that this evidence can be substantiated by valid statistical comparisons.
- **Construct validity** refers to the extent to which dimensions on different tests relate to one another. Two factors that correlate highly on a personality test are not necessarily identical, but do provide reassurance that they are related and are a "construct" or part of the makeup (like honesty, dependability, sociability) of an individual, as related to actual job performance. Construct validity is the extent to which a selection device measures a theoretical construct, characteristic, or trait. Typical constructs are intelligence or mechanical comprehension. Because a hypothetical construct is used as a predictor in establishing this type of validity, personality tests and tests that measure other such constructs are more likely to be questioned for their legality and usefulness than other measures of validity.[8]

After ensuring reliability and validity, the next task for the HR professional is to determine **required qualifications** versus **desired qualifications**. Many times a hospitality company will only identify one or a few qualifications for a job. This process limits the ability of the HR professional to find the "best match" for the job. Through the job analysis process, the company has identified the necessary KSAs; now the HR professional must decide which qualifications are a requirement for the job, and which qualifications are desired for the job. To help in the selection process, many times the requirements are kept to a minimum, thus keeping as many applicants as possible in the applicant pool.

Checking References

Checking references is a vital part of the selection process. References can be personal, professional, or educational. Many companies have eliminated the personal reference, thinking it is a waste of time because the personal reference will know very little about the professional abilities of the applicant. Professional references can relate directly to the work history, and will also be able to provide information on the KSAs of the applicant. Educational references may not know the actual work history of the applicant, but they can provide valuable information about the KSAs of the applicant in the classroom. This can help the HR professional determine the fit of the applicant.

The company must set policy and procedures on what to provide during a reference check. This is integral to avoid legality issues because of defamation of character. In general, the company will provide answers to three reference check questions: (a) What were the dates of employment? (b) What was the pay rate? and (c) What was the final job title? Today's current trend is to have applicants sign waivers that grant permission to contact references, check court records, and verify educational histories. These waivers include a statement releasing the company from all liabilities associated with the reference check. Even if an applicant signs a waiver, the company is not required to release more information than the answers to the three required reference check questions.

Two other types of reference checks are credit reference checks and third-party background checks. To obtain a credit reference check, the company must first get permission from the applicant, and then contact a credit bureau and provide the bureau the social security number of the applicant. This practice has been highly scrutinized because it can violate an applicant's right for privacy under the provisions of the Fair Credit Reporting Act. An applicant must be given a copy of the credit report, and must be given time to correct any discrepancies. Third-party background checks can be costly, depending on the depth of information accessed by the company. The hiring company pays for the expertise of the company providing the background check, because of the possible serious nature of finding the best person for the job.

Professional reference checkers are changing to a different tact. They are taking advantage of the opportunity to learn more about their candidates by using a new technique that includes "judgment-neutral questions." Judgment-neutral questions yield helpful information and significant insights because they form a new framework that avoids asking the reference giver to make good/bad judgments of the potential hire. For example, a reference giver is unlikely to give a candid answer to a question such as "What are Sally's weaknesses?" for any number of reasons. However, if a reference checker asks an alternative set of judgment-neutral questions, he or she can elicit helpful information about a candidate. Judgment-neutral questions can also help to immunize the reference giver from harm.[9] Figure 5.4 includes some sample judgment-neutral questions.

Finally, there are four methods to collect reference information. Probably the simplest but least successful is the telephone reference checks. Many references are reluctant to give information over the phone to someone they don't know. One way to avert this is to have the applicant contact the reference and tell them someone may be calling. Written reference checks can be initiated by the applicant or the company. These forms contain some type of waiver of an individual's Privacy Act rights, and are completed by the applicant before being delivered to the reference provider. The type of reference check used most seldom is the personal interview. The time and cost of this approach prevent many companies from using this method. The last method is the use of the World Wide Web. A reference check can be conducted via the Internet, but the information may not be accurate or credible.

Interviewing Errors and Biases

Having the best employees is essential for any business. A company spends many hours and many dollars recruiting potential employees, so the task at hand is selecting applicants to become its perfect employees. Employment interviews are the most common method to the selection process. Before discussing the types of interviews, problems with interviews should be revealed.

1. Tell me about your professional experience with Sally. In what capacity did the two of you work together? What was the outcome of that experience?

2. Name the three most important things you would tell someone about Sally in preparation for an initial meeting with her.

3. If you were to rehire Sally, what type of role would you offer her?

4. Think back to a time when you've seen Sally most committed and fired up about her work. What was it that seemed to motivate her?

5. When you've seen Sally least committed or fired up about her work, what was it about the task at hand that seemed to dampen her motivation?

6. On a scale of one to ten, would you describe Sally as a one, which is more of a consensus decision maker (i.e., she consults others before making decisions), or a ten, which is a completely independent decision maker (i.e., she prefers to make decisions on her own, without the need for consensus)?

7. Think back to Sally's biggest success. Did she do the majority of the work herself, or did she delegate the majority of the work?

8. When Sally gets lost or stuck on a problem or is unsure of something (such as what to do next), is she likely to ask for help sooner, or later? Or will she continue trying to figure it out for herself on her own?

9. Under what level of supervision does Sally operate best? That is, does she thrive by having more interaction with her boss, or by having less interaction in order to get the job done consistently well?

10. During the time you've known or worked with Sally, what is the most significant area of professional learning and growth you have seen in her?

11. What type of job do you think Sally would best be suited to do?

12. What type of job do you think Sally would be least suited to do?

FIGURE 5.4   Twelve Judgment-Neutral Questions to Ask References.[10]

Interviews can be impacted by the interviewer, the interviewee, the company, the situation, or the environment. Thus the possibilities of selecting the best person for the job can be taxing.

The first major problem is **inter-rater reliability**. This occurs when two people interview the same applicant and they do not arrive at the same decision using the same qualifications. Interviewers can also make **similarity errors**. The interviewers are likely attracted to candidates

Nonverbal communication.   *Credit*: Hasloo Group Production Studio / Shutterstock.

Nonverbal Message	Typical Interpretation
Making direct eye contact	Friendly, sincere, assertive
Avoiding eye contact	Cold, insecure, nervous, concealing
Shaking head	Shocked, disbelieving
Patting on the back	Congratulatory, encouraging
Scratching the head	Bewildered, disbelieving
Smiling	Understanding, encouraging
Biting the lip	Fearful, nervous, anxious
Tapping feet	Nervous
Raising the eyebrow	Surprised, disbelieving
Narrowing eyebrows	Angry, resentful, disapproving
Wringing hands	Nervous, anxious, fearful
Leaning forward	Attentive, interested
Slouching in seat	Bored, relaxed
Sitting on the edge of seat	Anxious, apprehensive
Shifting in seat	Restless, bored
Hunching over	Insecure, passive
Erect posture	Assertive, self-confident

FIGURE 5.5   Interpretations of Nonverbal Communication Cues.[11]

who are similar to them in terms of outside interests, personal background, or even appearance. With similarity errors, an interviewer can also have **race, sex, and age biases**. Title VII of the Civil Rights Act and age discrimination laws try to protect the interviewee, but this bias can be difficult to eliminate from the interviewer. Also, many interviewers can make a **first impression error**. As the saying goes, first impressions are lasting impressions; the interviewer usually focuses on the positive aspect of the applicant. First impression errors can also be referred to as the halo effect. The **halo effect** occurs when an interviewer views the favorable side to the interviewee. Because a company commonly interviews several applicants for one position, it is very easy for the interviewer to compare the applicants, or have **contrast errors**. The applicants should not be compared to each other; rather the applicants should be compared to the standards set by the company in the job description. Human nature can be designed to note negative information over positive information. This is a bias known as **overweighing negative information**, and is a common practice for the interviewer to note the negative aspects to the interview. Another negative error is the **devil's horn**; that is, the interviewer puts emphasis on a single negative trait. Sometimes interviewers do not always hear what is said or intended, nor do they remember everything that is said. This is known as **faulty listening and memory**. An interviewer can also remember the most recent behavior or response of an applicant, or have recency errors. The interviewer can also **dominate the interview** and not allow the applicant to speak during the interview. Finally, the interviewer must be concerned with **nonverbal communication** on his or her part, as well as the applicant's. Many researchers have shown that someone's clothing, smile, speech, or habits can influence the interview in a positive or negative fashion. Examples of nonverbal messages and how they are interpreted by others are given in Figure 5.5.

INTERVIEWING AND TESTING CANDIDATES

Types of Interviews

There are three categories of interviews: unstructured, semi-structured, and structured. The **unstructured interview** questions are not planned; the interviewer directs the questions down any path he or she may want. This means that interviews with different applicants will likely

Structured or semi-structured interview.   *Credit*: Ambrophoto / Shutterstock.

be entirely different. Opinions vary on the value of this style of interview. Some experts believe the unstructured interview has little merit because of the low inter-rater reliability, while other experts believe that using this method can achieve a better understanding of the applicant because all possibilities can be explored (unlike the structured and semi-structured).

The second type of interview is the **semi-structured interview**. As the name implies, some preparation of questions takes place, usually for traits that need to be explored, but depending on the applicant's response, there is also flexibility built into the interview. Usually the interviewer prepares very broad questions, and then will ask the applicant to speak specifically about the applicant's experience. A critical feature to the semi-structured (and the unstructured interview) is the use of open-ended questions, and wanting more than a "yes" or "no" response.

The third interview type is the **structured interview**. Questions for this type of interview are prepared in advance, asked in the same way to each applicant, and asked in a specific sequence. Very little flexibility is allowed with this process. The results of the structured interview allow the interviewer to compare the responses of the applicants. Because of this aspect, many experts believe structured interviews to have more reliable and valid information. The disadvantage to this approach is the tendency to produce very shallow information, and strengths and weaknesses of the applicants may not be revealed.

Of course, there are techniques to the types of interviews. A **situational interview** is a variation of the structured interview, and uses different types of questions. The interviewer can ask situational questions ("What would you do when two servers call in sick on a busy Friday night?"), knowledge questions ("What do you mean by REVPAR?"), or performance questions ("Are you willing to take the general manager's position at a poor performing restaurant?"). Another type of variation to the structured interview is the **behavioral interview**. Here the interviewer establishes an area of discussion, and then asks about the behavior of the applicant ("Tell me about the most difficult shift you worked on your last job. Why was it so difficult?"). The interviewer is trying to link past behavior to a predictive behavior pattern. Sample questions for the situational and behavioral interviews are included in Figure 5.6.

A third type of technique is the **stress interview** (also known as the group interview). The applicant is interviewed by a panel of interviewers. The intent is to put the applicant under stressful session of discussion. Once the interview is over, the panel members must come to a group decision, sometimes a difficult task in its own right.

The purpose of a **screening interview** is to save the company (and managers) time and money by limiting the number of applicants. Determining the requirements for the job position usually helps in screening. The rough screening uses a limited number of specific criteria. A common bias to this method is that the interviewer might get very specific with the applicants. The screening should be done rather quickly to determine the best applicant fit, and then to perform a more in-depth interview. The **data-gathering interview** is usually conducted by someone with very little input in the hiring decision; the goal is to gain as much knowledge about the

General Question	Situational Question	Behavioral Question
What do you like about being in customer service?	How do you say no to a customer's request?	Tell me about a time you went out of your way to give great customer service.
What is the difference between coaching and discipline?	How would you handle an employee who is not working as expected?	What was the most challenging employee performance issue you have handled? How did you handle it?
What methods do you use to make decisions?	How would you react if an employee collapsed on the floor?	Give me an example of a decision you made that was not effective. Why do you think it was not effective?
What policies do you feel are necessary to support you when disciplining employees?	How would you handle a situation where you encountered employees arguing?	Describe a situation where you handled a disagreement between employees.

FIGURE 5.6   General, Situational, and Behavioral Questions.

applicant as possible. And finally, the decision interview is conducted with the person who will actually make the hiring decision.

Besides the types of interviews and the techniques of interviewing, the interviewer must also consider the approach of the interview. The interviewer needs to set the tone of the meeting. This can be done in three ways. The **direct approach** usually requires yes/no responses, thus leaving little ability to collect an abundance of information. With the **nondirect approach**, the interviewer encourages the applicant to talk freely about his or her experiences in former jobs, educational experiences, or expectations at work. The objective is to gain more personal information about the applicant. The eclectic (or mixed) approach emphasizes open-ended questions and yes/no responses. The interviewer looks for detailed information with the open-ended questions, and specific background information with the yes/no responses.

In all cases, the questions that are asked during an interview must be based on the job requirements and not discriminatory. For example, it is acceptable to ask an applicant what hours and days he or she is available to work. It is not acceptable to ask how many children or what type of child care the applicant has. Questions that ask about race, age, religion, sexual orientation, and national origin are to be avoided. Figure 5.7 has examples of acceptable and unacceptable questions.

Making the Decision

As discussed in Chapter 2 of this text, human resource management is defined as legal discrimination. This is most evident in the selection process. The company, and especially the hiring manager, must practice legal discrimination. The HR professional knows that he or she must select the best applicant for the job, thus discriminating against those individuals not chosen for the position. The HR professional must stay legal, and have up-to-date knowledge of all employment laws. To remain in the legal realm, the HR professional must consider bona fide occupational qualifications in the job design process. An employer has to discriminate based on a characteristic associated with the nature of the job; it is the job of the HR professional to follow the laws in the process, starting with job design.

Before the selection process starts, the HR professional should develop an evaluation form, based on the requirements and desirable traits as advertised in the position. This form should mirror the advertised traits, and then these criteria should be quantified with some type of numeric scale.

Topic	Acceptable	Unacceptable
Attendance	Are there specific times or days you cannot work?	What religion are you?
Attendance	Do you have a reliable method of getting to work?	Do you own a car?
National origin	Are you eligible to work in the United States?	What is your national origin?
Disabilities	Can you perform the duties of the potential job?	Have you ever filed a workers' compensation claim?
Education	Do you have a high school diploma? (if required for the job)	What year did you graduate from high school?

FIGURE 5.7 Examples of Acceptable and Unacceptable Interview Questions.

The reason for the evaluation form is to try to remove subjectivity from the decision process. There are ways to avoid subjectivity:

- Each interviewer should know his or her biases, and try to eliminate them from the process.
- Do not mistake a calm person for someone not interested in the position.
- Do not mistake the talkative person for someone who is truly prepared for the interview.
- Do not look for a friend, or someone who is similar to you.
- Do not assume that a specific trait makes an individual more qualified (i.e., a graduate of Harvard is better than a graduate of UCLA).
- Do not be impressed with an applicant just because the applicant knows the jargon of the position.
- Do not focus on one or two strengths while overlooking obvious weaknesses.[12]

A tool that can help in the evaluation process is the **MAU** (multiattribute utility) **model**. The **MAU model** is set up to identify the criteria that will be used to evaluate the applicants and weights for importance of each of the criteria.[13] In the decision situation, the model is used as an aid to judgment and not as a substitute for judgment. In relating the MAU model to the selection process, the first step is to identify criteria that will be used to evaluate each applicant. Using the job specifications in Figure 4.4, the criteria would be as follows:

- Professional, good interpersonal skills
- Ability to sell menu items and meet guest needs
- Ability to understand menu items and describe to guests
- Basic reading, writing, and math skills
- Ability to transport food and beverage items
- Legal age to serve alcoholic beverages

The next step is to determine the utility or importance weight between 1 and 99 associated with each of the criteria. The importance weights should add up to 100. This number indicates the relative importance of each of the criteria to the others. If each of the six criteria mentioned earlier were equally important, each would be assigned a weight of 100/6 or 16.7.

The next step is to develop a points-if table for each of the criteria. These tables will be used to assign points when evaluating the application materials. Figure 5.8 includes a sample points-if table for one of the criteria. Next, points are assigned for each applicant and a total is calculated by multiplying the weight times points and summing up all criteria. The completed MAU table is included in Figure 5.8. The applicant with the highest number of points is selected. In this case, applicant B will be offered the position. Many times the actual offer is made in person or over the phone. Once the offer has been tendered, a written offer should be sent to the candidate.

Essential skills or criteria and weights (in parentheses):
1. Professional, good interpersonal skills (20)
2. Ability to sell menu items and meet guest needs (20)
3. Ability to understand menu items and describe to guests (20)
4. Basic reading, writing, and math skills (10)
5. Ability to transport food and beverage items (10)
6. Legal age to serve alcoholic beverages (20)

Sample Points-If Table for Criteria 1: Professional, good interpersonal skills:

Points	If
10	Easily establishes rapport during interview. References document good skills.
7	Easily establishes rapport during interview. Unable to document skills in reference checks.
5	Average ability to establish rapport. References confirm ability.
3	Difficult to establish rapport. References confirm ability.
1	Difficult to establish rapport. Unable to document skills in reference checks.

MAU Table:

Applicant	Criterion 1 (20)	Criterion 2 (20)	Criterion 3 (20)	Criterion 4 (10)	Criterion 5 (10)	Criterion 6 (20)	Total Score
A	7	10	5	5	10	10	790*
B	10	10	10	7	7	10	940
C	7	7	7	10	10	5	720
D	7	7	10	7	7	5	720

* Total score for Applicant A = Sum of $(7 \times 20) + (10 \times 20) + (5 \times 20) + (5 \times 10) + (10 \times 10) + (10 \times 20)$.

FIGURE 5.8 **MAU Model Example.**

THE BOTTOM LINE

Recruitment refers to the search of individuals both inside and outside of hospitality companies. There are many ways to recruit employees, and it is up to the hospitality manager to use as many of these as possible to ensure an adequate applicant pool. Hospitality managers should review the process for selecting employees to assure that the right applicant is matched to the right job. Job specifications and job descriptions should be used as the basis for screening applicants, interviews, and selection. Hospitality managers should make sure they use appropriate methods for confirming the backgrounds of applicants, interviewing candidates, and selecting among qualified applicants.

The selection process is critical to the success of the company. By completing a thorough job analysis, the HR professional starts with a strong foundation to the process. The HR professional should take a step in the right direction by analyzing the needs of the company and by having an accurate forecast of these needs. By recruiting an internal or external candidate, the HR professional should get qualified individuals into the applicant pool. By legal discrimination, the HR professional should select the best applicant for the job, and extend an offer. With all of these components in place, the company is well on its way to profitability.

Discussion Questions

1. How do KSAs impact the hiring decision?
2. What are the basic steps in the recruitment process?
3. How does seasonality influence the labor applicant pool?
4. Why is the people plan so important to companies?

5. What are the advantages and disadvantages to internal recruiting? To external recruiting?
6. What tools can the HR professional use to ensure a large applicant pool?

7. What is the difference between reliability and validity?
8. Describe the different types of validity.
9. Why is the issue of validity so important in the selection process?
10. How can the HR professional use the application form to better the company?
11. What are the advantages and disadvantages to testing?
12. How can an HR professional remove inter-rater reliability?
13. How could the HR professional remove errors and biases from the selection process?
14. Differentiate between an unstructured interview, a semi-structured interview, and a structured interview.
15. What is the advantage of the stress interview? The disadvantage?
16. By using the MAU model, how can the HR professional better the selection process?

Application Exercise

1. You have worked as a front-desk manager for 12 years and feel pretty good about the staff that you've hired in the past. Due to a promotion of your assistant manager to a sales position, you find that a critical position in your team will be vacant in two weeks. Describe the process you will use to identify both internal and external candidates for the assistant manager position. Develop the timeline for accepting applications, checking references, interviewing, and selecting the final candidate. Develop a list of interview questions and other selection tools you will use to select your final candidate for the position.

Endnotes

1. U.S. Bureau of Labor Statistics (2012). Hires in the accommodation and food service industries. Accessed from http://data.bls.gov/timeseries/JTU72000000HIL?data_tool=XGtable
2. Society for Human Resource Management (2013). Executive brief: Differences in employee turnover across key industries. Accessed from www.shrm.org/research/benchmarks/Documents/Assessing%20Employee%20Turnover_Final.pdf
3. U.S. Bureau of Labor Statistics (2012). Employment Projections 2010–2020. Accessed from http://www.bls.gov/bls/newsrels.htm#OEP
4. Grensing-Pophal, L. (2002). The do's and don'ts of recruiting from within. Accessed from www.shr.org/hrdisciplines/staffing management/Articles/Pages/CMS_000357.aspx
5. Ibid.
6. Weatherley, L. (2005). *Selection tests: Employee testing series part II*. Alexandria, VA: Society for Human Resource Management.
7. Weatherley, L. (2005). *Reliability and validity of selection tests: Employee testing series part I*. Alexandria, VA: Society for Human Resource Management.
8. Peck, D. (2007). High yield reference checking: Adding new value to the hiring equation. *Employee Relations Today*, doi: 10.1002/ert (online journal).
9. Ibid.
10. Ibid.
11. Arthur, D. (June 1995). The importance of body language. *HR Focus*, 72, 23.
12. Harvard Business School Press (2002). The hiring process: Attracting the best people. Boston, MA.
13. Huber, G. P. (1980). *Managerial Decision Making*. Glenview, IL: Scott, Foresman and Company.

Key Terms

Behavioral interview   An interview technique that focuses on a candidate's past experiences, behaviors, knowledge, skills, and abilities by asking the candidate to provide specific examples of when he or she has demonstrated certain behaviors or skills as a means of predicting future behavior and performance.

Concurrent validity   The means of determining a test's or other assessment tool's validity by comparing test scores against actual job performance.

Construct validity   The extent to which a test or other assessment instrument measures a particular trait.

Content validity   The degree to which a test or other assessment instrument used during the selection process measures the skills, knowledge, and abilities or other related job qualifications.

Contrast errors   Interviewers compare applicants to each other, either positive or negative traits.

Criterion-related validity   A procedure that uses a test as a *predictor* to determine how well a person will perform on the job.

Data-gathering interview   An interview conducted by someone with very little input in the hiring decision.

Desired qualification   A trait that a hiring company would like to see in its future employee.

Devil's horn   An interviewer puts emphasis on a single negative trait.

Direct approach   A technique used by an interviewer to collect applicant information, and usually requires yes or no responses, thus leaving little ability to collect an abundance of information.

Dominate the interview   A negative technique used by an interviewer. The interviewer does not allow the interviewee to talk during the session.

Faulty listening and memory   An interviewer does not always hear what is said or intended, nor does he or she remember everything that is said.

First impression errors   The interviewer usually focuses on the first, positive aspect of the applicant.

Halo effect   A form of interviewer bias, occurring when the interviewer rates or judges an individual based on the individual's positive or strongest traits, allowing his or her overall perception of the person to overshadow any negative traits.

Inter-rater reliability   The degree to which observations made by different interviewers about the same applicant agree.

Labor force population   The number of individuals in a targeted population.

Labor market   Individuals who possess the knowledge, skills, and abilities needed to perform the tasks required for each position in an organization.

MAU model   Shows a decision maker how to aggregate the satisfaction derived from each of the various attributes into a single measure of the overall utility of the multiple attributes.

Nondirect approach   A technique used by the interviewer to encourage the applicant to talk freely about his or her experiences in former jobs, educational experiences, or expectations at work.

Nonverbal communication   The process of communication through sending and receiving wordless messages.

Overweighing negative information   The process of noting negative information over positive information.

People plan   A plan designed to maximize a company's investment in human capitol or human resources.

Predictive validity   The degree to which a score on a scale or test predicts scores on some criterion measure.

Race, age, and sex biases   A tendency or preference by an interviewer toward a particular perspective, ideology, or result, when the tendency interferes with the ability to be impartial, unprejudiced, or objective.

Reliability   A measure of the ability of a test or other appraisal instrument to evaluate what is being measured on a consistent basis.

Required qualification   A trait that a hiring company deems absolutely necessary in its future employee.

Screening interview   Usually the first step taken during the interviewing process, involving reviewing prospective candidate applications/resumes, verifying information supplied by the candidate, conducting interviews, and examining test results.

Semi-structured interview   An interview style that allows both planned and unplanned questions. Typically, the unplanned questions allow interviewers to ask more specific questions about a broad issue raised by the structured questions.

Similarity errors   A type of error in an interview (or performance appraisal) that results when a manager or interviewer is attracted to an applicant because of personal or professional similarities.

Situational interview   Situational-type scenarios that are designed to gauge how an applicant would respond to certain situations that could occur in the workplace. These are often hypothetical, or "what if" style questions.

Skills inventory   A document that includes the knowledge, skills, and abilities for each employee. The management inventory lists the critical-thinking, problem-solving, and prioritizing abilities for each manager.

Stress interview   An interviewing style whereby the interviewer subjects a candidate to pressure or stress to ascertain how the candidate reacts under such conditions.

Structured interview   A structured interview asks the same questions of each candidate, so that valid comparisons of the quality of responses can be obtained. The questions generally take four job-related forms: situational, observational, personal, and behavioral.

Succession planning program   A plan that identifies the next step in the career ladder for each employee.

Unstructured interview   An interviewing style in which no questions are planned in advance. Instead, an interviewer directs the interview down whatever path seems appropriate at the time.

Validity   The general concept of validity is traditionally defined as "the degree to which a test measures what it claims, or purports, to be measuring." Validity is normally subdivided into three categories: content, criterion-related, and construct validity. Validity is an essential characteristic for all tests and test ratings.

Training and Development Systems

KEY TERMS

ADDIE model
Attitude survey
Behavior modeling
Brainstorming
Business games
Case study training
Coaching
Combined method
Computer-based training (CBT)
Conference training
Demonstration
Diversity training
Formative evaluation
General property orientation
In-basket training
Individual analysis
Job instruction training (JIT)
Job/task analysis

Lecture
Off-the-job training
On-the-job training (OJT)
Organizational analysis
Programmed instruction
Return on investment (ROI)
Role-playing
Sensitivity training
Simulations
Specific work group and job orientation
Structured discussion
Summative evaluation
Training criteria
Training needs assessment
Training objectives
Vestibule training
Web-based training

OBJECTIVES

- Explain the purpose of an orientation program
- Distinguish between a general property orientation and a specific job orientation
- Identify proper approaches to orientation and those approaches that should be avoided
- Define the stages of a training program
- Describe training methods and how to select the appropriate method
- Explain implementation and evaluation of a training program
- Explain the employee development process

> **Consider This**
>
> You are an assistant manager in a high-volume, training restaurant. It is Mother's Day, and the restaurant general manager has asked a newly hired employee to start on this day. You decide to have the employee stay in the break room and roll silverware for the restaurant. The restaurant is packed, but so far, all the customers seem to be happy, and all seems to be going very well. After about 3 hours, you notice a server rolling silverware at an empty table, so that more guests can be seated. You are furious because the new trainee should have this done. You head back to the break room, and find it empty. What happened to the new employee? And why isn't the new employee rolling silverware?

INTRODUCTION

Strategic hospitality managers recognize the need for developing human capital. Training is one of the tools an organization uses to develop employees, which leads to accomplishing objectives. Assessing organizational training needs is the diagnostic phase of the training process. Many organizations recognize the link between the profitability of an organization and the effectiveness of its training programs. The reasons for the relationship between profitability, improved staff retention, and recruitment success seem obvious when you consider the results of a professionally planned and executed training program. Good training

1. increases the skills of managers and employees
2. decreases duplication and waste
3. increases customer service and guest satisfaction
4. improves the quality of products, safety, and sanitation
5. improves employee satisfaction and decreases turnover
6. increases productivity and profits

If the planning and execution phase is not conducted in good faith and in an efficient and effective manner, the organization could experience one or more of the following consequences:

- Training may be used incorrectly—that is, the problem may actually be related to a performance issue, not training.
- Training programs may have the wrong objectives, course content, or training approach.
- Training program participants may not have the correct skills or competencies to be successful on the job.

Training. *Credit*: Constantine Pankin / Shutterstock.

- Training program may not be able to deliver on its promise—that is, the expected change in employee productivity, employee knowledge, skills, and abilities (KSAs), or measurable financial results anticipated by the organization may not be possible due to deficiencies in program design.
- Financial resources will be spent incorrectly or unnecessarily because they are not properly aligned with the company's business strategy.
- Lack of training programs may hinder the development of future leaders in the organization.

NEEDS ASSESSMENT

A **training needs assessment** is the process used to determine if training is necessary. It is the first step in the instructional system design process. Although there is no universally endorsed instructional systems development model, the training process is often referred to as the **ADDIE model** because it includes analysis, design, development, implementation, and evaluation. The ADDIE model is presented in Figure 6.1.

There are three levels of needs assessment—organizational analysis, job/task analysis, and individual analysis.

- **Organizational analysis**—Organizational analysis considers the appropriateness of the training process based on the context in which the training will occur. An important aspect of organizational analysis involves strategic planning and the identification of the KSAs that will be needed in the future. Both internal and external forces will influence the training process and must be considered when performing and updating an organizational analysis. The organizational analysis should identify the following:

  - Environmental impacts (new laws such as ADA, FMLA, and OSHA)
  - State of the economy and the impact on operating costs
  - Changing workforce demographics and the need to address cultural or language barriers
  - Changing technology and automation
  - Increasing global marketplaces
  - Political trends such as sexual harassment and workplace violence
  - Organization goals and the effectiveness of meeting these goals
  - Resources available (money, facilities, materials on hand, expertise)
  - Climate and support for training (management support, employee willingness to participate, and assigned responsibility for outcomes)

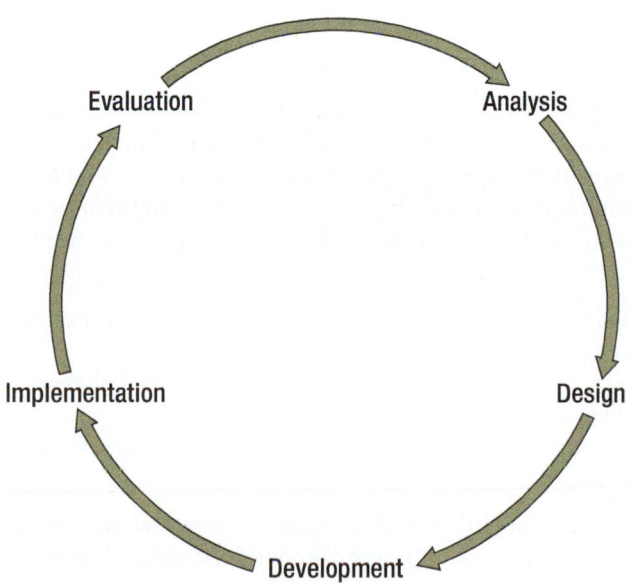

FIGURE 6.1 The ADDIE Model.

Organization-Wide Sources	Job-Based Sources	Individual Employee Sources
Customer service records	Engagement indices	Assessment center tests
Engagement indices	Job certification criteria	Attitudes surveys
Equipment records	Job descriptions	Certification records
Exit interviews	Job evaluation records	Critical incident records
Grievances	Job performance standards	Job knowledge tools
Process delays	Job procedures	Performance appraisals
Quality records	KSAs	Personnel records
Supervisory observations	Questionnaires	Position questionnaires
Training observations		Role clarification records
Training records		Training records
Worker injuries/illnesses		Skills tests

FIGURE 6.2   Possible Sources of Training Needs Assessment.[1]

- Job/task analysis—The second way an organization may elect to diagnose training needs is through a job or task analysis. The company can compare the requirements of certain jobs with the KSAs of employees who perform these jobs in an exemplary manner versus the KSAs of those who have difficulty performing these jobs. Training professionals can make recommendations about modifications to job requirements and, or changes to training objectives and, or curricula to differentiate high-potential performers on the job.
- Individual analysis—A third level of assessing training needs is to focus on how individuals perform their jobs. This is the most personalized level of needs assessment. The use of employee performance evaluations is the most common approach in this instance. Based on the employee performance evaluation, a recommendation would be made by the employee's supervisor regarding the area for performance improvement and the need for specific training. Another way of assessing an individual's training needs is through a career development recommendation at the time of the individual's performance evaluation.

Sources that can be used for training needs assessment for each of the three levels are presented in Figure 6.2.

ORIENTATION

Training actually begins with the orientation of the new employee to the company and to the work environment. On the first day of the job, the employee is put into a new environment, meets the boss, meets fellow employees, and encounters new policies. This can be a daunting experience for newly hired employees, and they can feel uncomfortable. If the goal is to make them long-term employees with the company, then orientation programs should be designed to reduce this stress associated with the new job. Hospitality companies need to provide the following information:

1. Job-related issues such as company standards, management expectations (including a performance evaluation), policies, and procedures
2. Cultural issues, acceptable norms of conduct, acceptable behavior, company traditions, company beliefs, and management philosophies
3. Specific job responsibilities (including a job description), technical job aspects, and equipment

Proper planning of the orientation program is essential, and the orientation program should guarantee that all topics are covered without duplication. Many times, hospitality companies divide the orientation program into two sections: (a) general property orientation and (b) specific work group and job orientation.

Orientation.   *Credit*: Image Team / Shutterstock.

General Property Orientation

General property orientation deals with the basic information an employee will need to understand the broader system of the hospitality company. General property orientation includes helping employees understand: (a) important policies and general procedures (nonjob specific), (b) information about compensation and benefits, (c) safety and accident prevention issues, (d) employee rights and responsibilities, and (e) physical facilities. Often at large hospitality properties, general property orientation can be conducted by the human resource department with a little help from the manager or immediate supervisor, because much of the content is generic in nature. At smaller hospitality properties, the general manager usually conducts the orientation session. Orientation can play a vital role in reducing turnover. In fact, some hospitality organizations calculate an average expense of turnover is over $6,000 per employee.[2] Benefits of a general property orientation are presented in Figure 6.3.

Specific Work Group and Job Orientation

The second kind of orientation is called specific work group and job orientation. This process is used to help employees understand the following: (a) function of the organization, and how the employee fits in job responsibilities, expectations, and duties, (b) policies, procedures, rules, and regulations, (c) layout of workplace, and (d) introduction to coworkers and other people in the broader organization. The employee's immediate supervisor and/or manager usually conducts the specific work group and job orientation because much of the content will be specific to the individual. Benefits of a specific work group and job orientation program are presented in Figure 6.4. Often the orientation process will be ongoing, with supervisors and coworkers providing coaching.

There are some key points to orientation. They are as follows:

1. Orientation should begin with the most important information (basic job survival).
2. Orientation should emphasize people as well as procedures and policies. Employees should have a chance to get to know people and their approaches and styles in both social and work settings.
3. Assign a new employee with an experienced person, but make sure the experienced person wants to mentor the new employee, and make sure the mentor has interpersonal skills. This relationship provides ongoing support.
4. Introduce employees to both information and people in a controlled manner. A new employee can't absorb everything at once, so don't waste your time. Remember to space out introductions.

Benefits for the Company

- Provides a consistent message to all new employees
- Employees get to know the company
- Provides introduction to the management team
- Provides a memorable first impression
- Builds a strong foundation of the company's values and philosophy
- Presents business goals and priorities
- Provides a chance to start building the concept of teamwork
- Lowers turnover

Benefits for the Employee

- Provides an understanding of the company's expectations about employee performance
- Enables the employee to understand his or her value to the company
- Builds self-esteem of the new employee
- Ensures new employees know their importance to the operation
- Provides a structured learning environment
- Establishes early commitment to teamwork
- Builds a foundation for employee motivation

FIGURE 6.3 **Benefits of General Property Orientation.**

Methods for Orienting Employees

The goal to orientation is for the new employee to be more comfortable with the new job. By creating a more relaxed and comfortable atmosphere, the new employee will become productive more quickly. The following steps will help the new employee start work in a more positive mindset.

Benefits for the Department

- Provides consistency in employee training and development
- Helps maintain resource availability
- Helps to ensure quality service and meeting guest expectations
- Ensures that standards are maintained
- Provides consistency in staff performance
- Ensures staff competencies
- Provides the basis for smooth operations

Benefits for the Employee

- Teaches the new employee how to do the job correctly
- Builds high morale among all the employees
- Builds self-esteem by employee knowing the specific tasks to the job
- Creates a team environment
- Helps employees become productive more quickly

FIGURE 6.4 **Benefits of Specific Work Group and Job Orientation.**

Step 1	Introduce the company in a way that makes the new employee feel confident about his or her decision to join the company.
Step 2	Review important policies/procedures such as standards of conduct and performance, and policies for discipline and safety.
Step 3	Review benefits and services that are provided by the company.
Step 4	Complete all benefit plan enrollment forms.
Step 5	Complete employment documents such as payroll withholding documents and I-9 verification forms.
Step 6	Review performance standards and provide a performance evaluation form.
Step 7	Set employee expectations about (a) training and development, (b) wage increases, (c) job security, (d) recognition, (e) working conditions, (f) promotions, (g) educational assistance programs, (h) counseling, (i) grievance procedures, and (j) other relevant expectations.
Step 8	Introduce coworkers and a mentor.
Step 9	Provide a tour of the entire facility.
Step 10	Show the new employee the workflow of the job.

FIGURE 6.5   Ten Steps in a Well-Designed Orientation.[3]

1. Welcome the new employee by showing him or her a relaxing environment. Do not create a tense or hostile environment.
2. Ensure the employee develops positive impressions about the company by having the correct person conduct the initial orientation session. The person conducting the initial session has to be knowledgeable about the company, well-spoken, and well-dressed.
3. Make sure the direct supervisor is present. This shows the new employee that the boss is interested in him or her as an employee.
4. Enforce the fact that the employee made the correct choice by choosing this company.
5. Show new employees the entire operation, not just their area. New employees need to understand their role in the entire organization. This will eliminate stress in the new employees.
6. Finally, get to the specific work group and job orientation.

The final key to a successful orientation process is following up with each employee. Orientation should be followed by a period of close supervision. During this time, the direct supervisor needs to observe the new employee, and assist with his or her learning process. The supervisor needs to give praise as well as constructive criticism. By spending time with the new employee, the supervisor is showing his or her interest in the new employee, and will reap the rewards of improved performance. The ten steps in a well-designed orientation are presented in Figure 6.5.

TRAINING AND DEVELOPMENT

Most experts agree that training needs to be a continuous cycle. For the newly hired employees, training is essential so that they quickly become productive in their new jobs. For the tenured employees, training is essential for their development. Figure 6.6 lists the seven steps in the training cycle.

Training begins with the **training needs assessment**. Once the need has been identified, the cycle begins. The second step to the training cycle is establishing **training objectives**, or establishing goals for the training program. The objectives will vary with the circumstances. Objectives are developed to improve service, improve productivity, or reduce costs.

The third step in the training cycle is establishing **training criteria**, or the benchmarks that are set by the company to measure effectiveness. Once a benchmark has been met, the training manager knows the trainee has met the KSAs of the training. The fourth step to the cycle is pre-testing the trainees. It is important to know their beginning level of KSAs. If the objectives are set too low, and the trainees are at a more advanced level, they will quickly become bored with the training, and become ineffective. If the objectives are set too high, then the trainees become disenchanted with the process, and again become ineffective. By knowing the beginning level of KSAs of the trainee, the training manager will be able to establish a challenging and motivating training program for the trainee.

The fifth step to the cycle is choosing the training methods. Training methods can be broadly categorized into **on-the-job training (OJT)** or **off-the-job training**. Training methods can be related to individuals or groups. The methods vary in how much the trainee is allowed to participate. More details about training methods are presented in the next section. The sixth step to the training cycle is implementing the training. The key to this step is to implement the processes established in the other steps. And finally, the seventh step is evaluating the training program. By evaluating the goals set forth in the second step, the training manager can determine the success of the training, and make appropriate changes for the next training cycle.

Delivery Methods

As stated earlier, training methods can vary for groups and individuals. Training methods will also depend on the type of employee, management, or time. OJT is primarily learning by doing, and is probably the most used (and abused) approach to training. Typically, one employee will be asked to teach the newly hired employee a skill. Many times this assignment will be made without taking into consideration the skill of the trainer. Because a person can perform the skill, he or she is chosen to teach the new person. Being good at a job does not necessarily mean someone is good at training or teaching. Another method used to teach task-oriented jobs is **job instruction training (JIT)**. JIT is a structured approach and requires the trainee to proceed through a sequential order of steps. The steps for JIT approach are as follows: (a) introduce the topic and prepare trainee, (b) assess trainee's level of knowledge or skill, (c) demonstrate the task, and (d) allow trainee to practice, providing adequate feedback. Many times, JIT is administered

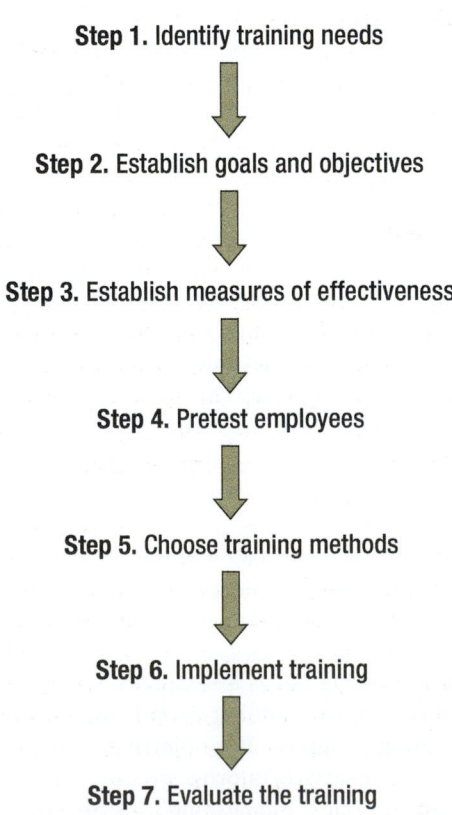

Step 1. Identify training needs

Step 2. Establish goals and objectives

Step 3. Establish measures of effectiveness

Step 4. Pretest employees

Step 5. Choose training methods

Step 6. Implement training

Step 7. Evaluate the training

FIGURE 6.6   The Training Cycle.

On-the-job training.   *Credit*: Goodluz / Shutterstock.

with **computer-based training (CBT)**. Here, workers train at their own pace, usually in training atmosphere, and not in the actual operations of the organization. This CBT can be conducted via the Internet (or **web-based training**), or through an intranet (an internal company website). The advantages to this type of training include the following: (a) accessibility, either time or distance with trainers, (b) cost, especially if there is an investment in hardware/software, (c) frequency, and how often the employee can access training, (d) pace, set by each trainee, (e) instruction, technology leverages the trainer's ability to do more training, (f) participation, everyone participates in training, where sometimes students in the class do not participate, and (g) overcoming the fear factor, some employees may fear sitting in a classroom, but not when they are behind a computer. While the emphasis is on developing technical skills, soft skills (discussed later in this book) should not be forgotten.

One of the most common off-the-job training methods is **lecture**. The trainer does the majority of the talking, making for a relative passive and restrained experience for the employee, unless the trainer has exceptional presentation skills. This method provides a large quantity of information, which makes it a good method to use when covering basic information. Some of the disadvantages are the lack of two-way communication, no allowance for the varying levels of KSAs of the trainees, and retention can be lower because the participation level is low. Another training method is **demonstration**. The trainer demonstrates how to perform a specific skill (e.g., checking in a guest at the front desk) to one or more trainees. This method is suitable for learning procedures or skills. Hands-on training by the trainees typically follows demonstrations. Hands-on training allows the trainer to use another method of training, or **coaching**. Coaching is providing constructive feedback on the performance of the trainee. It helps the overall development of the trainees. After providing constructive feedback, the coach allows the trainee to repeat the performance till he or she obtains the desired skill. A trainer can also use the **combined method**—tell (lecture), show (demonstration), do (hands-on training), and finally, review (coaching). This combination method is excellent for teaching new skills or behaviors. When teaching new behaviors, it is also called **behavior modeling**. In behavior modeling, the desired behavior is explained (lecture), then the trainer demonstrates the behavior, next the employee performs the behavior, and finally, the trainer provides feedback. This method requires time investment and needs a skilled trainer to impart this training.

Programmed instruction uses a manual or a computer to present training material, which will be divided into modules. After the trainee is given the first module, the trainee is asked to complete a questionnaire (or generally by clicking a correct key on the computer). If the trainee is correct, then the second module is presented, and the same process is repeated. Eventually the trainee completes all the modules of the training. Programmed instruction allows trainees to move at their own pace. **Simulations**, sometimes referred to as **vestibule training**, duplicate a real-life situation. An example is a simulation of the front-desk task of helping a guest through the process of checking into the hotel. Many times the trainee is placed just outside the actual

Programmed instruction.
Credit: Andrey_Popov / Shutterstock.

work environment. The advantages are that the training does not interrupt the normal flow of business, and it usually results in a high level of learning. The disadvantage is the expense to this method, primarily duplicating the work environment. **Business games** are a form of simulation; the difference is that games create a competitive environment. Business games can be developed for groups or individuals. Their success depends on the creativity of the training, and the interactions of the simulation. Another type of simulation is **role-playing**. Employees simulate a specific real or hypothetical situation involving two or more people. This method examines current behavior, or tries to build new skills and confidence. Role-playing is usually followed by discussion and analysis.

Structured discussions are conversations between employees (trainer and trainee) aimed to meet specific, predefined objectives. An example would be training a class on kitchen safety. The trainer would divide the class into small working groups and ask each group to develop ideas on how to make the kitchen a safer environment. Once the groups have been given some time, the trainer gets them back into the larger group, and asks them to share their ideas. The key is for the trainer to keep the numerous smaller groups on track. Another form of discussion is **brainstorming**. Here the trainer asks employees to spontaneously generate ideas about a topic. The key is not to evaluate the ideas, leaving this for a later time.

Case study training uses a series of events, either real or hypothetical, in the business environment. This method challenges the employees to decipher the problem, and then to propose action steps to rectify the problem/situation. One of the downfalls to this type of training is that the training happens in a protected environment, and not in the real business environment. In the hospitality industry, problems occur in all shapes and sizes, and not in neatly packaged case studies. Another type of training for managers is **in-basket training**. Here the trainees are given a "basket" of tasks/situations. The trainee must sort the material into priorities. The goals of in-basket training are as follows: (a) to train participants to identify the biggest issues that require immediate attention, (b) to teach participants how to delegate these issues, and (c) to teach participants how to work on several items simultaneously. Research has found that in-basket training is significantly and positively correlated with predicting future management behavior.[4] **Conference training** is a one-on-one discussion between trainer and trainee. Conference training permits virtually any topic to be discussed. The advantage is the reinforcement of the trainer, while the disadvantage is the cost of the individualized training.

Finally, as the workforce becomes more and more multicultural, emphasis is placed on sensitivity training and diversity training. **Sensitivity training** was first developed by Kurt Lewin, and is often used to enhance interpersonal skills. Sensitivity training normally occurs in small groups, generally four to ten participants. Typically each participant is confronted about his or her behavior, and then each participant is given the opportunity to express his or her feelings about the group process. The key to this type of training is the trainer; he or she must keep strong emotions out of the process, and make sure the focus is on the behavior. The advantage enables the trainee to see how others perceive him or her in the workplace. The disadvantage is that the process can become very personal, unless the trainer is very skilled in the process. Diversity training educates employees to be more sensitive to their coworkers' (and guests') needs, usually racial and religious. To be effective, diversity training should aim at the following:

- Motivate the trainee to improve his or her performance
- Clearly demonstrate desired skills
- Provide for active trainee participation
- Provide timely feedback on the trainee's performance
- Provide for trainee positive reinforcement
- Structure tasks from simple to complex
- Be adaptable to specific problems
- Encourage positive transfer of KSAs[5]

Research has shown that diversity training is successful when it is voluntary and it is supported by mentoring.[6]

Cross Training

Cross training occurs when employees are trained to perform job duties other than those normally assigned. Cross training may be a short-term temporary fix or an ongoing planned process. It can take many forms, from one- to two-day temporary assignments to a sophisticated process of job rotation typically lasting six or more months. Historically, cross training has focused on broadening employees' skills to reduce costs and provide job coverage. Along with on-the-job training, it was often used in trade jobs and administrative functions as a way for employees to learn new skills. Originally, cross training provided backup help when the primary jobholder was unavailable for a day or two. It filled the void and allowed the manager to juggle priorities. It was also invaluable if a jobholder left the organization, as someone else was able to cover until the position was filled.

Today, the reasons organizations implement cross training go beyond these traditional needs. Cross training has many more benefits for employees and organizations. Along with improving productivity, it increases employee commitment and motivation. Cross training increases employees' knowledge and abilities to perform different tasks by using current skills or by learning new skills. It is a good way to add variety to employees' workdays, to add new challenges to their jobs, and/or to try out new skills for future career development. It offers the opportunity to work with different employees and supervisors, adding to enhanced self-esteem in both the employee learning the new skill and the employee teaching the skill. In addition to enlarging jobs—performing different but relatively equal tasks—cross training may be designed to enrich jobs. Job enrichment adds more responsibility to an employee's work. Through exposure to a variety of jobs, the employee gains a better understanding of the interrelationships between jobs and work groups and can develop a "bigger" picture of the operation of the organization.

Today's employers are looking for versatile and flexible workers. They want team players willing to accept or even volunteer for duties or projects outside their normal job responsibilities. The last thing they want to hear is "that's not my job" or "I don't know how to do it." By accepting cross training assignments, employees show management that they are willing to learn new skills. Employees can then demonstrate the KSAs needed for future advancement by showing how quickly they learn and how well they carry out new tasks. Cross training usually does not result in immediate promotion or advancement to a higher pay grade, but it does indicate that the employee is interested in learning new skills and the skill diversity may help the person meet the qualifications for future career advancement. Also, if downsizing, rightsizing, or restructuring initiatives occur, employees with broader skills and the ability to assume larger roles are more valuable and so are often the ones who are retained.[7]

Training Evaluation

The last step in the training cycle is the evaluation of the training. Many times organizations ignore this last step, thus wasting their valuable training dollars. The key is to evaluate the training objectives. This evaluation should not only occur at the end, rather it should occur during every step to make the training more valuable. Formative evaluation is the ongoing evaluation process, and is completed with observation, interviews, or surveys. Summative evaluation

Result Area	Sample Methods
Employee Reaction	On a scale of 1 to 5, rate each of the following: subjects covered, teaching methods, trainers, and training facility. Would you recommend the training to other employees? Yes or No.
Knowledge Gained	What information did you learn from this session? May also observe performance or give a test on the topic.
Behavior	A performance appraisal by supervisors, peers, subordinates, and/or guests can be conducted to evaluate changes in behavior.
Attitudes	An attitude survey may be conducted to determine employee opinions, feelings, and perceptions.
Productivity	An evaluation of productivity as measured by a decrease in employee turnover, an increase in employee satisfaction, or increase in guest satisfaction. May also measure productivity through a decrease in costs and waste, decrease in labor costs, and increased profit.

FIGURE 6.7   Categories of Results for Summative Evaluation with Sample Methods.

measures the results of the training program. Categories of results and sample evaluation methods are presented in Figure 6.7.

The most effective method for evaluating a training program uses at least one measure for each of the five categories of results—employee reaction, knowledge gained, behavior, attitudes, and productivity. Strategic managers will calculate a **return on investment (ROI)** for every training program. To do this, the benefits or the summative evaluation results should be converted to dollars. Some of the benefits that are harder to convert to dollars include employee reactions and attitudes. Other benefits of a training program may include cost savings through increased productivity, increased sales, or decreased turnover. Direct and indirect costs of the training program include design and development, delivery method, materials, facilities, and student costs. Once costs and benefits have been identified in terms of dollars, the ROI can be calculated using the following formula:

ROI = Benefits/Costs

It is expected that this number be greater than 1 and a larger number indicates a more effective training program.

Return on investment.   *Credit*: Stuart Miles / Shutterstock.

EMPLOYEE DEVELOPMENT

Once the initial training program is completed, the focus should turn to the continued development of employees. The goal of training now becomes the promotion of employees to levels of more responsibility and more authority. The process for employee development includes five steps as presented in Figure 6.8.

The first step in the employee development process is to identify business needs for employees with specialized KSAs. A process for moving through the management hierarchy of the organization can be used to identify needs for employees with supervisory skills and abilities. A career ladder or career lattice may be used to help employees identify potential promotion opportunities. Feedback from customers during customer service interactions can also be a source for improving employee skills. Another source of needs includes plans for new services, which may require new skills for current employees.

The second step is to identify the KSAs of current employees. Supervisors may use a checklist or performance evaluation form to assess current levels of KSAs. A self-evaluation by employees may also be used to identify areas of weakness and interest in developing new skills and abilities. The next step is a gap analysis where business needs are compared to employee skills to identify areas for knowledge and skills development. This gap analysis should result in a list of KSAs needed to carry out the goals of the organization.

Once the gap analysis is completed, the employees who are interested in obtaining new skills and abilities should be contacted and a training program should be developed. The training program may include a variety of coaching, mentoring, cross training, job rotation, and educational experiences. Feedback should be used to help employees develop the needed KSAs. A full evaluation of the effectiveness of the development program will lead back to a revision of business needs and the cycle repeats.

THE BOTTOM LINE

Formal training and development programs are important for every organization. However, most hospitality managers are involved in training employees every day. Informal performance reviews during a shift with immediate feedback on correct ways to handle a task are typical. Using these immediate training opportunities is important in a successful operation.

The easiest way to apply training and development to hospitality management is to look at a company, well-known for its training. In 2007, the Ritz Carlton (a two-time winner of the Malcolm Bridge National Quality Award in the years 1992 and 1999) was voted the number one training company out of 125 companies. The Ritz Carlton values training so much, that at

Evaluate training effectiveness. *Credit*: Bannosuke / Shutterstock.

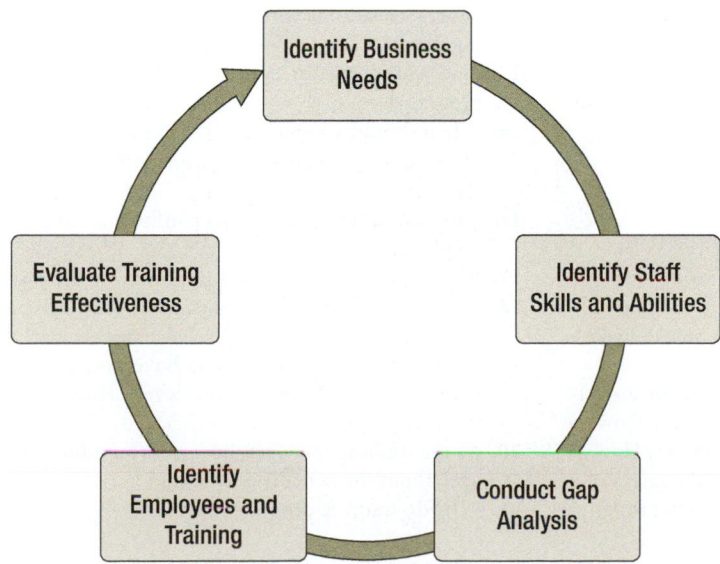

FIGURE 6.8 **Steps in Employee Development.**

the beginning of every shift, a 15-minute "refresher" training meeting takes place. During this meeting, the leader focuses on one of the following 12 "service values."

1. Create lifelong Ritz Carlton guests, by building strong relationships
2. Respond to the expressed and unexpressed wishes and needs of all guests
3. Create unique, memorable, and personal experiences for the guests
4. Each employee must understand his or her role in the "key success factors"
5. Seek opportunities to innovate and improve the Ritz Carlton experience
6. Owning and immediately resolving guests' problems
7. Create an environment of teamwork
8. Find opportunities to continuously grow and learn
9. Employee involvement in all aspects of the work environment
10. Employee pride in professional appearance, language, and behavior
11. A commitment to protect the privacy and security of each guest, other employees, and the company's assets
12. Taking responsibility for uncompromising levels of cleanliness, and creating a safe, accident-free workplace

Ritz Carlton is known for its attention to detail. With this emphasis on the guests, and on training, it is sure to continue its success in the hospitality industry.[8]

The overall goal of training is to bring about a desired level of knowledge, skills, and abilities with all employees of the company, whether the employee is new or tenured. Most hospitality companies value training, and in some cases, companies take training and development as the most pressing issue within their operation. In time of economic crisis, with stiff business competition, demanding customers, and concerns of a safe working environment, a good training program can be a valuable tool to retain employees and provide excellent customer service.

Training is the primary responsibility of every manager in the hospitality operation. The training manager is the professional guide in the training cycle. This individual facilitates the needs assessment, the orientation program, the training program design, training methods, the evaluation of the training program, and the career development of all employees (cross training). Finally, the training manager must conduct a cost/benefit analysis to justify the investment of organization resources (people, facilities, and money) into the training process.

Discussion Questions

1. Why do training managers need to assess the different levels of training?
2. What type of information can be used to design a training program? And why is this important?
3. What are the goals to an organization's orientation program?
4. How does general property orientation differ from specific work group orientation?
5. What should be included in an orientation kit?
6. What should the orientation leader avoid?
7. How is orientation different from mentoring?
8. Why is training considered a cyclical process?
9. What are the steps in the training cycle? And how is each one dependent on the other?
10. If you were asked to train a small group of adults in how to make a bed, what techniques would you use?
11. What training methods would you use to teach KSAs for the following situations: (a) What to do in case of a fire? (b) How to handle a credit card sale at the front desk of the hotel? (c) How to handle a customer complaint? (d) How to tell the doneness of a steak? (e) How to know when equipment is functioning properly?

or (f) How do I receive dry, frozen, and perishable goods into the hotel?

12. When are attitude surveys an effective method of analyzing training needs?
13. How can a pretest be helpful in the assessment of a training program?
14. When should a trainer decided to conduct behavioral modeling?
15. How can a company benefit from computer-based (or web-based) training?
16. How can a training manager influence the career growth of an employee?
17. Why is career development important to the organization?
18. In times of financial crisis, is it wise to pare the training programs?
19. As the training manager, you have noticed a spike in customer comments about poor service levels. How should you adjust the training program?
20. As the training manager, how can you influence the general manager about the benefits of training?
21. Why do training programs succeed?

Application Exercise

You are an assistant manager in a high-volume, training restaurant. It is Mother's Day, and the restaurant general manager has asked a newly hired employee to start on this day. What can you do to make this employee feel less stressed about starting his new job? How would you implement his training for this day? What would you avoid doing with this newly hired employee? What would you suggest you tell the restaurant general manager?

Endnotes

1. Weatherly, L. (December 2004). Human resource development series part II: HRD and training needs assessment. Accessed from http://www.shrm.org/Research/Articles/Articles/Pages/Human_20Resource_20Development_20Series_20Part_20II__20HRD_20Training_20Needs_20Assessment.aspx
2. Mulvey, Janemarie (March 2005). Employee turnover rises, increasing costs. Employment Policy Foundation. Retrieved from www.epf.org/pubs/factsheets/2005/fs20050317.pdf
3. Cascio, W. F. (1989). *Managing Human Resources: Productivity, Quality of Work Life, Profits*. New York: McGraw-Hill.
4. Mulvey. Employee turnover rises
5. Cascio, *Managing Human Resources*
6. Kalev, A., Dobbin, F., & Kelly, E. (2006). Best practices or best guess? Assessing the efficacy of corporate affirmative action and diversity policies. *American Sociological Review*, 71(4), 589–617.
7. Asselta, C., & Sperl, C. (2002). Cross training—value in today's environment. SHRM White Paper, 11/1/2001.
8. Gordon, J. (March 2007). Redefining elegance. *Training*, 14–20.

Key Terms

ADDIE model   The training process that includes analysis, design, development, implementation, and evaluation.

Attitude survey   A tool used to solicit and assess employee opinions, feelings, perceptions, and expectations regarding a variety of managerial and organizational issues.

Behavior modeling   This method explains (lecture) the desired behavior, then the trainer demonstrates the behavior, next the employee shows the behavior, and finally, the trainer provides feedback.

Brainstorming   A decision-making approach in which group members suggest alternative potential causes and/or solutions to problems for group consideration.

Business games   A form of simulation creating a competitive environment.

Case study training   A situation or circumstance relating to the workplace described in writing and the trainee is asked to read and respond either verbally or in writing.

Coaching   A training method in which a more experienced or skilled individual provides an employee with advice and guidance intended to help him or her develop skills, improve performance and enhance the quality of his or her career.

Combined method   A training method that uses several approaches, such as tell (lecture), show (demonstration), do (hands-on training), and finally, review (coaching).

Computer-based training   The use of a computer to deliver training content either via CD-ROM, Internet, or corporate intranet.

Conference training   A one-on-one discussion between trainer and trainee, which permits virtually any topic to be discussed.

Demonstration   A training method in which the trainer shows trainees how to perform all or part of a task.

Diversity training   A fundamental component of a diversity initiative that represents the opportunity for an organization to inform and educate senior management and staff about diversity. The purpose of training is not only to increase awareness and understanding of workplace diversity, but also to develop concrete skills among staff that will facilitate enhanced productivity and communication among all employees.

Formative evaluation   The process of ongoing evaluation, and is completed with observation, interviews, or surveys.

General property orientation   A method designed to relay basic information that an employee will need to understand the broader system of the hospitality company.

In-basket training   A training method where the trainees are given a "basket" of tasks/situations and are then asked to prioritize them.

Individual analysis   A means of assessing training needs by focusing on how individuals perform their jobs.

Job instruction training   Very similar to on-the-job training, where training is delivered directly at the workplace.

Job/task analysis   The systematic process of gathering, examining, and interpreting data regarding the specific tasks comprising a job.

Lecture   A training method where the trainer, or lecturer, delivers a large amount of information to either a single trainee or a group of trainees.

Off-the-job training   Training methods where instruction is delivered away from the actual job, perhaps in a classroom setting either onsite or offsite.

On-the-job training   Training methods where the instruction is delivered directly on the job.

Organizational analysis   The training process that includes analysis, design, development, implementation, and evaluation.

Programmed instruction   A training method using a manual or a computer to present training material.

Return on investment (ROI)   A method for evaluating training effectiveness that requires costs and benefits be identified and used in the formula: ROI = benefits/costs.

Role-playing   A training method in which each participant purposely acts out or assumes a particular character or role.

Sensitivity training   A form of individual counseling geared toward increasing self-awareness and sensitivity to others. It aims to assist key employees in developing their leadership skills surrounding issues of diversity and harassment prevention.

Simulations   An instructional method used to teach problem solving, procedures, or operations by placing learners in situations akin to reality.

Specific work group and job orientation   A more detailed aspect of introducing the new employee to the organization. Here, more specifics are provided to the new employee.

Structured discussion   Asks the same questions of each employee, so that valid comparisons of the quality of responses can be obtained. The questions generally take four job-related forms: situational, observational, personal, and behavioral.

Summative evaluation   A process using several methods to measure the end results of the training program.

Training criteria   The benchmarks that are set by the company to measure training effectiveness.

Training needs assessment   The process used to determine if training is necessary; it is the first step in the instructional system design process.

Training objectives   The outcomes desired from the training and development process; objectives should state the desired behavior and the conditions under which it should occur.

Vestibule training   A form of training conducted outside of the workplace to acclimate newly hired employees with procedures and equipment or tools to be used in their jobs.

Web-based training   A training method that is usually off-the-job training and is conducted via the Internet.

Performance Management Systems

OUTLINE

KEY TERMS

360° feedback

Alternative ranking

Behavioral observation scale (BOS)

Behaviorally anchored rating scales (BARS) method

Contrast effect

Counseling

Critical incident method

Cross-cultural bias

Devil's horn effect

Discharge

Discharge interview

Employment at will

Error of central tendency

Exit interview

Forced distribution

Graphic rating scale

Guest (customer) evaluations

Halo effect

Hierarchical appeal process

Hot stove approach

Inter-rater reliability

Leniency bias

Management by objectives (MBO)

Multiple rater evaluations

Narrative essay

Ombudsman appeals process

Open door policy appeals process

Oral warning

Paired comparison

Peer appeals process

Peer evaluations

Personal prejudice

Preventative discipline

Progressive discipline

Public policy

Recency effect

SARA

Self-evaluation

Similar-to-me bias

Simple ranking

Strictness bias

Suspension

Written warning

Wrongful discharge (or dismissal) suit

OBJECTIVES

- Describe general performance evaluation (appraisals) issues
- Summarize the functions of performance evaluation
- Identify and discuss potential problems with performance management
- Define the types of rating systems
- Describe methods of appraising performance
- Identify the raters in performance management
- Discuss the potential for legal issues in performance management
- Define and discuss the counseling process

Consider This

Kamil has just been promoted to district manager for a pizza company, and has been given six restaurants to supervise. These pizza restaurants are mainly inner-city stores in a large metropolitan area. His manager has confidence in his ability to turn these restaurants around, and have these restaurants become profitable again. After one month, Kamil realizes the challenges, and doesn't think there is enough time in the day to accomplish his goals. He schedules a meeting with his boss. What should he say to the boss?

INTRODUCTION

Conducting employee performance appraisals is an essential part of hospitality managers' jobs. For many managers, it is an unpleasant task that is often done without the proper investment of time in the preparation and execution. It is never an easy task to judge the competence of another; nor should we minimize the difficulties that can arise in conveying the results to the employee. This difficulty is compounded when the manager is poorly trained in communication skills.

Satisfactory performance appraisals demand the following:

1. Well-trained managers
2. Well-designed appraisal instruments
3. Clearly stated performance objectives (for the employees)

These formal appraisals should have the following criteria:

1. Appraisals should be conducted once or twice a year.
2. Appraisals should be in written form and documented.
3. Adequate prior notice should be given to the employee.
4. The method and objective of the appraisal should be properly explained to the employee prior to his or her starting to work for the company.

Informal appraisals should be an ongoing, even daily event. A good manager should show interest in the daily tasks of his or her employee by encouragement and praise, and by offering help. He or she should not be afraid to tactfully point out specific errors in an employee's performance.

PERFORMANCE EVALUATION SYSTEMS

Before an evaluation is attempted, there must be a clear statement of expectation, or in other words, a detailed written job description. Preferably this job description should be the mutual effort of managers and employees. It is best that it be compiled early in the employment period and cannot be too detailed. This gives management an objective tool to work with and helps to eliminate any perception of bias or subjectivity on the part of the manager. Appraisals should be designed with a specific purpose in mind. Several systems may be in use at the same time in order to assess different aspects of the business.

Performance appraisal.
Credit: Auremar / Shutterstock.

Uses of performance appraisals include the following:

1. To supply feedback to employees and to alert management to strengths or weaknesses in its operation
2. To identify the need for additional training for both managers and employees
3. To help in developing career goals, and to help in career counseling to employees
4. To be used as an administrative tool to determine when reward or punishment may be appropriate for an employee (i.e., merit pay should relate to outstanding work, as should demotion (or termination) for poor performance)
5. In the case of grievances, the performance appraisal can be invaluable documentation and help protect the organization in a lawsuit or EEO (equal employment opportunity) discrimination charge
6. Performance appraisals can gauge the effectiveness of a training manager by evaluating personnel before and after the training session
7. As an effective tool to determine the strengths and/or weaknesses in the selection process

As discussed in Chapter 5 (Selecting Employees), validity and reliability are important elements in performance management systems. Performance appraisals have construct validity, which means they must measure what they intend to measure in all aspects of the employee's performance. The performance evaluation process must have reliability, and it must consistently deliver the same results for all employees with similar KSAs (knowledge, skills, and abilities). Finally, the performance evaluation process must be concerned with inter-rater reliability. When two or more raters are rating the performance of an employee, they must agree on the same rating, this is said to have high inter-rater reliability.

The Evaluation Form

The key to managing performance is the evaluation form. This form must be in writing, no oral evaluation should be allowed. The organization must add this documentation to the employees' personnel files. The format that is selected depends on the purpose of the performance appraisal; the need to collect different types of information requires different formats and methods. A manager generally judges performance in three ways: (a) what is achieved (results), (b) what the employee does (behavior), and (c) what the employee has (KSAs).

Many evaluation forms have two types of input—subjective and objective. The performance appraisal process wants to quantify the results, behavior, or knowledge of the employee, and to rate this performance in an objective way. This allows the evaluator to give the performance a number rating. Though subjectivity is not a required attribute, we must realize that it is very difficult to totally eliminate subjectivity. Suppose for example, you have taken over

Evaluation form.   *Credit*: Mert Toker / Shutterstock.

as a district manager for a large restaurant chain, and you are responsible for six restaurants. The restaurants are not performing well financially, so you implement actions to correct the issues within each restaurant. After the first year, you have made some strides, but the financial numbers are not meeting budgeted levels, thus, the district manager will receive below-average ratings for objective (financial) criteria. But recognizing the improvements in the six restaurants, the manager's supervisor gives the district manager above-average ratings for the subjective criteria.

When completing the evaluation form, the evaluator should avoid using vague words such as adequate, reasonable, or approximately. It is by stating specific results, behaviors, and knowledge that the evaluator will be able to clearly communicate with the employee.(An example: The general manager is given a target of 10 percent increase in sales over the same time period as last year.) This clear communication will motivate the employee to improve performance in the future. Finally, the evaluation form needs to be practical and acceptable to raters and employees. To be practical, the evaluation form must be easy to understand and easy to use. In order for it to be acceptable, the evaluation form must be reliable and valid.

Methods

There are several methods used to evaluate performance. Each method has unique advantages and disadvantages. This section will discuss the most commonly used methods, and discuss each method's strengths and weaknesses. The most popular method is the **graphic rating scale**. This scale delineates rating factors for a certain job, and then formulates rating responses, usually in the form of unsatisfactory to outstanding. The three most common types of graphic rating scale are (a) simple or straight ranking, (b) alternative ranking, or (c) paired rankings. **Simple ranking** is the method in which the evaluator ranks all employees from best to worst. This method provides a simple order for consideration of the performances of employees. The disadvantages are the choice of the ranking criteria, which does not distinguish between different aspects of the job's responsibilities. Typically, the evaluation only considers one responsibility. To improve this aspect, the evaluator needs to identify the job's different responsibilities and should rate each employee on these separate responsibilities. Although very similar to simple ranking, the **alternative ranking** is the method in which the evaluator lists each employee's name on a different piece of paper. The evaluator then chooses the best employee first and puts that name at the top of the list. The evaluator selects the worst employee second and places that name at the bottom of the list. The evaluator selects the second best employee and places that name following the best employee. The evaluator selects the second worst employee and places that name above the worst employee. The process of alternating between best and worst continues until all employees have been ranked. This method allows the evaluator to make comparisons between similar employees

Criterion	Employee in this column is better	Than employee in this column
Work performance	Johnson	Smith
Customer service	Smith	Taylor
Teamwork	Taylor	Abernathy
Communication with managers	Smith	Abernathy
Attendance	Johnson	Taylor
	Johnson	Abernathy
Overall	Johnson has the largest number in this column, so he is ranked as first. Smith is second, Taylor is third, and Abernathy is fourth.	

FIGURE 7.1   **Paired Comparison Ranking Method. Employees to be ranked: Johnson, Smith, Taylor, Abernathy**

as the extremes are removed from consideration. This method has the same advantages and disadvantages as the simple ranking method. The **paired comparison** method involves the direct comparison of employees to each other on each job criterion. An example of this is found in Figure 7.1. By counting the names on the left side of the list, the employee whose name is listed first the most number of times is the employee with the highest ranking. Again, the advantages and disadvantages are similar to the simple ranking method.

Forced distribution uses the theory behind a bell curve and evaluates most employees in the middle as medium performers, a few top performers, and a few poor performers. Statistically speaking, this method will put 10 percent of the employees as outstanding performers, 20 percent as good, 40 percent as average, 20 percent as marginal, and 10 percent as unsatisfactory performers. Figure 7.2 presents an example of a normal curve. This method eliminates some leniency and severity biases, but creates a central tendency bias. Another disadvantage is the possible lowering of employee morale because the employees are categorized into specific job performance levels.

A type of rating method that uses both formal and informal performance evaluations is the **critical incident method**. Here, the evaluator keeps an individual log on each employee, and places emphasis on employee behavior. The advantages of this method are the availability of specific behavior for the entire evaluation period and the ability of the evaluator to create better goals and objectives for the evaluation. A disadvantage is that the evaluator must be diligent in

Paired comparison.   *Credit*: Dusit / Shutterstock.

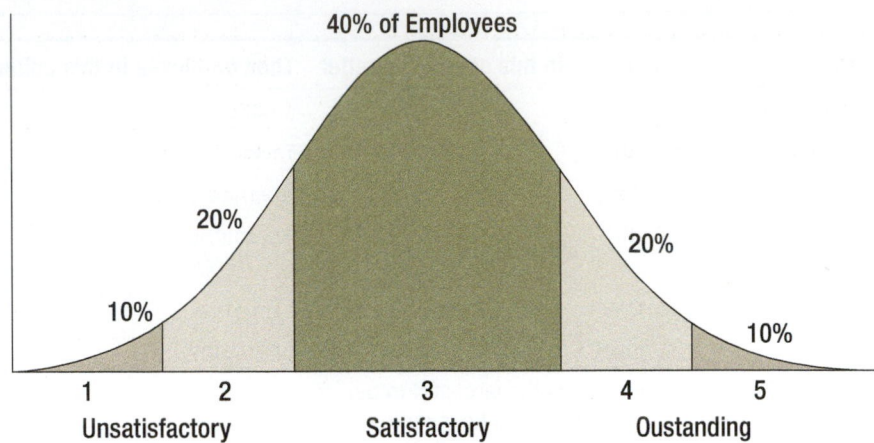

FIGURE 7.2   **Normal Curve.**

keeping the critical incident logs because of the time-consuming tasks involved in this method. Another version of this method is the **narrative essay**. With this method, the evaluator simply writes an essay describing the employee's behavior. The advantages and disadvantages are similar to the critical incident method.

Next, behavioral approaches use the same concept as the critical incident. **Behaviorally anchored rating scales (BARS) method** uses specific descriptors of desired and undesired behaviors in a checklist form. Figure 7.3 includes an example of a BARS evaluation form. The evaluator observes the work-related incidents and records them to portray an accurate measure of the employee's performance. Normally a committee of employees and managers develops the BARS. Since employees are also involved, the work group usually accepts BARS, and usually BARS provides a very accurate rating of overall performance. The weaknesses are the amount of time it takes to develop and the expense involved in developing the descriptors.

Similar to BARS, and developed in response to concerns with BARS, was **behavioral observation scales (BOS)**. This type of appraisal system also judges employee performance on the number of observable behaviors, either good or bad. But the difference is that the BOS allows for a number of observations, whereas BARS allows only one behavior rating. Many times the descriptors used with the BOS scale include "always" to "never." This is an advantage of the BOS method. The disadvantages of the BOS method are similar to BARS. A sample BOS form is presented in Figure 7.4.

There are advantages and disadvantages in each method of performance evaluation. As a result, one method is typically selected by a company and is used for all positions. Figure 7.5 presents advantages and disadvantages of all the six methods.

Management by objectives (MBO) is a combination method of performance evaluation and goal setting. This method involves meetings between employee and manager (or manager and his or her supervisor) in which goals are established, and agreed upon by both parties. Once the goals are established, specific plans are developed to achieve these goals, and then methods are selected to measure progress toward these goals. An MBO system is accomplished by establishing regular meetings to assess the performance and, if necessary, adjust plans to ensure goal attainment. The steps to a MBO are as follows:

1. Employee develops goals for the evaluation period.
2. Employee and manager meet to discuss goals, modify the goals (if necessary), and agree on the goals; the goals are then put into writing.
3. Next, the parties agree to the specific plans of attaining goals, and they establish the methods of measuring the progress.
4. At the end of the evaluation period, employee and manager meet to discuss goal achievement, and performance rating is given.
5. The process is repeated for the new evaluation period.

The advantage of the MBO rests in the agreement of both parties to clearly establish goals that help the individual and the company. The disadvantages are: (a) the amount of time

Employee:		Department:
Supervisor:		Date:

Performance Category: Apply interpersonal skills to develop the team

Circle the
appropriate rating

Behavior Anchor	Rating Scale	Behavior Anchor
	5.00	(a) Lead, influence, motivate, and persuade others to achieve company goals (b) Develop constructive and cooperative working relationships with others (c) Employ leadership skills to facilitate workflow (d) Observe and coach others for improved performance
(a) Often leads others to achieve company goals (b) Most working relationships with others are constructive (c) May need to be reminded to use leadership skills (d) Often coaches employees for improved performance	4.00	
	3.00	(a) Leading others is achieved most of the time (b) Some problems in working relationships with others (c) Coaching employees is not a priority
(a) Problems in working with employees and leading them to reach company goals (b) Many problems exist in working relationships with others (c) Many employees need direction and training	2.00	
	1.00	(a) Shows no interest in developing positive working relationships with others (b) Does not give employees direction on how to improve

FIGURE 7.3   BARS Example: Apply Interpersonal Skills to Develop the Team.

involved, (b) the need to stay away from short-term goal setting, (c) the potential for employees to agree to all goals recommended by the managers, and (d) different goals are set for each employee, and the possibility of one employee seeing the MBO system as not being fair. An example of an MBO format is in Figure 7.6.

Employee:	Department:			
Supervisor:	Date:			
Behavior Observation: Management Soft Skills				
Behavior/Skill	**Frequency**			
Scale	**Always**	**Frequently**	**Occasionally**	**Seldom**
Acts creatively/tries new ideas				
Asks questions of supervisors and subordinates				
Delivers presentations to necessary individuals				
Gets commitment from supervisor and subordinates				
Influences subordinates in a positive manner				
Negotiates important details that will have a positive impact on the business				
Persuades supervisor and subordinates of the importance of the task at hand				
Seeks information to make better decisions				
Shows enthusiasm for the job at hand				
Takes rejection and builds upon it				
Updates skill level to become a better performer				
Uses humor to diffuse a difficult situation				

FIGURE 7.4 **BOS Example: Soft Skills Competencies in Managers.**

Who Conducts the Performance Evaluation

In a performance management system, usually the supervisor is the only one who evaluates the hourly employee. In hospitality management companies, usually this supervisor does have direct contact with the employee. When this supervisor does not have direct contact, it poses a serious problem to the evaluation process. Those supervisors who have direct contact with the employees are the best evaluators of performance. While performance evaluations are primarily a management task, they can also include many other options. Some of those options are discussed next.

Self-Evaluation—Employee input can be an effective component of the evaluation process. Many times a manager will ask an employee to provide a self-rating of his or her performance. This style of evaluation can lead to defensiveness, disagreements, and bad feelings between the employee and manager, so it is essential that the evaluator ask the employee to provide key results of performance. This gets the employees to focus on their accomplishments. Employee input has a number of positive results. First, it involves employees in the process, enhancing ownership and acceptance. Second, it reminds managers

Performance Appraisal Method	Advantages	Disadvantages
Graphic Rating Scale	Simple to use - Provides a quantitative rating for each employee	Standards may be unclear - Often has problems with halo effect, central tendency, leniency, and bias
Paired Comparison	Simple order for comparison	May consider only one responsibility
Forced Distribution	Ends up with a predetermined number or percentage of employees in each group	Results depend on the choice of cutoff points
Critical Incident	Identifies what is right and wrong about performance - Requires evaluation on an ongoing basis	May be time consuming to keep logs during entire period - May be difficult to rate or rank employees
BARS	Provides behavioral anchors and is very accurate	Takes time to develop - May be difficult and expensive to develop
BOS	Performance is evaluated on a number of behaviors - Uses a scale of always to never	Takes time and is difficult to develop

FIGURE 7.5   Advantages and Disadvantages of Performance Appraisal Methods.

Restaurant:	Name:	
Review Period:	Reviewer:	
Performance goals	**Measures of Results**	**Results**
(1) Market share	Sales	Increase by 3%
(2) Guest comments	Ratio of positive comments	Increase to 90%
(3) Profit	Profit as a percentage of sales	Increase by 5%
(4) Labor costs	Total labor as a percent of sales	Decrease by 5%
(5) ServSafe certified managers	Number of completions	90% of managers
(6) Health and safety conditions	Sanitation inspection ratings	Above 100
(7) Employee turnover rate	Turnover as a percentage of employees	Decrease by 5%

FIGURE 7.6   MBO Example.

of the results employees have delivered and of how they were achieved. Third, employee-generated accomplishments can be included in the formal appraisal, decreasing managers' writing requirements. Fourth, employee input increases communication and understanding. Managers and employees usually review and discuss the accomplishments before they become part of the appraisal, resulting in fewer disconnects between the manager's view and the employee's view of the contribution of the employees. Finally, employee accomplishments can be retained and used as input for pay or promotion decisions. Research has shown that employee accomplishments are effective predictors of how successfully employees will perform at higher job levels, and they thus provide useful input for promotion decisions.[1]

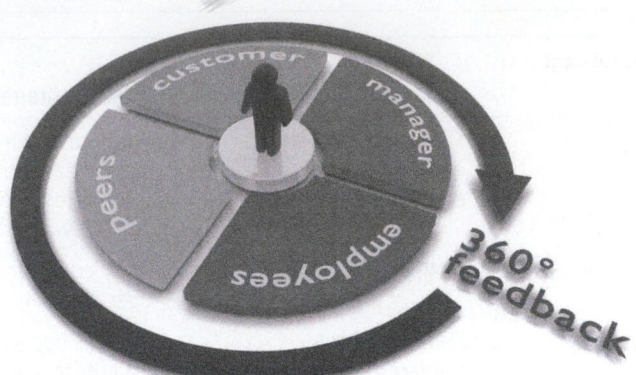

360° feedback. *Credit*: S. John / Shutterstock.

Peer Evaluations—An employee usually works very closely with his or her peers, and among everyone in the work environment, it is usually one's peers who have the most contact with the employee involved in the evaluation. Hospitality organizations also focus on teamwork within their environments. Here again it is the employees who have the most contact with their peers and their teamwork abilities. Similar to self-evaluations, peer reviews can lead to defensiveness, disagreements, and bad feelings between employees. It is probably best to use peer evaluation as one of the components of the performance management system.

Guest (Customer) Evaluations—Almost every hospitality operation asks for feedback from its customers. The purpose of this feedback is to correct any issue that may arise within the operations of the company. Many times, these customers' comments can also help with employee evaluations and, as stated in Chapter 6 (Training and Development), can help identify training needs. Many times a manager can incorporate the positive customer comments into the evaluation. Likewise, the manager can also use negative comments to help improve an employee's performance. Again, it is probably best to use guest evaluations as one component of the performance management system.

Multiple Rater Evaluations—As hinted earlier, a combination approach is probably best when it comes to the performance management process. Using a multiple rater system can increase the accuracy of the evaluation system, and generally, the person being evaluated perceives the multiple ratings as fair and equitable. Thus, contributions from different perspectives can be especially interesting and valuable. This multiple rater system is referred to as **360° feedback** (also called multisource feedback, full-circle appraisal, or group performance review). Possible participants in 360° feedback include supervisors, subordinates, peers, employees from other departments, customers, and even suppliers. It has been said that 90 percent of Fortune 500 companies use 360° feedback.[2] Some recommendations for using the 360° feedback method are included in Figure 7.7.

When 360° feedback is integrated successfully, it can remedy some of the flaws in the traditional performance management system. It must be noted that feedback is only one component of the evaluation; it is not the entire evaluation. Other considerations are as follows: (a) ensure the collection of relevant data, (b) ensure that one rater cannot dominate the results of the evaluation, and (c) train raters in the process.[4]

- Feedback must be confidential and anonymous, but it is acceptable to state the appraiser's level within the company
- State the length of relationship between the rater and person being rated
- Follow-up is essential - a discussion concerning those criteria receiving the biggest variance between ratings should take place
- Develop a plan of action from the results
- Combine objective ratings (quantitative) with subjective (narrative) ratings
- Avoid fatigue - don't evaluate everyone at once[3]

FIGURE 7.7 Recommendations for Using 360° Feedback.

When to Conduct Evaluations

Performance appraisals are most beneficial when conducted frequently. Though this seems obviously, ironically this is not the widespread practice. The norm for performance appraisal is twice yearly, but often once annually. In fact, a national survey of employers revealed that December 24 is the most popular date for managers to conduct their annual performance.[5] Annual performance appraisals present many problems, even to the most conscientious of managers. Memory fades and it is often difficult to remember even the general event of 12 months ago, let alone the details involved. Managers can minimize, but not eliminate, this problem by being assiduous in their note keeping throughout the period. Although it may be difficult for managers to give daily feedback to the employees, feedback should be given frequently.

The hospitality industry often experiences another hurdle to effective performance appraisals and that is rapid managerial turnover. This makes it very difficult for the practice of biannual or annual performance appraisals to be effective within the industry. In many companies, managerial turnover can be anywhere between 50 and 100 percent. This means in practice, in the course of a year, an employee may work under several managers. Unless very good notes have been taken and accurate records kept, severe distortions may result in appraisals. This is not fair to the employee or the company.

How to Handle Evaluations

Feedback to the employee is at the heart of performance appraisals. Yet obvious as this may seem, it is often neglected. In a 2002 survey in the Chicago area of 25 companies, over 50 percent of respondents claimed that the feedback they received from their supervisors was so slight that it was of little or no value.[6] A larger international survey of over 10,000 persons found 50 percent of respondents were frustrated by the outcome and claimed that their supervisor was not clear, frank, or complete when discussing their performance appraisals with them. Further indications found that 17 percent were left unsure of what their managers thought of their work, 22 percent were unclear on the objectives they were to achieve, and another 33 percent complained that their managers gave them little or no assistance in improving their performance and were not forthcoming in discussing their performance with them. Despite this lack of interest or know-how on the part of management, 90 percent of respondents claimed to be enthusiastic about the process and welcomed detailed, objective feedback.[7]

Feedback sessions should be given to employees as soon as possible and should include the following:

1. The specific behavior the employee has exhibited
2. The impact of the behavior on others—the team and the business
3. What the employee should do to improve
4. Discussion on the next steps the employee will have to take and deadlines for the same

Finally, it is wise to be aware of SARA. Usually when a supervisor has to give constructive criticism (negative feedback), the employee will generally go through four emotional phases. First, the employee will be shocked (S) by the feedback, and usually deny the level of performance. Second, the employee will be angry (A) with the feedback and might feel anger toward the evaluator. Third, the employee will resent (R) the feedback, and might start to plot reactions (resulting in termination). But finally, the employee needs to accept (A) the constructive criticism. When the evaluator can get the employee to this level, the employee will be ready to improve performance.[8]

SOURCES OF DEFICIENCIES

A well-designed performance appraisal system will provide an accurate picture of an employee's daily performance. It will emphasize the good and the bad. It must be job related, be specific, set standards, and use dependable measures. The performance appraisal is job related when it addresses critical behaviors that make for employees' successful job performance (i.e., an appraisal of the dishwasher does not emphasize a "big" personality, rather an attention to detail). The performance appraisal should provide specific details on observable acts. The performance appraisal should arise from the clear performance expectations that have been written in the employee's job description. There must be a written record of standards. Both managers and employees should develop these standards. Employers should be apprised of these standards before the evaluation occurs. The standards set must be attainable in the normal performance of the job. Finally, a performance measure should use a dependable method easily understood by the manager and the employee. A too complicated system causes confusion and resentment, and ultimately does not achieve its goals. A performance appraisal system that has dependable measures is one that allows all evaluators to arrive at the same conclusion. This demands that rating criteria are objective and verifiable by more than the administering manager or agent.

One of the first biases that can occur is the **halo effect** or **devil's horn effect**. This occurs when the supervisor's personal relationship with the employee influences the assessment of the employee's performance. If you like the individual, you are more favorable (halo effect); if you dislike the person, you tend to view his or her performance with disfavor (devil's horn effect). Personal bias skews the manager's thinking and personality. The **error of central tendency** occurs when a supervisor favors making all performance ratings as average. He or she avoids the extremes of "very poor" or "excellent," and thus does not give a fair evaluation of the employee's performance. In this case, the manager fails to point out areas that need improvement, or areas that exceed expectations. With the **leniency** and **strictness biases**, some managers want to be liked and viewed positively by their employees, so they rate everyone high, and give favorable feedback to mediocre or even poor performers. On the other hand, a supervisor with a strictness bias tends to rate in the opposite direction, and is too harsh in his or her evaluation. These supervisors or managers often want to be viewed as tough or challenging. Both of these biases can be checked by appraisal standards that are objective and measurable rather than vague or subjective. The **recency effect** happens when managers easily recall the more recent actions of an employee and this can lead to unfair appraisals of the same employee's overall work ethic. Managers should keep good notes on employee performance and behavior over the total appraisal period. This will help in giving a fair evaluation of the total output of all employees. The **contrast effect** is when managers compare the performance of one employee to another.

In today's workplace, employees come from diverse, cultural backgrounds, and consequently their belief systems and social habits are diverse. Thus, managers bring a **cross-cultural bias** into the evaluation process. Managers must guard against demanding uniform thinking or speech mannerisms in employees. They must educate themselves about the cultural differences in the organization's employees. A manager can also bring a **personal prejudice** into the evaluation process. Personal biases stem from many sources—family background, political ideologies, level of education, class, stereotypical generalities, and even religious notions. Therefore, to be truly professional, supervisors must honestly examine themselves regarding their personal prejudices and insure that each employee is regarded as an individual apart from whatever group or ethnic origin he or she may belong. A **similar-to-me bias** occurs when the manager treats those who hold his or her views and judgments as superior to those who differ from him or her. This bias impacts the results of the evaluation. Again, a good manager should overcome personal feelings and be objective in the evaluation of all employees. Some other unintentional errors that may cause inaccurate ratings are the following:

- Rating an individual's personality rather than performance
- Attractiveness (as seen by the evaluator) can lead to higher ratings
- Not taking the time to observe performance
- Viewing the evaluation process as bureaucratic, and the evaluator's interest is in the process, regulation, and legalities of the performance appraisal
- Manager overload—with downsizing of the organization, more evaluations are placed on the remaining managers
- Technological increases can lead to less time to interact with the employees[9]
- With the increase in task complexity, an employee may have numerous supervisors; thus input from several individuals will need to be garnered.[10]

DISCIPLINE

By and large, people carry their concept of discipline from childhood. We remember the discipline within our homes and schools. Perhaps this is one reason why some managers feel uncomfortable when disciplinary action is needed. Yet discipline is an indispensable management tool.

It is best to look on discipline as an investment in the future, rather than as a punishment for a past transgression. Discipline should be used primarily to encourage desired conduct and correct processes.

Laying the Foundation for a Discipline System

The primary focus for managers is establishing rules of conduct and setting boundaries for their work environment. These rules and boundaries should then be clearly communicated to the employees. This can be done in writing, orally to the individual, collectively at a management/staff meeting, within training sessions, or in employee manuals. The important thing is not the method of communicating as the clarity and thoroughness of the process. The following examples of disciplinary problems show that the need for clear communication of rules and expectations cannot be overemphasized.

- The employee did not know what to do.
- The employee did not know how to do what he or she was supposed to do.
- The expectations were not realistic.
- The employee was not suitable for the task he or she was being asked to perform.
- The employee was not motivated to do a good job.

This short list shows that the lack of clear communication on the part of management is the root cause for poor performance and for the lack of enthusiasm on the part of their employees.

Understanding the purpose of discipline should be an essential prerequisite for every manager with the responsibility of the disciplinary process. Therefore it is essential for managers to do the following:

A. Establish reasonable rules
B. Make sure the rules are understood by their employees
C. Enforce the rules firmly and impartially
D. Clearly and immediately document behavior that warrants discipline

Administering Discipline

Normally the discussion is over three approaches to discipline: (a) hot stove approach, (b) progressive discipline approach, and (c) preventative discipline approach. In practice, these three approaches may overlap, or a manager may use elements of all three. Many times, the hot stove approach and progressive are considered reactive because they react to negative behaviors. Preventative is proactive, with the focus on good behavior.

The **hot stove approach** rests on the notion that if employees touch a hot stove, then they get burned. In other words, if they infract a rule, they are subject to disciplinary action. The key points are as follows:

- Immediacy—The disciplinary action must occur immediately so that there is an obvious link between the disciplinary action and the rule/policy infraction.
- Warning—The manager must have clearly communicated the rules and policies of the company to the employee with the warning that disciplinary action follows an infraction.
- Consistency—Corrective action must be consistent and impartial, so that all will be burned to the same degree for the same infraction.
- Impersonal—The disciplinary action should focus on the behavior and not on personality.
- Appropriate—The punishment must be commensurate with the gravity of the infraction.

This system makes sense to most, as it seems to treat everybody with the same yardstick. It appears fair to all employees. Yet its weakness is that it makes no allowance for different circumstances or individual differences. An example is an infraction by a new hire and the same infraction by a tenured employee; should they both receive the same punishment? The tenured employee can be presumed to have a greater understanding and appreciation of the policies than the newly hired employee.

The **progressive discipline** approach also depends on communication that clearly defines the actions that will be penalized and the consequent disciplinary action that will be taken. An example of progressive discipline would be when an employee arrives to work late. The first occurrence would warrant an oral warning, the second a written warning, the third a suspension, and the fourth would result in termination. Most progressive disciplinary approaches include these four steps.

1. An **oral warning** is informal, but does include documentation.
2. A **written warning** is a formal warning that is documented and placed in the employee's personnel file.
3. A **suspension** is where an employee is given a period of no work, usually without pay.
4. A **discharge** is determined when the company no longer wants the services of the employee.

Documentation of each stage of the process should be maintained. It should include the reason for the action, behaviors that were demonstrated, the step of the process, and the counseling that was provided. The employee should have an opportunity to indicate assistance needed to improve, and the form should be signed by the employee. The supervisor should sign and date the form with a copy placed in the employee's file and a copy given to the employee.

Many managers prefer this approach. The managers annunciate clear rules and nondiscriminatory treatment of rule breakers. Any discrimination or partiality in this approach (or any approach) can give rise to grievances, discrimination charges, and ultimately lawsuits. The one major criticism is that results may be short term and deal more with the symptoms instead of the cause of poor work performance.

Preventative discipline approach puts the emphasis on the positive qualities to be found in each employee. Here the focus is on the cause rather than on the symptoms involved in the unsatisfactory behavior. Figure 7.8 includes some guidance for managers when using preventative discipline.

Stages in this disciplinary system include the following:

- Oral reminders
- Written reminders
- Paid decision-making leave
- Discharge

Again encouraging good behavior is the emphasis. Reminders are an encouragement to do the task correctly rather than spotlighting only what was done wrong. Critics of this approach think it naïve to have paid leave as part of a disciplinary process. This they claim is rewarding bad performance with a paid vacation and might easily be an encouragement to continue the bad behavior rather than an incentive to improve. Yet research seems to support a "paid decision day." Research found that most employees view a suspension even with pay as an embarrassment and indeed punishment. The objective of a "paid decision day" is to allow the employee time to reflect on whether he or she wants to correct the recognized problem and improve his or her performance or seek employment elsewhere. The decision becomes the employee's and avoids conflict or lawsuits. This may be why many of the most successful companies in the United States use this approach.[11]

Traditional disciplinary approaches are basically reactive; however, the preventative approach is proactive. Preventative discipline appeals to managers who believe that today employees respond better to positive encouragement than to negative sanctions. Preventative discipline also leads to better teamwork and a sense of shared responsibility. It also places the responsibility and the decision for improvement on the individual. Thus it develops overall accountability and it can help in preventing lawsuits. Because this method is nonadversarial, it is nonthreatening for managers and thus they are more likely to approach poor performance issues early and bring about a change in behavior before serious issues arise. In any organization, early correction of bad behavior is a most important and has a significant contribution.[12]

---

1. Establish a good professional rapport with his or her employees
2. Have the ability to relate on a consistent level without blurring their professional roles
3. Place the emphasis on solving the problem at hand rather than on punishment
4. Have a positive attitude toward his or her employees and should assume that given the opportunity, the employee will correct the problem once it is brought to his or her attention
5. Focus on praising and reinforcing good performance rather than on punishing bad performance

FIGURE 7.8 Guidance for Using Preventative Discipline. The manager must do the following:

Appeals Mechanism

An essential element in any discipline program is an appeals system. This system must of course be communicated and fully understood by the employees. The system serves two major functions: (a) it allows each party the opportunity to present its side of the issue, and (b) it gives the employees a voice at the discipline table. The presence of an appeals mechanism gives evidence of management's sincere efforts during a litigation to provide due process for its employees. There are four types of appeal processes.

First, the hierarchical appeals process is based on the organization's chain of command. Employees who feel they have been unjustly treated must first appeal to their direct supervisor. If this appeal fails, the employee should appeal to the next level of supervision within the organization. The process can thus continue to the highest management level. Appeals should be made in writing.

Second, the open door policy appeals process allows an aggrieved employee to appeal to any manager within the organization, regardless of the manager's level or area of responsibility. This often proves to be an ineffective system, as it is less structured and managers are often reluctant to get involved in other manager's areas, much less overrule their decision. The appeal is often referred back to its original starting point. It also gives way to inconsistencies, as some managers may be diligent in their efforts to give voice to the employee while others may take the issue less seriously.

Third, the peer appeals process demands that a grievance committee is established. This committee is made up of employees and managers. Normally his or her peers elect the representative of the employee, while management representatives are appointed. The advantage of this system is that it allows the employee's participation in the appeals process. This can create better relations between employees and management and it will become easier for an employee to accept the decision. When unionized employees are involved, managers must ensure that the terms of collective bargaining agreements are not violated.

Fourth, the ombudsman appeals process is used mainly in government and university settings. This process involves the use of an ombudsman or a mediator who investigates the complaint by listening to both sides and endeavors to reach a decision that is acceptable to both parties. However, the ombudsman does not have the authority to issue a final judgment in the case when the sides remain in disagreement.

Discharging the Employee

Some managers view discharge as the ultimate form of punishment. Most experts in the field of human resources disagree with this view. It is true the employee must seek new employment, and the manager not only loses a worker, but must now spend the time and pay the expense to find and train a replacement. In some cultures (i.e., Japan), managers rarely terminate an employee as it is seen as a failure on their part in their not being able to mold the individual into a productive member of their staff. Discharging is often the easy way out for an uninspiring manager. Many companies in the United States are adopting this approach as it becomes more costly to replace lost employees. Discharging an employee should only happen when all other remedies have been exhausted. It must be approached with caution and after deep deliberation. Hasty or improper handling of a discharge can sometimes result by bringing the employer to court.

From what has preceded, it must be abundantly clear that managers must be very circumspect and be thoroughly familiar with the facts of the situation involved. Before the dismissal of an employee can be sanctioned, many companies demand that the manager has complete documentation of the grievance and has involved progressive discipline in the process. This is demanded to avoid a wrongful discharge (or dismissal) suit. Companies are anxious that their managers don't dismiss employees wrongfully. Wrongful termination lawsuits account for 13 percent of all lawsuits in the United States. Currently three out of five companies report being sued for wrongful discharge.[13]

Wrongful discharge suits can have a serious impact on an organization's finances and reputation. Employees can sue for a host of infractions on the part of a manager and can claim back pay, front pay, and punitive damages. This litigation is based on the Civil Rights Act of 1991, which allows wrongful dismissal cases to be tried before a jury. The act has capped liability awards at $300,000. Then in 1995, the U.S. Supreme Court added a clarification that ruled after-acquired evidence, or information acquired after the dismissal, cannot be used by the defense.[14]

- Did the employee know what was expected?
- Were the policies clearly communicated?
- Did management explain the importance of the policies/rules?
- Were the rules that were broken reasonable and important to the company?
- Is there substantial evidence to support the discharge?
- Is discharge proportionate to the infraction?
- Was the performance appraisal fair and complete?
- Did management monitor the performance diligently and try to remedy and correct the behavior?
- Is this rule or policy and its infraction applied consistently to all employees?

FIGURE 7.9 **Critical Questions Regarding Discharge.**

Wrongful dismissal suits may also include cases where a manager pressures the employee to quit by demoting the employee or by transferring him or her to a different department or section. If a transfer can be seen as a way of avoiding termination, it is viewed as wrongful dismissal or discharge; a demotion can be viewed as wrongful discharge if no documentation of wrongdoing can be provided. Courts normally view demotions and transfers as wrongful discharge if they involve a significant cut in pay and benefits, diminished responsibilities, a significant change in travel schedules, or being passed over for promotions. Even in cases of voluntary resignations, employers can be liable if it can be shown that management deliberately made working conditions so burdensome that it brought about the resignation. In such cases, deliberate intent is the key issue for the court and the burden is on the employers to prove that they could not have foreseen the resignation.

Before managers exercise the final option to discharge, they must question themselves regarding how well they communicated with the employee and how well they monitored his or her performance. The answers to the questions in Figure 7.9 will help a manager decide if discharge is the best option. If the answers are "yes" to the questions, then a discharge may be in order.

A "no" answer indicates that the situation should be corrected before a discharge may be warranted. Whether these questions are critical to litigation or not, they should be part of a manager's day-to-day relationship with his or her employees.

The golden rule for managers is to be just and fair to all employees. The most frequent litigation won by employees is one where the rules were enforced unfairly. To illustrate, take this often given example:

Employee A is a nice, cheerful person liked by managers, customers, and fellow employees. However, his weakness is tardiness. Employee B has an introverted personality, is a poor performer, and is not well liked by most. He also is often tardy. A manager who terminates employee B, but keeps employee A is setting himself or herself up for a wrongful discharge suit.

In the previous section on discipline, we noted that managers must:

1. Understand the purpose of discipline and discharge
2. Realize the importance of establishing reasonable rules
3. Clearly communicate the rules
4. Justly and fairly enforce the rules
5. Maintain complete files on the behavior of each employee that could lead to discharge or discipline

It is always wise for a manager to consult with a third party when contemplating the discharge of an employee. This brings an independent voice to the table and bolsters the case before a court. It shows that the decision to dismiss was not made lightly, but rather with diligence and objectivity.[15]

Finally, the best protection a company can have against wrongful discharge litigation is the development of a proactive program with the following criteria:

- Clearly communicate the company's employment practices
- Aggressively monitor employee performance

- Thoroughly investigate any problem that could potentially lead to litigation
- Periodic public audits of company policies that involve employees and customers
- Adopt a strict code of ethics within the entire organization
- Adopt procedures that facilitate in-house whistle-blowing
- Purchase employment practices liability insurance
- Actively lobby for reforms to prevent unfavorable proposals to wrongful discharge litigation[16]

Another method of discharging an employee is using **employment at will**; that is, management can terminate an employee at any time and for any reason. Until recently, this doctrine has guided all relationships between U.S. employers and employees. It was generally recognized that an employee could terminate employment at any time; thus, an employer could as well. Both parties have considered the labor relationship between employers and employees expendable. However, the present view predicates an implied contract between employer and employee. The chief events that sustain this view are in the National Labor Relations Act of the 1930s, the Civil Rights Act of 1991, and the Family and Medical Leave Act of 1993. Because of this legislation, employers have found the courts less willing to uphold employment at will. Even in states that continue to carry employment at will laws, the fact that employees have a right to a jury trial diminishes the power of employment at will. A jury is inclined to seek sufficient cause for termination. Where sufficient cause is not present, the jury invariably sides with the employee. Though some companies still use employment at will, the climate in labor relations has changed more in favor of the employee. As a result, many employee relation experts claim that managers no longer have the right to enforce employment at will.

On the other side, there are experts who claim that employers can retain the employment at will policy simply by clearly stating to the employee that this is company policy. These experts suggest that, during the hiring process, the employer request the potential employee to sign a waiver of rights, which should be included in the employee handbook. However, this practice also faces hurdles. In 1983, the U.S. Supreme Court in the case of *Pine River State Bank v. Metille* ruled that the existence of an employee handbook constituted evidence of an implied employment contract between employer and employee. Many state courts have also ruled in this fashion. These rulings were made primarily because of the language found in the manuals. The language speaks of benefits, grounds for disciplinary action or probation, EEO, affirmative action policies, and also suggests that the employee can work for the company as long as he or she does a good job. These, according to the courts, implied employment contracts. The ruling of these cases concerning employment at will tells managers that this practice is very difficult to sustain in today's culture. If a case ends up in court, it can cost the company thousands of dollars.

A third method of discharging employees is **public policy**. This concerns the rights of employees given to them by law. This means that employees cannot be dismissed because they become involved in following activities: for filing workers' compensation claims, doing jury duty, serving in the National Guard, refusing to commit perjury, or whistle-blowing. All these activities fall under what is known as public policy.

There are other federal and state laws that impact employees. An example is the Employee Retirement Income Security Act of 1974 (ERISA), Section 510, prohibiting discharge in order to avoid paying benefits to employees. Again, the burden of proof rests with the employers who are obliged to prove that they did not discharge an employee for the purpose of not paying benefits.

The final task in the discharge process is the **discharge interview**, which is similar to an exit interview (the next section), but is usually an unpleasant task. Discharge is the ultimate penalty, and should only be taken after all other avenues have been explored. The purposes of the discharge interview are as follows:

1. Relate the history of events that has led to this discussion
2. Give an explanation why this severe action must be taken
3. Complete the process of disciplinary action

A manager will be conscious of the consequences of discharge in the life of the employee and perhaps his or her family. However, managers who face the task with professionalism and objectivity should find the task less stressful.

> - Gently probe to find what went wrong during the period of employment
> - Be familiar with all the evidence supporting the discharge and have all documentation available at the interview - (The documentation should include complete records of all disciplinary action concerning the employee and also the terms and conditions of these actions)
> - Explain very clearly and specifically all the reasons for the discharge
> - Be respectful of the employee - (The fact that he or she proved not to be a good employee for the organization does not mean that he or she won't excel in another organization)
> - Avoid all confrontation and do not get angry
> - Assure the employee that the reason for dismissal will remain confidential
> - Have a witness present to ensure an accurate account of the proceedings in the event there should be litigation
> - Law requires that an employee be paid in full at the time of the discharge (some, but not all, states require this procedure)
> - Make known the appeal process available to the employee
> - Advise the employee, that if asked for a reference by a future employer, management can answer only the three questions required by law: (a) job position, (b) dates of employment, and (c) salary

FIGURE 7.10 Critical Questions Regarding Discharge.

Managers should observe the following guidelines in Figure 7.10 during discharge interviews. These guidelines should help managers to expedite the interview with grace and humanity.

The Exit Interview

When an employee leaves, either voluntary or involuntary, it is essential that the company gain as much information as possible from this individual. Managers can learn much about the company's operations from a well-conducted **exit interview**. It can also be a source for making necessary changes for improvement in the operation. The exit interview affords disgruntled employees the opportunity to vent their frustration with the way the managers operate, or with the policies of the organization. Because some exit interviews can be emotional or confrontational, it is always better to have someone other than the employee's immediate supervisor conduct the interview.

Employees leave for all kinds of reasons. Some will be more forthcoming than others. If the real reasons are to be ascertained, the manager conducting the interview must be capable of creating an atmosphere conducive to an open conversation between two equal adults. Typically, an employee will tell his or her employer that he or she is leaving because he or she has found a better job, or a job with more opportunity for advancement. But this is not always the case. Most leave because of dissatisfaction either with their boss, coworkers, or the conditions of their employment. It is important for a company to know why its employees leave, as this costs the company money, and potentially profit. If information gathered at these interviews is used to prevent further loss, then it will serve the company well.

Recognizing the importance of exit interviews is very important, but conducting the exit interview in an open, communicative, trustworthy fashion will truly benefit the organization. Someone other than the employee's immediate supervisor should conduct exit interviews. An external source is best. Some companies hire consultants to collect this information or it may be done via the Internet (but this method also leads to some other potential problems, such as overstating a grievance). The following guidelines may be helpful:

- Conduct the interview in the final week of employment, and avoid the last day
- Ensure the employee of confidentiality
- Probe for the real reason for the departure
- Schedule a follow-up interview (With the lapse of time, a former employee is apt to give a more complete and more accurate reason for his or her leaving. A third party should do this interview. One can also use this follow-up interview to determine the possibility of the employee returning to your organization.)
- Close with a warm, sincere "thank you"

COUNSELING FOR PERFORMANCE IMPROVEMENT

In this chapter, the discussion was the link between performance evaluation and discipline. Organizations strive to be the best in their field; therefore, they need the best employees. Chapter 10 of this text will discuss coaching and teambuilding, which is usually associated with the higher performing employees. What happens to those employees who have not attained this level? Do we discharge them without an opportunity to improve? When employees have poor performance, or unwanted behaviors, it is up to the manager to help resolve this issue. The manager should ask himself or herself: Does this employee know/understand the desired behavior, does this employee know how to perform to the standard, or does the employee just want to perform according to company standards? The first case can be corrected with a thorough explanation of the desired behavior; the second case will likely require some training; the third case is part of the progressive discipline process, and requires counseling.

Effective employee counseling requires the manager to assist in the process of helping the employee overcome poor performance. The one question managers should ask themselves before deciding on counseling is, "Is the process of counseling likely to succeed?" If the answer is yes, then it is time to prepare for counseling. To prepare for a counseling session aimed at overcoming the employee's poor performance, the manager will need to (a) document the poor performance with dates, times, behaviors, and any other information pertinent to the performance, (b) schedule an uninterrupted time period, and (c) make sure the employee is given sufficient notice. After the preparation is completed, the counseling manager must be aware of five objectives that are essential for effective counseling. They are as follows:

1. Win the employee's agreement for the need to improve
2. Assess and identify the root cause of the problem
3. Agree on specific actions that will improve performance
4. Followup, followup, and followup with the employee to ensure progress toward the goal
5. Recognize the improvement in performance in order to reinforce the positive performance (or preventative discipline)[17]

By accomplishing these five goals, the employee should start to deliver a better performance for the organization.

One thing a manager must also remember is that not all poor performance is caused by work-related events. The old saying of "leave your troubles at the door" is tried and true, but for some employees, this can be difficult to achieve. The counseling manager needs to consider this possibility when counseling, and therefore must be ready to help with personal problems that may be affecting the employee's performance at work. This recognition can lead the manager to suggest using the company's employee assistance program (EAP), thus helping the employee with the external factors affecting performance.

APPLICATIONS TO HOSPITALITY MANAGEMENT

Performance management can be an important factor in the success of a hospitality organization. Some HR personnel would say that ignoring performance management can doom the company. HR's job is to create a performance evaluation process that requires managers to (a) give constructive feedback, (b) train these managers on how to deliver this feedback, and (c) insert checks and balances into the performance management system in order to ensure reliability and validity, as well as objectivity (and of course, some subjectivity). An effective performance management system will have three components:

1. Beginning with a period of goal setting
2. Mid-period reviews
3. End-of-period evaluations

An example of an effective performance management system is Destination Hotels & Resorts. The company had an active 360° feedback program, but it wasn't aligned with the company's business strategy. The company did an in-depth analysis of its strategy. Through a SumTotal platform (technology company), Destination Hotels & Resorts launched a 360° feedback program and multiple rater feedback system to evaluate individuals within its organization.

Managers elected to participate in succession planning, in which they created (and updated) an online repository of information about their career, geographic preferences, interest in task force assignments, educational history, and career path aspirations. This information formed a talent profile from the employee perspective. The company's philosophy was not to figure out what was wrong with its employees, but rather to focus on the positive aspects of its managers, and to exploit this in a productive way that should work for all involved parties. Destination Hotels & Resorts derived the following benefits from this new technology platform:

- Control the number of people being transferred or promoted
- Assess the availability of managers capable of participation on a specific task force
- Identify personnel capable of filling key positions internally, saving a significant amount in cost and in lost productivity
- Increase the identified people's ability to groom internal talent

Destination Hotels & Resorts now has a succession planning program that genuinely helps the company's performance. The company estimates the number of managers ready for the next step to be 5 out of 30; it has also seen a steady increase in the number of managers ready for promotion in 6 to 12 months; the real benefit is the continuous cycle of its 360° feedback program. Succession planning is now its business strategy, and this strategy is what helps the company have growth in its business.[18]

THE BOTTOM LINE

The mission of any organization is to perform in such a way that customers return, thus ensuring expanding profitability. To make this happen, the organization's employees must be better than average. An effective performance evaluation system is key. This system must be valid and reliable, must be subjective and objective, and has to be fair to all employees. Managers must be aware of human factors that enter into employees' performance, and be ready to address any deficiencies. Managers who are willing to address performance concerns help not only lower-performing employees, but also the performance of the entire team. By providing constructive feedback, and the willingness to counsel employees, managers ensure a better working environment for all.

Discussion Questions

1. What are the basic necessities of a performance evaluation?
2. What are the minimal characteristics of performance evaluations?
3. List the potential uses of performance evaluations?
4. How does an evaluator assess performance?
5. What are the principal differences between graphic rating scales and behaviorally anchored rating scales?
6. What are the advantages (and disadvantages) of using narrative essays?
7. Why do companies use a behavior observation scale?
8. What are the advantages and disadvantages of using 360° appraisals?
9. How frequently should we conduct performance evaluations on hourly employees? On salaried employees? Why?
10. Why is it difficult to remove unintentional errors from the rating process?
11. What is essential to the discipline process?
12. What must be done when administering discipline?
13. What are the advantages and disadvantages of progressive discipline versus preventative discipline?
14. How can an employee appeal discipline?
15. Why does the government use an ombudsman approach to appeal disciplinary procedures?
16. What process should a manager use before discharging an employee?
17. Why is a paid suspension good when it relates to discipline?
18. Under what circumstances might an employee file a wrongful discharge lawsuit that would be difficult for managers to defend?
19. When would an employee feel he or she has an implied contract to work for a company?
20. What advantages are there to employment at will for the company? For the employee?
21. List the effective processes of an exit interview.
22. Why does a manager use counseling?
23. What "tool" do most companies use to assist in the counseling process?

Application Exercise

Kamil has been a high performing restaurant general manager for four years, and has just been promoted to district manager for a pizza company, and has been given six restaurants to supervise. These pizza restaurants are mainly inner-city stores in a large metropolitan area. His manager has confidence in his ability to turn these restaurants around, and have these restaurants become profitable again. After one month, Kamil realizes the challenges, and doesn't think there is enough time in the day to accomplish his goals. He is getting frustrated with his lack of success with the six restaurants. And to top it off, his boss is coming along for an area visit tomorrow, and wants to inspect at least three of the restaurants.

Well, the first visit is not the best. The boss recognizes some improvement, but still sees a major opportunity to improve. The second visit is the worst ever. The restaurant is poorly staffed, poorly trained, and is in need of a major cleaning effort. Kamil's boss stops the visit, and asks Kamil to talk to him at a neighboring McDonald's restaurant. What does the boss do? What does Kamil do?

Endnotes

1. Hough, L. M., Keyes, M. A., & Dunnette, M. D. (1983). An evaluation of three "alternative" selection procedures. *Personnel Psychology*, 36, 261–276.
2. Carruthers, F. (November 14, 2003). Nothing but the truth. *Australian Financial Review*, 78. (Note: This reference pertains to U.S. companies, not Australian companies.)
3. Vinson, M. (1996). The pros and cons of 360-degree feedback. *Training & Development*, 50, 11–12.
4. Lepsinger, R., & Lucia, A. (1997). 360-degree feedback and performance appraisal. *Training*, 34(9), 62–70.
5. Schellhard, T. (December 24, 1996), Mr. Cratchit, let's have a word before you go home tonight. *Wall Street Journal*.
6. Brown, G. (2002). Re-evaluating evaluation. *Canadian HR Reporter*, 15(7), 5.
7. Pickett, L. (2003). Transforming the annual fiasco. *Industrial and Commercial Training*, 35(6), 237–238.
8. Adapted from Rogel, C. (2010). Using the SARA model to learn from 360° feedback. Accessed from http://www.decision-wise.com/blog/2010/06/04/using-the-sara-model-to-learn-from-360-degree-feedback/
9. Neal, Jr., J. (2003). The #1 Guide to Performance Appraisals: Doing It Right! (4th ed.), Perrysburg, OH: Neal Publications, Inc.
10. Sumer, H., & Knight, P. (1996). Assimilation and contrast errors in performance ratings: Effects of rating the previous performance on subsequent performance. *Journal of Applied Psychology*, 81, 436–443.
11. Sunno, B. B. (1996). Positive discipline—sending the right or wrong message. *Personnel Journal*, 75, 109–111.
12. Guffey, C., & Helms, M. (2001). Effective employee discipline. *Public Personnel Management*, 111–127.
13. Autor, D., Donohue, J., & Schwab, S. (2002). The costs of wrongful discharge laws, MIT department of economics working paper No. 02, 41.
14. Barlow, W. (1995). The after-acquired evidence defense: Where do we stand now? *Personnel Journal*, 74, 152–156.
15. Baxter, Jr. R. (1994). Protecting against exposure. *National Law Review*, 16, 1.
16. Gardner, S., Gomes, G., & Morgan, J. (2000). Wrongful termination and the expanding public policy exception: Implications and advice. *S.A.M. Advanced Management Journal*, 38, 44.
17. Stone, F. (2007). Coaching, counseling, & mentoring, New York: American Management Association.
18. Whitney, K. (May 2007). Destination hotels: Leveraging technology for effective succession planning. *Chief Learning Officer*, 32–35. Retrieved on July 9, 2011, from http://www.nxt-book.com/nxtbooks/mediatec/clo0507/index.php

Key Terms

360° feedback   A method of performance appraisal that utilizes input from supervisors, peers, subordinates, guests, and others to provide a comprehensive evaluation of a staff member's performance.

Alternative ranking   A rating method used in job evaluation and performance evaluation whereby the evaluator is asked to select the best and worst employees from a listing of all employees and then rank them accordingly.

Behavioral observation scale (BOS)   A form or method used to conduct a formal performance evaluation where the evaluator is required to rate the frequency of identified job behaviors.

Behaviorally anchored rating scales (BARS) method   A form or method used to conduct a formal performance evaluation where the evaluator is required to rate the employee along a continuum using specifically determined job behaviors.

Contrast effect   A type of rater bias when the evaluator contrasts characteristics (positive or negative) of his or her employees.

Counseling   Actions or interactions in one or many forms, which serve to provide direction, guidance, or advice with respect to recommendations, decisions, or courses of action.

Critical incident method   A form or method used to conduct a formal performance evaluation where the evaluator is required to maintain a log of positive and negative employee performance.

Cross-cultural bias   A rating bias brought into the evaluation process because of cultural circumstances (background, beliefs, or habits).

Devil's horn effect   A type of rater bias that occurs when the rater allows a negative attribute to cloud the objectivity of the overall employee performance appraisal.

Discharge   The termination of an employee based on previous disciplinary proceedings or for violating a major work rule or policy.

Discharge interview   A meeting between an employee and an employer in which the purpose is to terminate the employee's employment.

Employment at will   A legal doctrine that states that an employment relationship may be terminated by the employer or employee at any time and for any or no reason.

Error of central tendency   A rating error occurring when the rater displays a propensity to assign only average ratings to all individuals being rated.

Exit interview   An interview conducted at the time of an employee's resignation, which is used to identify the underlying factors behind an employee's decision to leave.

Forced distribution   An appraisal rating method intended to prevent rater errors by requiring the rater to force ratings into a bell-shaped curve.

Graphic rating scale A rating system in which evaluators rate employees on specific measurable criteria.

Guest (customer) evaluation A performance appraisal strategy where the company's customers have an opportunity to examine the individual's job performance.

Halo effect A type of rater bias that occurs when the rater allows a positive attribute to cloud the objectivity of the overall employee performance appraisal.

Hierarchical appeal process A process that employees who feel they have been treated unfairly can use to take their concerns to succeeding levels of the chain of command.

Hot stove approach An approach to discipline based on immediate punishment for each offense.

Inter-rater reliability A rating system where two or more evaluators rate the performance of an employee in the same manner, and agree upon the same rating.

Leniency bias This bias occurs when the evaluator is not as critical of the employee.

Management by objectives (MBO) A process for setting employee performance goals through meetings between an employee and a manager. The goals are used for performance evaluation at the end of the established time period.

Multiple rater evaluation A performance appraisal strategy whereby an employee is reviewed by many other parties (supervisor, peers, subordinates, guests, or suppliers) who have sufficient opportunity to examine the individual's job performance.

Narrative essay A rating system in which the appraiser writes a narrative essay that describes the strengths and weaknesses of each employee.

Ombudsman appeals process A neutral third party helps individuals or groups in conflict resolve disputes by mediating, coaching, and facilitating communication between the parties and recommending an appropriate resolution.

Open door policy appeals process A company policy whereby the manager's door is always open to employees who may wish to voice a complaint or state an issue.

Oral warning A verbal warning given to an employee by a manager or supervisor as a means of correcting inappropriate behavior or conduct.

Paired comparison A form of rating, in which the rater compares, one by one, the performance of each member in a group with the performance of every other member in the group.

Peer appeals process An appeal process where an employee is reviewed by his or her peers who have sufficient opportunity to examine the individual's grievance.

Peer evaluations A performance appraisal strategy whereby an employee is reviewed by his or her peers who have sufficient opportunity to examine the individual's job performance.

Personal prejudice A rating bias stemming from the evaluator's personal beliefs or life events.

Preventative discipline Actions that management can take to encourage employees to follow standards and rules so that infractions are prevented before they occur.

Progressive discipline An approach to discipline that begins with sanctions that increase in severity as the violation increases in severity. The typical sequence of disciplinary actions consists of a verbal warning followed by a written warning followed by suspension and then termination.

Public policy Rights given to employees because of legislation, and a form of protection to employees for unlawful termination of employment.

Recency effect A type of rater bias that occurs when the rater allows a recent event—either negative or positive—to cloud the overall objectivity of the employee performance appraisal.

SARA A sequence of emotions felt by an employee receiving a poor performance report; the emotions are: shock, anger, resentment, and acceptance. (Also seen in grief counseling as SARAH, adding hope.)

Self-evaluation A form or method used to conduct a formal performance appraisal where the employee evaluates his or her own job performance in writing.

Similar-to-me bias A rating bias where the rater gives positive results to employees who have like characteristics to the evaluator.

Simple ranking A method of ranking all employees in a single list; also called straight ranking.

Strictness bias This bias occurs when the rater is too critical of the employee.

Suspension A period of time during which the employee is not allowed to work within the operation and receives no pay.

Written warning A more formal warning that is provided to the employee in writing and that usually details the violation as well as what the employee could expect if such violations were to continue.

Wrongful discharge (or dismissal) suit Firing an employee for reasons that violate public policy, terms of a contract, or a covenant of good faith and fair dealing.

8

Reward and Compensation Systems

OUTLINE

Introduction to Topic
Salaries and Wages
Tipped versus Nontipped Employees
Determining Pay Ranges and Scales

Benefits
    Mandatory Benefits
    Voluntary Benefits
Incentives
    Nonfinancial Compensation
The Bottom Line

KEY TERMS

401(k) retirement plans
AD&D insurance
Assistance benefits
Bonuses
COBRA
Consumer price index
Cost-of-living adjustment
Deferred compensation
Dental plans
Direct compensation
Downsizing
Employee assistance programs (EAPs)
Employee stock ownership plan (ESOP)
ERISA
Exempt status
Extrinsic rewards
Group incentive plans
HMO
Hospitality-specific benefits
Immediate compensation
Incentives
Indirect compensation
Individual incentive programs
Intrinsic rewards
Knowledge-based pay system
Leveraged ESOP

Mandatory benefits
Medical insurance benefit
Meet the competitor
Merit pay system
Ordinary ESOP
Pay follower
Pay leader
Pay ranges
Pension plans
Perquisite
Piecework wage system
PPO
Prescription drug plans
Retirement benefits
Service charge
Skill-based pay system
Social security benefits
Stock option plan
Time-off benefits
Tip credit
Tip pool
Unemployment compensation
Vesting
Vision care plans
Voluntary benefits
Workers' compensation

OBJECTIVES

- Describe the steps in establishing pay ranges
- Identify options for establishing pay structures
- Define types of compensation
- Explain the difference between tipped and nontipped employees
- Identify categories of employee benefits
- Describe the factors to consider when developing benefit plans
- Identify the characteristics and advantages of effective incentive programs
- Describe common individual and group incentive plans
- Explain the impact of reward and compensation systems on the labor budget

Consider This

Sarah and Bill have been two of your company's best employees for ten years. Their performance evaluations have always been above target, and this year is no different. To coincide with their performance evaluations, you as the HR (human resource) director have to decide on their salary increase. After reviewing your company's salary history, you have noticed a distinct gap between male and female wages, with the male average substantially larger. You decide to give Sarah an 8 percent increase, and Bill a 4 percent increase to start narrowing the gap. Is this an ethical gesture by the HR director?

INTRODUCTION

When the term compensation is used, people think about wages or salaries they earn for their work. These dollars only represent part of their compensation. Compensation is commonly divided into **direct** and **indirect compensation**. These two types of compensation are then categorized into **immediate compensation** or **deferred compensation**. Direct compensation involves an employer's payment of money (either in the present or in the future) for an employee's productivity while at work. This can include base pay (salary or hourly), merit pay, incentive pay, or bonuses. Direct deferred compensation refers to money earned in one period, but paid in a

Tips. *Credit*: Tootles / Shutterstock

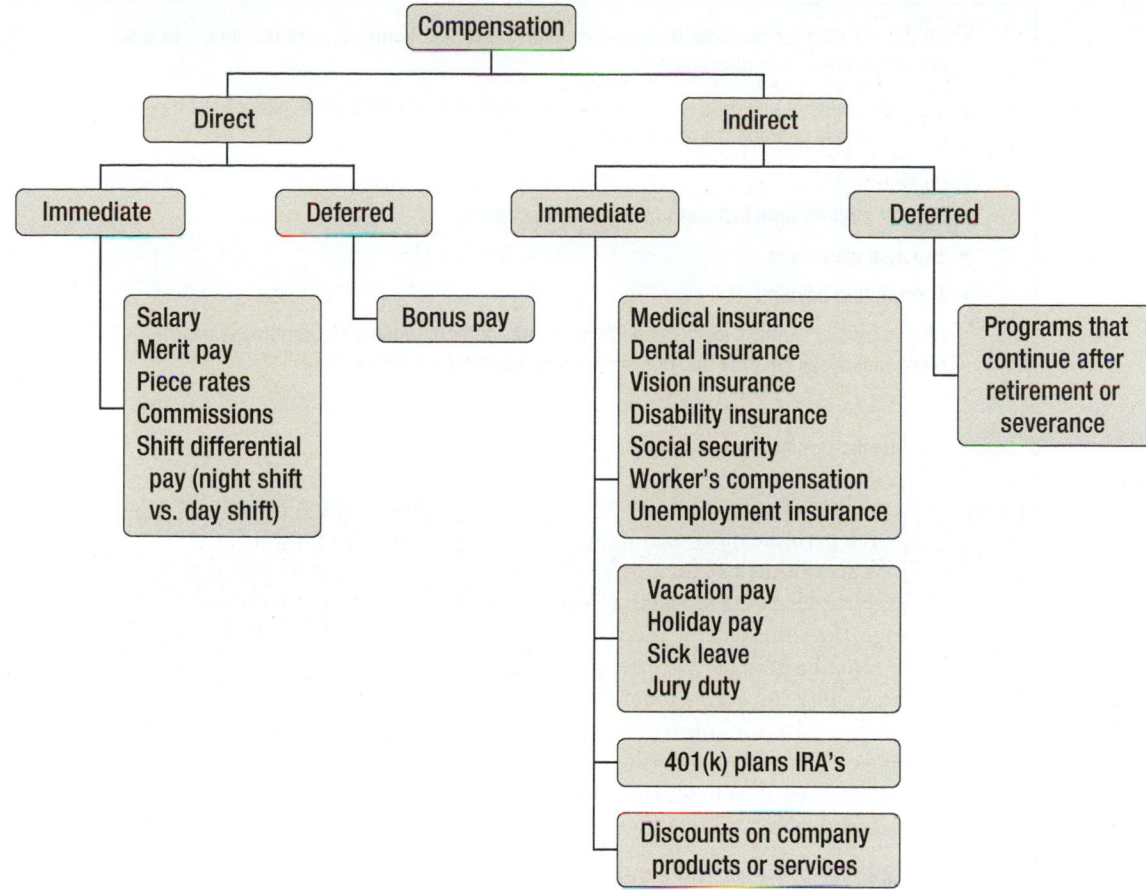

FIGURE 8.1   Types of Compensation.

future period. A classic example is the bonus structure of most companies, with the employee earning a bonus for the period, but paid in the next period. Indirect compensation is given as a condition of employment rather than for direct exchange for productivity. In some cases, the federal government mandates this indirect compensation. Examples of indirect compensation are medical insurance, dental insurance, vision care insurance, disability insurance, social security, workers' compensation, unemployment insurance, vacation pay, national holiday pay, sick leave, jury duty, retirement pay (401[k]), individual retirement accounts, discounts on company products, or a company car. Figure 8.1 shows the basic relationship of a compensation system.

The type of compensation is important to the overall compensation package. Employees usually think of their wages and the amount of tips earned as their total compensation. In contrast, the HR manager recognizes the entire compensation package. There are also two other types of rewards included in compensation: **extrinsic rewards** and **intrinsic rewards**. An extrinsic reward is a financial or nonfinancial compensation offered by the employer. An extrinsic reward could be the salary offered or meal privileges. An intrinsic reward is a self-initiated compensation, such as pride in one's work, or a sense of professional accomplishment. The HR manager is concerned with both extrinsic rewards and intrinsic rewards. It is to be noted that not all employees react to rewards in the same fashion. Rather, all employees exchange work for some type of reward.

SALARIES AND WAGES

In industry, there are two types of compensation: salaries and wages. Managers and higher-level supervisors are typically paid a fixed amount of money, or a salary. Employees are typically paid an hourly rate of pay, or a piecework wage (defined later in the chapter). The advantage of the salary system is that such employees are not subject to overtime provisions of the Fair Labor Standards Act of 1938 (FLSA). The term wage is used in a variety of contexts and may include

> - All dollars paid for personal service—including salaries, bonuses, commissions—to workers of all ranks, including officers
> - The cash value of any perquisite of the job (an example of a perquisite, also called a perk, is an automobile given to the chief executive officer)
> - All tip income
> - Monies paid for time lost due to sickness or accident
> - Expense allowance
> - Termination payouts
> - Money paid to workers for items such as board, lodging, union dues, employee payments to pensions, social security tax, or premiums on insurance policies

FIGURE 8.2   Items Considered as Wages.

any of the items listed in Figure 8.2. For the purpose of this chapter, salary will refer to a fixed amount paid on a periodic basis, and wage will refer to an hourly amount.

The FLSA sets guidelines for employers. It states that employees be paid at least the federal minimum wage for all hours worked. (Note: Some state and local governments have a higher minimum wage than the federal rate.) For any hours worked above 40 for a weekly period, the employee must be paid at 1.5 times the hourly rate. FLSA does make exclusion for exempt employees. To qualify for exempt status, employees must meet certain criteria regarding their job duties, and be paid a minimum salary, currently $23,660 per year, or $455 per week. Job titles do not determine exempt status. In the hospitality industry, most exempt jobs fall into executive, administrative, or outside sales classifications (usually hotel sales and marketing positions). To qualify for executive status, an employee must meet the following criteria:

- The employee must be paid a minimum salary of $455 per week.
- The employee's primary duty must be managing the operation, or managing a department/subdivision of the operation.
- The employee must direct the work of at least two or more full-time employees.
- The employee must have the authority to hire/terminate other employees, or the employee's suggestion/recommendation for hire/promotion/termination must have significant weight.

To qualify for administrative status, an employee must meet the following criteria:

- The employee must be paid a minimum salary of $455 per week.
- The employee's primary duty must be the performance of office or nonmanual work directly related to the management of the general business operations of the employer.
- The employee's primary duty includes the exercise of discretion and independent judgment with significant matters of the operation.

To qualify for outside sales exemption, the following criteria must be met:

- The employee's primary duty must be making sales (as defined by FLSA) or obtaining orders/contracts for services or use of the company's facilities (and a payment must be received).
- The employee must be customarily and regularly engaged away from the employer's place of business.

These exemptions do not apply to manual laborers or blue-collar workers who perform repetitive physical work, or who do major tasks of physical skills. However, the following conditions allow employers to deduct wages in daily increments from exempt employees:

1. Absent for one or more full days for reasons other than illness or disability
2. Absent for one or more full days for illness or disability provided the deduction is made in accordance with a policy that provides compensation for time lost
3. To offset amounts received for jury duty, witness fees, or military pay
4. Per diem payments in the initial and last weeks of employment
5. Good faith penalties for violations of major safety regulations
6. Good faith unpaid disciplinary suspensions (for one or more full days for violation of workplace conduct policies)

While most hospitality employees (such as cooks, dishwashers, servers, bell men, front-desk clerks) are paid an hourly wage and are sometimes tipped by customers, some hotel managers use a **piecework wage system**. The best example is the hotel room attendants who are paid by the number of rooms cleaned. This system has both advantages and disadvantages. The advantage can be in the number of rooms cleaned, as a more skilled employee may be capable of cleaning more rooms, thus earning higher wages. The disadvantage is the possible lack of quality work, and not really getting the rooms cleaned satisfactorily. Another disadvantage is the employee does not have control over the occupancy percentage, the seasonality of the hotel, the total number of room attendants employed by the hotel, or the scheduling of room attendants. It is important that HR managers understand federal, state, and local provisions for compensation payments. An employer must comply with the standard that is most beneficial to the salaried employee. More information about the qualifications can be found at the Department of Labor website.

TIPPED VERSUS NONTIPPED EMPLOYEES

In the hospitality industry, the practice of tipping is common. A tip is a gift of money given directly to someone for performing a service or task, and is also known as gratuity. As a form of compensation, tips are often controversial. The customer gives tips directly to the employee, and the business is not involved. But if the business were not there, the employee would not have the chance to get the tip, thus the business is indirectly involved in the tipping process. There is federal legislation concerning the topic of tipping. The FLSA defines a tipped employee as one whose monthly tips (currently $30) exceed the minimum established by the Wage and Hour Division of the U.S. Department of Labor. Currently, tips received by employees may be credited as wages for up to 50 percent of the minimum wage. Plus, the Wage and Hour Division also stipulates the minimum wage of $2.13/hour for a tipped employee. If the employee's hourly tip earnings (averaged weekly and called the **tip credit**) added to the hourly minimum wage do not equal the federal minimum (or state minimum), then the employer is responsible for paying the difference between the minimum wage and the tip credit. The employer is prohibited from using an employee's tips for any reason other than as a credit against its minimum wage obligation to the employee or in furtherance of a valid **tip pool**. Only tips actually received by the employee may be counted in determining whether the employee is a tipped employee and the amount of the tip credit. Thus, the maximum tip credit that an employer can currently claim under the FLSA is $5.12 per hour (the minimum wage of $7.25 minus the minimum required cash wage of $2.13).

Tips.   *Credit*: CandyBox Images / Shutterstock

1. The amount of cash wage the employer is paying a tipped employee, which must be at least $2.13 per hour.

2. The additional amount claimed by the employer as a tip credit, which cannot exceed $5.12 (the difference between the minimum required cash wage of $2.13 and the current minimum wage of $7.25).

3. The tip credit claimed by the employer cannot exceed the amount of tips actually received by the tipped employee.

4. All tips received by the tipped employee are to be retained by the employee except for a valid tip pooling arrangement limited to employees who customarily and regularly receive tips.

5. The tip credit will not apply to any tipped employee unless the employee has been informed of these tip credit provisions.[1]

FIGURE 8.3   **Information Provided to Tipped Employees.**

The requirement that an employee must retain all tips does not preclude a valid tip pooling or sharing arrangement among employees who customarily and regularly receive tips, such as servers, bellhops, counter personnel (who serve customers), bus people, and service bartenders. A valid tip pool may not include employees who do not customarily and regularly receive tips, such as dishwashers, cooks, chefs, and janitors. Tip pooling is a complex area, and employers should be aware of the difficulties that may arise. Employers are legally allowed to assist employees in developing a tip pooling arrangement that is fair and that is based on the specific duties of each service position. The employer should document participation in the employee's personnel file. The information that the employer must provide to the employee is found in Figure 8.3.

Another area of potential conflict is **service charge**. A compulsory charge for service, for example, 15 percent of the bill, is not a tip. Such charges are part of the employer's gross receipts. Sums distributed to employees from service charges cannot be counted as tips received, but may be used to satisfy the employer's minimum wage and overtime obligations under the FLSA. If an employee receives tips in addition to the compulsory service charge, those tips may be considered in determining whether the employee is a tipped employee and in the application of the tip credit.

When tips are charged on a credit card and the employer must pay the credit card company a percentage on each sale, the employer may pay the employee the tip, minus that percentage. For example, where a credit card company charges an employer 3 percent on all sales charged to its credit service, the employer may pay the tipped employee 97 percent of the tips without violating the FLSA. However, this charge on the tip may not reduce the employee's wage below the required minimum wage. The amount due to the employee must be paid no later than the regular payday and may not be held while the employer is awaiting reimbursement from the credit card company.

Another area of concern for employers is overtime pay with a tipped employee. When the employer takes the tip credit, overtime is calculated on the full minimum wage. The employer may not take a larger tip credit for an overtime hour than for a straight time hour. To determine the overtime rate of pay, use the following three steps:

1. Multiply the prevailing minimum wage rate by 1.5 ($7.25 × 1.5 = $10.875)
2. Compute the allowable tip credit (50%) against the standard hour rate ($7.25 × .5 = $3.625)
3. Subtract the number in step 2 from the result in step 1 ($10.875 − $3.625 = $7.25 is the overtime rate)

DETERMINING PAY RANGES AND SCALES

The goal of any organization's reward and compensation program should be fair and equitable in order to attract, motivate, and retain employees. This program has to consider the organization's profitability as well. In many hospitality programs, this compensation package is the largest expense. Thus it is important that the HR department manage the compensation program in such a manner that the employees determine it to be fair and equitable. To devise this compensation program, the HR manager must include five important aspects. These are listed in Figure 8.4.

1. Job categories
2. Competitive pay
3. Internal pay equity
4. Pay linked to performance
5. Open communication

FIGURE 8.4   **Important Components of a Compensation Program.**

1. Job categories—Not all employees do exactly the same job, so pay differences do exist. Most employees accept this rationale for pay variations, and can easily see that a supervisor should make more than an hourly employee. When employees understand real differences between job responsibilities, they understand the differences in pay. The HR manager often accomplishes this by offering **pay ranges** within the same job. For example, a trainee, an intermediate desk agent, and a senior front-desk agent are considered to be different levels of management at the front desk of a hotel. Each classification would have its own pay range. Next, employees need to be aware of the skills and the experience needed for advancement to a higher-level position.

2. Competitive pay—Comparisons need to be considered in the local labor market, as well as in the entire labor market. The HR manager will want to compare rates of pay with competing local companies (e.g., assessing the rate of pay for the front-desk position). Generally, a company can position itself in three ways: (a) **pay leader**, paying more than the market average so that the company will attract the better employee, (b) **pay follower**, paying below the market average so that the company will generate larger profits, or (c) **meet the competitor**, paying the prevailing wage of the market. Likewise, the HR manager must consider the company's global market, assessing the difference of pay between New York City and Raleigh, North Carolina. The HR manager completes this task by conducting periodic salary surveys. This is accomplished by talking to the counterparts in other hospitality organizations. These surveys can help establish pay ranges for jobs, show how your organization compares to the local market, and help in establishing the number of job categories. A HR manager does not necessarily have to merely match the market. The salary survey may be used to justify higher salaries when there is a shortage of critical employees.

   Pay rates are often adjusted upward due to **cost-of-living adjustments** (COLAs). Usually COLAs are based on the **consumer price index** (CPI), a governmental measure of the average change in prices for goods and services purchased by the company's employees over a certain period of time. The Bureau of Labor Statistics, an agency in the U.S. Department of Labor, issues the CPI monthly. The CPI varies according to many different environmental and economic factors. As the CPI increases, the value of money, or the purchasing power of the individual, goes down. It is often referred to as inflation.

3. Manage internal pay equity—Most HR managers think that managing internal pay equity is more important than managing external pay equity. Employees are more likely to know the amount paid to their fellow workers, than the amount paid to the employee of a competing firm down the street. Also, employees realize that it is difficult to compare to other companies because of the benefits offered by the other company. Employees typically make comparisons with their coworkers, and also typically compare their performance with the performance of their fellow coworkers. These factors can create a morale problem and lead to a turnover problem. The best way to control this concern is to pay employees within the established pay ranges, and to pay for identifiable measures in job performance. An example of this pay difference may be to pay more to an employee working the front desk at unconventional times, say from 11 p.m. to 7 a.m. This is an example of paying for the shift worked rather than the tasks completed.

4. Linkage of pay to performance—Most employees and most managers agree that employees who perform their jobs better than their coworkers should receive larger pay increases. Measurable employee effort, difficulty of work, shift assignments, and current pay all play important roles in helping the HR manager develop a **merit pay system** that reflects the appropriate levels of pay for employees. Some managers do not agree with this practice of linking pay to performance because in their view it causes the eroding of teamwork. On the other hand, since paychecks are not issued to groups, but to individuals, most employees

feel they deserve to be compensated for their efforts. This is why it is so vital to have an effective performance management system in place (as discussed in the previous chapter).

Another method companies use is the skill-based pay system. This system assumes that the company can pay more for those who do more. According to this method, the company pays more for the knowledge or skills each employee has (or acquires), rather than the job alone. A variation of this system is also called the knowledge-based pay system. This pay system can be useful when technological advancements create a need for new skills or knowledge. This skill-based system has the advantage of improving staff performance and reducing unwanted turnover, helps improve the company's recruitment,[2] and in effect helps to create additional rungs on the company's career ladder. Some disadvantages include: (a) lengthy time to establish, (b) increase in labor costs, (c) some employees learn the new skills, and then have no advancement within the organization, (d) creation of false expectations, and (e) how to categorize skills outdated by technology.[3]

5. Open communication—Some HR managers find it uncomfortable to discuss pay issues with employees. However, most HR managers know pay and compensation issues are a much-discussed topic between employees. Therefore, it is critical that the HR manager communicate to the employees the mechanics of the compensation plan. Discussing employee pay is delicate, but helping employees understand how their pay increase was determined, why a particular amount was given, and how the employee can earn more will help the workforce of the organization to become less stressful, and hopefully achieve greater profitability for the company.

BENEFITS

While most employees focus on direct benefits, or dollars received, the HR manager realizes this is only a part of the compensation expense. HR managers know that the total cost of compensation to their company can range from 20 to 40 percent of the total amount of expenditures of their operations. In most countries, compensation is more than just the monetary amount paid to employees. Compensation includes mandatory and voluntary benefits. In the United States, federal, state, and local governments have passed laws requiring employers to provide more benefits than just the monetary amount. In addition, many companies also offer voluntary benefits to help attract top-notch employees to their companies.

Mandatory Benefits

The listing of benefits provided by employers in Figure 8.5 indicates that most benefits are provided on a voluntary basis. Figure 8.5 also includes the mandated benefits that employers must

Mandatory Benefits	Voluntary Benefits
Workers' compensation	Health insurance
Unemployment compensation	Life insurance
Social security	AD&D insurance
COBRA benefits	Pension plans, 401(k)
FMLA	Leaves of absence
ERISA	Paid holidays
	Paid vacations
	Paid sick/personal time
	Education assistance
	Child care assistance
	Social and recreational benefits
	Hospitality specific benefits

FIGURE 8.5 Comparison of Benefits.

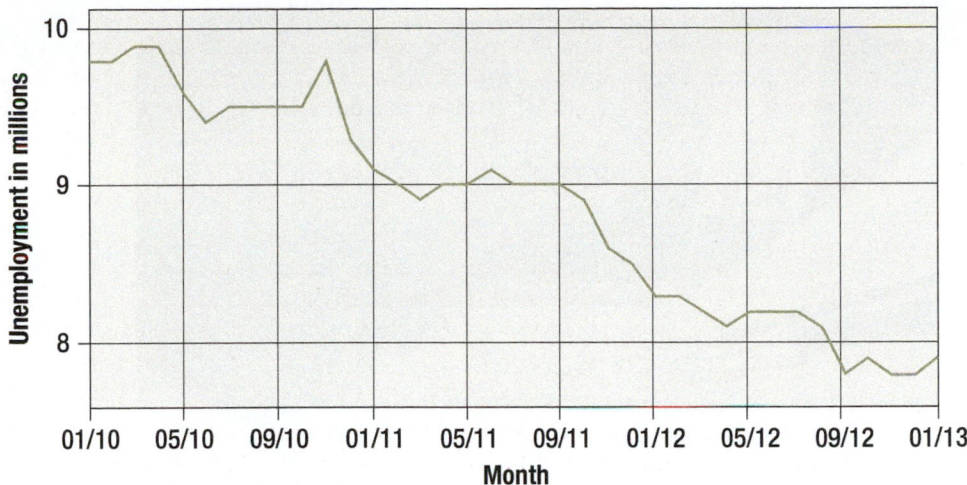

FIGURE 8.6 Trends in U.S. Employment.

provide. **Workers' compensation** is a benefit that provides medical care, disability payments, and death benefits resulting from a work-related accident or illness. The employer usually hires a workers' compensation insurance carrier to provide these benefits. In the case of large firms, the HR department will manage this benefit. Workers' compensation laws vary by state; however, in most states, the premium paid is based on four years of claim experience. Because of this, it is important for an organization to be proactive with workplace safety, thus lowering this expense. Another factor that plays a role in workers' compensation premiums is the risk assigned to industries. The hospitality industry has been identified as a high risk workplace; thus, even more emphasis needs to be placed on workplace safety.

In today's economic climate and the elevated unemployment levels of workers, employees have an interest in unemployment compensation. See Figure 8.6 for the trend in U.S. unemployment between 2010 and 2013.[4]

Unemployment compensation is also a state-enforced mandatory benefit that provides compensation payments to employees who have been laid off, or have become unemployed due to **downsizing** situations. Like workers' compensation, the amount paid for unemployment compensation is also based on claim experience. Hence, HR departments must be diligent when enforcing policies concerning involuntary separations from the organization, in order that costs be kept to a minimum. These organizations are also very protective in their defense of unemployment compensation charges.

Initially signed into law in 1935 by Franklin D. Roosevelt, **social security benefits** became integral aspects of compensation, for both the employer and the employee. It is formally known as the federal Old-Age and Survivors Insurance Trust Fund and the federal Disability Insurance Trust Fund program (OASDI), in which *OA* references old age, *S* for survivors' (widow/widower) income, and *DI* for disability insurance. Today, the term social security is used to only mean benefits paid out for retirement, disability, or death. In this program, an employer's contributions are matched by employee contributions. The amount is established by a specified formula set by the legislation. This benefit is administered by the U.S. Social Security Administration, a federal agency. It is important to note that social security was never intended to provide total retirement to individuals in their later years of life, rather the intent was to supplement their other retirement income.

FMLA (Family and Medical Leave Act of 1993)provides for mandatory leave of absence to employees with a qualifying family or health care need. The usual extent of a mandatory leave is 60 days, and the employee must be returned to the same type of position with equivalent pay levels. Many companies offer variations on this mandatory benefit, but these companies must comply with the minimal level established by the legislation.

Many employers offer voluntary group health insurance options to employees. The Consolidated Omnibus Budget Reconciliation Act of 1985 (**COBRA**) mandated the continuation of this health insurance option to a terminated employee (termination, voluntary leave, or in case of a business closing). These provisions cover employers with 20 or more employees. It is noted that this provision is provided to the terminated employee at their cost (100%), and for a period of 18 months.

Social security benefits.
Credit: NikP / Shutterstock.

Similar to COBRA provisions, and since employers offer a voluntary pension program, the Employee Retirement Income Security Act of 1974 (ERISA) governs the actions of employers concerning pension plans. If employers offer pension plans, ERISA requires the compliance with a wide range of reporting and disclosure requirements.

Voluntary Benefits

All employers must offer certain benefits as required by law. These same employers offer voluntary benefits in order to create employee loyalty, and to compete with other organizations for potential recruits. HR managers need to recognize these aspects of compensation, and they need to recognize the importance of these benefits to current and future employees. For instance, older workers place more emphasis on retirement benefits, younger workers on flexibility (schedules, working at home, travel), and workers with families place more emphasis on family benefits (child care, elder care, or company perquisites). These voluntary benefits are designed to enrich the lives of the organizations' employees, in the hope they create a happier, more motivated employee, and maybe a more productive employee.

Most individuals are familiar with insurance benefits, the more popular ones being medical, prescription drug, dental, and vision insurance. Many other insurance options are available, but the one important aspect is tax saving for the employee. These benefits are paid pretax deductions, meaning employees do not pay social security and FICA (Federal Insurance Contributions Act) tax on that portion of their income, thus lowering their tax expense.

Medical insurance—Health care coverage is the most costly insurance program for the employer. It customarily equals 7 to 8 percent of the organization's payroll and, in some cases, equates to even more. In most cases, the companies pay a certain percentage of the cost and the employee pays the other percentage (usually 50/50 plan). It has been noted that if an employer is willing to pay 100 percent of the cost, it could equate to a dollar amount equal to or greater than $8,000 (depending on the coverage offered). Most organizations offer two types of plans: HMO (health maintenance organization) and PPO (preferred provider option). Originally, a health maintenance organization provided preventive care to individuals before they became ill, but over time, administrators began to seek the most inexpensive means to provide health care. A PPO usually has the insured employee pay a deductible up to a certain amount.

Prescription drug plans—These plans allow employees to purchase prescription drugs through a network of providers at a substantially lower cost. In a typical plan, employees pay $30 to $50 for a prescription drug, or $10 to $20 for a generic drug. The balance is picked up by the insurance carrier.

Dental plans—A typical dental play has a fixed deductible (usually $40 to $100) per visit and an annual maximum payout amount by the insured employee (usually $1,000 to $2,000 per year). Routine dental care (6-month checkup and cleaning) is covered 100 percent, and usually

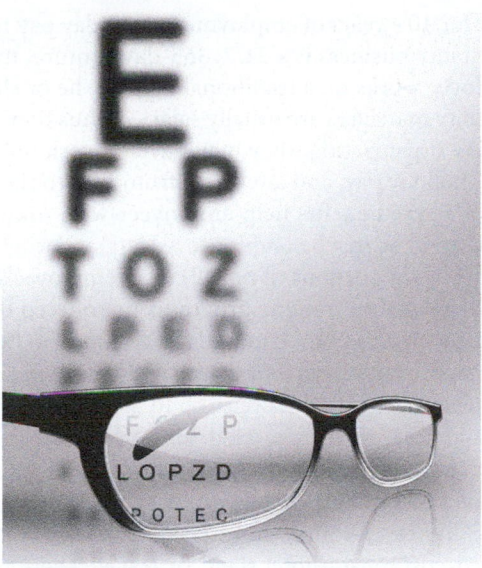

Voluntary benefits— vision care plan.
Credit: Zffoto / Shutterstock

50 percent of major work (bridge and crowns) is covered. Again, this varies greatly by each provider's plan.

Vision care plans—These plans are usually very popular, and most employees participate in vision care. Typically vision care plans have a fixed deductible (similar to dental plans) for eye exams, and also subsidize the cost of eyeglasses and contact lenses. The premiums for these plans are usually very low.

Accidental Death and Disability (AD&D) insurance—Many employers offer their employees life insurance and disability insurance. Life insurance pays a benefit to beneficiaries in the event of the death of a worker. These payments are intended to provide for final expenses and to provide a small portion of income for remaining family members. There are two types of disability insurance: long term and short term. Disability insurance provides income to individuals who are unable to work due to illness or accidents. This is differentiated from workers' compensation because the accident (or illness) does not occur at work. Usually employees pay nothing for the life insurance premium, but pay more when they elect to have more coverage than the minimum established by the organization. When it comes to disability insurance, many times the employee covers 100 percent of the expense. Long-term disability policies continue employee pay beyond that provided by the short-term policy.

Retirement benefits—Retirement plans typically cost organizations about 3 to 5 percent of payroll. They are usually offered as a pension plan or a 401(k) plan. Pension plans have lost their popularity and, in times past, were funded 100 percent by the company. These plans are highly regulated and, therefore, can be difficult to manage. However, 401(k) retirement plans are popular. These plans offer employees the option to contribute to their retirement plans at a pretax rate. Many times, the employer will match the employee contribution, usually at a predetermined rate (100%, 75%, or 50%). The advantages to these plans are: (a) they are portable, meaning the employee can take them to a new employer, (b) employees typically choose where to invest their money, or they chose their investment options (usually dependent on their willingness to accept risk—the more risk, the greater the potential payout), and (c) they are relatively easy to administer for the employer. Finally, these plans have a vesting period, usually five years. Vesting refers to the amount of time that employer contributions cannot be accessed by the employee. For example, if the vesting period is five years, then any funds contributed by the employer cannot be taken by the employee until after five years of employment. This helps the employer build employee retention and, hopefully, employee loyalty.

Time-off benefits—The employee is paid for time that is not actually worked. These include paid holidays, vacations, and sick/personal days. Most hospitality organizations allow for two weeks of paid vacation for years 1 to 5, three weeks of vacation pay for years 6 to 10, and four weeks of vacation pay for 10+ years of employment. Holiday pay is different for hospitality companies. Since the hospitality business is a 24/7, 365-day venture, many times holiday pay is not offered; and if an employee works on a traditional holiday, he or she is paid at 1.5 times the normal rate of pay. Hospitality managers are usually salaried, thus they realize that upon accepting a job within a hospitality organization, they may have to work on holidays. Nonhospitality companies offer six days of holiday pay, and anywhere from four to six personal days of pay.

Assistance benefits—These benefits help employees with uninsured expenses, such as educational expenses, child care, or maybe employee assistance programs (EAPs). An educational assistance benefit will pay for portions (if not all) of an employee's tuition for a hospitality-related class, or for expenses related to training programs not offered by the company. Another potential assistance benefit is with child care. Though not common in hospitality companies, this type of benefit generates more loyalty from employees with children. EAPs provide counseling for employees encountering a variety of issues relating to alcohol, drugs, health, legal, financial, housing, mental health, child care, elder care, grief, abuse (spousal/child/parent), career planning, or retirement. Finally, some hospitality companies have social and recreational facilities for their employees, in order to maintain or increase employee wellness.

Hospitality-specific benefits—Some hospitality companies can offer their employees benefits such as reduced-cost meals, hotel stays, or travel. These benefits offered at highly reduced amounts are very popular with employees, and can be offered by the company at a relatively low cost.

INCENTIVES

In addition to salary, wages, and benefits, many hospitality organizations offer compensation designed on work performance, or financial performance. These are often referred to as incentive programs, and are based on the financial performance of the company. Researchers have documented that pay-for-performance systems improve employee motivation and productivity, and usually improve the financial performance of the company. Figure 8.7 presents the characteristics of an effective incentive program. When designed carefully, performance-based incentives can increase employee income and lead directly to improvements in guest services and product quality.

Linking a component of pay to performance has critical advantages. The first advantage is the retention of quality employees. When companies link compensation to performance, they usually find that those employees who perform the best receive the greatest pay. These employees are motivated to remain a member of the team, and to keep performing at a higher level. Over a long time period, these companies are likely to have an entire team of high performers. Likewise, lower-performing employees are likely to leave the company, and usually go to companies without the pay-for-performance compensation.

Second, companies that link performance to pay see an increase in productivity from their high-performing employees. These employees have a reason to work harder and produce higher results either in service or in production. Third, there is a cost savings to linking pay for performance. When the company sees financial success, it will pass some of this success to the

---

1. The program goals must be understood by the employee, and directed to the employee.
2. Goals must be fair, reliable, and valid.
3. The goals must have room for improvement in performance.
4. The goal must be attainable.
5. The goal must be attached to a reward, whether money or merchandise.
6. Rewards must be attached to productivity, not time spent on the task.
7. Rewards must be administered quickly to reinforce the desire for improvement in performance.
8. Since the goals are attached to improvement in performance, they must also be attached to the possibility of climbing the career ladder.

FIGURE 8.7 Characteristics of Effective Incentive Programs.

higher-performing employee. When the company does not see financial success, the employee does not gain the additional financial incentive. Finally, linking pay to performance will increase the higher-performing employee's focus on the company's goals. When properly linked to the company's goals, the employees of the company will work toward this common goal, resulting in the successful completion of the goal. If a company has not been successful in matching the eight characteristics of pay for performance, it will probably not have an effective compensation program.

Performance-based pay includes incentives (monetary or nonmonetary), which are sometimes called bonuses. An incentive or bonus program may be designed to compensate an individual, a work team, a department, or every member of the operation. Incentive and bonus programs are very common within the hospitality industry and especially in food service operations, because managers believe that by implementing these programs they can increase quantity and quality of the products/services offered.

Individual incentive programs are most helpful when the work involved is not overly interdependent, or when individual improvement will help the company the most. Some potential disadvantages to these programs are the cost of administration. In some cases, this cost outweighs the improvement in productivity. Another potential disadvantage is the timing of the reward. If the reward lags too far past the performance, the employee's motivation to succeed will diminish. Finally, the incentive program must be perceived as being fair for all employees. If the program is not deemed as being fair for all, the employees will quit trying to increase their performance.

Group incentive plans are most helpful when cooperation and coordination are critical to the success of the operation, or where teamwork is essential. There are also disadvantages to group incentive plans. Employers have to be cautious about turning above-average performance into mere-average performance. This will lead the group to not trust the employer. Also, if employees continue their improved performance but the company has a bad year and does not offer the reward, the employees will lose faith in the employer, thus lowering their productivity. Employers should have systems in place to identify the free riders in the group. Some employees will continue to have average performance, and hope that this is not noticed so that they will still receive a part of the group's reward. One way to offset this disadvantage is to allow peer evaluation. By allowing peers to have a voice in the evaluation process, the average-performing employee will not gain the advantage of the group reward.

In hospitality companies, the most popular incentive plan is the bonus plan. Bonus plans are numerous. They can be based on sales (overall or an individual item), on quality control audits, on service audits, on loyalty programs, on guest retention rates, on employee retention rates, on effective training programs, and of course, on profit. These are just a few examples, and as shown numerous times, bonuses can be tailored to any situation.

Another financial incentive offered by companies is the employee stock ownership plan (ESOP). An ESOP establishes an account for each employee in a company. Typically the company distributes stocks (sometimes cash) into these accounts based on predetermined attainment of goals or on company profits. Usually these plans have been established for managers, but recently, these have been established for hourly employees as well. There are two common types of ESOPs:

1. Ordinary ESOP—A company contributes an annual amount into the employees' accounts to purchase stock. The employee receives the asset upon retirement from the company (or termination).
2. Leveraged ESOP—The ESOP borrows money from a bank (or lending institution) and provides a guarantee to make contributions back to the institution. The company uses these funds for capital use projects. The company repays the ESOP, which then repays the bank.

Several features make ESOPs unique as compared to other employee benefit plans. First, only an ESOP is required by law to invest primarily in the securities of the sponsoring employer. Second, an ESOP is unique among qualified employee benefit plans in its ability to borrow money. As a result, leveraged ESOPs may be used as a technique of corporate finance.[5] ESOPs also have the potential to increase employee productivity, lower turnover, reduce absenteeism, and hopefully lower costs. Owners can defer taxes on their gains if the ESOP owns 30 percent or more of the company's stock. Employees do not have to pay taxes on ESOP earnings until they receive monetary funds from their ESOP account.

Nonfinancial compensation—
working from home.
Credit: Chatursunil / Shutterstock.

Another financial incentive that is offered by companies is the **stock option plan**. A stock option plan gives the holder the right to purchase stock at a price preset at the time the option is awarded. Usually the price is lower than the current price of the stock. Usually stock options are only given to salaried managers, and commonly the amount is 20 percent of their annual salary. If the company continues to prosper, and the stock price increases, the value of the stock option also increases, thus motivating the manager to keep performance at a high level. Most financial managers advise employees to keep stock options until their retirement (or termination). This allows for the greatest financial reward. One disadvantage to stock options is that tax rates apply to gains. Since the Tax Reform Act of 1986, stock options gains are treated as ordinary income (rather than long-term capital gains), thus they are taxed at a higher rate.

Nonfinancial Compensation

Earlier in the chapter, intrinsic rewards were mentioned as part of a comprehensive compensation plan. Intrinsic rewards can be a powerful motivator for employees. These rewards are designed to enhance an employee's self-respect. These rewards can include a financial component, but many times, they do not need to have a financial component. Some common and effective intrinsic rewards are presented in Figure 8.8.

- More job freedom
- Increased responsibility in decisions
- Flexible work hours
- Flexible work stations (stay at home)
- Diversity in tasks
- Recognition events
- Thank you notes
- Birthday card (or recognition)
- Prime employee parking space
- Reward for perfect attendance
- Clothing items (with corporate logo)
- Employee planned outings

FIGURE 8.8 **Examples of Effective Intrinsic Rewards.**

When employees provide input into this type of system, they will feel more motivated about the reward. Employees know when their input is recognized and valued. By communicating the rationale behind these rewards, the HR manager should see an increase in employee motivation, and hopefully an increase in employee retention.

THE BOTTOM LINE

An example of the impact of compensation is seen in Burgerville, a Vancouver, Washington, based company. This company has offered health insurance to its employees since the early 1970s. In 2005, only 34 out of 1,500+ employees were enrolled in the program. Part of the reason was costs; monthly premiums were $94 for individuals and $299 for families, with $200 and $500 deductibles, respectively. It was clear that the company's health care plan was not accessible for its employees, hence the search for other options. The company eventually decided on Kaiser Permanente, with monthly premiums of $15 for individuals and $60 for family, with no deductibles. It was now the HR department's responsibility to show employees the benefits of the new health insurance. With the help of the company's general managers, the HR department was able to show this value and as a result got 90 percent enrollment. The company's return on investment came in the decreased turnover. In 2005, its turnover percentage was 128 percent, dropping to 54 percent in 2006, and holding steady at 52 percent. The same was seen in salaried turnover percentage, an 18 percent decrease. This is important for Burgerville because it estimates that a single "turn" costs the company $20,000, given recruiting, selecting, and training costs. This was a savings of $22+ million (1,500 × 128% = 1,920 employees needing to be replaced in 2005, to 1,500 × 54% = 810 employees needing to be replaced in 2006, or a difference of 1,110 employees × $20, 000 = $22.2 million).[6]

Wages and salaries are affected by many factors, both internal and external. In order for compensation systems to be effective, the basics of the operation have to be in place. Besides being leaders and managers within the operation, HR managers must know employment laws, they need to recruit/staff the operation, they need to have effective training and development systems, and they must have effective performance evaluation systems in place. Having these basics in place, a hospitality management company should have a very effective compensation system that helps it become more successful. These companies will have success in the retention rates of their employees, and an increase in productivity due to the increase in the motivation of all employees.

Discussion Questions

1. What external and internal factors impact compensation systems? What recommendations would you make to ensure an effective compensation system?
2. What are the types of compensation?
3. Define the difference in compensation for a tipped versus a nontipped employee.
4. How are wages different than salary?
5. What role does motivation play in compensation?
6. What factors or policies should a hospitality company consider when establishing pay grades?
7. What are the most common types of benefits offered by hospitality companies?
8. How is a pension plan different from a retirement plan? What impact did the Tax Reform Act of 1986 have on these benefit plans?
9. Given the demographic makeup of hospitality employees, what types of benefit plans would be the most important for them? Why?
10. What are some of the services offered through EAPs?
11. What are the principal differences between a pay for performance plan and a seniority plan?
12. What are some of the limitations associated with compensation systems?
13. How do individual and group incentives differ?
14. What are the advantages and disadvantages to an effective compensation system?

Application Exercise

Sarah and Bill have been two of your company's best employees for ten years. Their performance evaluations have always been above target, and this year is no different. To coincide with their performance evaluations, you as the HR director have to decide on their salary increase. After reviewing your company's salary history, you notice a distinct gap between male and female wages, with the male average substantially larger. You have also noticed a distinct difference between the amounts of salary offered to diverse employees. As the HR manager, you realize that Sarah is a female employee, and Bill is a diverse employee. You have a strict budget of labor dollars to dispense to all employees. How are you going to determine salary increases?

ndnotes

1. http://www.dol.gov/whd/regs/compliance/whdfs15.pdf
2. Gustafson, B. (January 2000). Skill-based pay improves PFS staff recruitment, retention and performance. *Health Financial Management*, 54(1), 62–64.
3. Luthans, F., & Fox, M. (1989). Update on skill-based pay. *Personnel*, 26–31.
4. http://www.data.bls.gov
5. http://www.esopassociation.org/about/about_whatis.asp
6. http://www.restaurant.org/pdfs/washingtonreport/2008/wreport_2008_03_24.pdf

Key Terms

401(k) retirement plans   A retirement plan that allows employees in private companies to make contributions of pretax dollars to a company pool that is then invested for them in stocks, bonds, or money markets.

AD&D insurance   Short for "accidental death and disability", a form of life and income replacement insurance.

Assistance benefits   These benefits are paid to the employee either immediately or deferred. An example would be an educational expense paid to the employee for completing a course directly aligned to the business's interest.

Bonuses   Financial rewards paid to employees for achieving predetermined performance goals.

COBRA   Under the Consolidated Omnibus Budget Reconciliation Act of 1985, if an employee terminates employment with the company, the employee is entitled to continue participating in the company's group health plan for a prescribed period of time, usually 18 months. (In certain circumstances, such as an employee's divorce or death, the length of coverage period may be longer for qualified dependents.) COBRA coverage is not extended to employees terminated for gross misconduct.

Consumer price index   An index of prices used to measure the change in the cost of basic goods and services in comparison with a fixed base period; also called *cost-of-living index*.

Cost-of-living adjustment   A COLA is an annual adjustment in wages to offset a change in purchasing power, as measured by the consumer price index. The consumer price index is used rather than the producer price index because the purpose is to offset inflation as experienced by the consumer, not the producer.

Deferred compensation   Payment for services under any employer-sponsored plan or arrangement that allows an employee (for tax-related purposes) to defer income to the future.

Dental plans   A monthly premium paid by the employer or employee for dental care (regular cleaning, x-rays, or more extensive work).

Direct compensation   All compensation (base salary and/or incentive pay) that is paid directly to an employee.

Downsizing   The process of reducing the employer's workforce through elimination of positions, management layers, processes, or functions.

Employee assistance programs (EAPs)   A work-based intervention program designed to identify and assist employees in resolving personal problems (i.e., marital, financial, or emotional problems; family issues; substance/alcohol abuse) that may be adversely affecting the employee's performance.

Employee stock ownership plan (ESOP)   A trust established by a corporation that operates as a tax-qualified defined contribution retirement plan, but unlike traditional defined contribution plans, employer contributions are invested in the company's stock.

ERISA   Employee Retirement Income Security Act of 1974 sets requirements for the provision and administration of employee benefit plans. Employee benefit plans include health care benefits, profit sharing, and pension plans.

Exempt status   Employees who meet one of the FLSA exemption criteria and who are paid on a fixed salary basis, thus not entitled to overtime.

Extrinsic rewards   Work-related rewards that have a measurable monetary value, unlike intrinsic rewards, such as praise or satisfaction in a job well done.

Group incentive plans   Compensation paid to a team of employees for successfully completing work toward a company goal.

HMO   A health maintenance organization

Hospitality-specific benefits   Compensation awarded to employees for work completed for the business; an example is a reduced price for a hotel room.

Immediate compensation   Money paid to the employee for time spent at work.

Incentives   Additional compensation used to motivate and reward employees for exceeding performance or productivity goals.

Indirect compensation   Compensation that is not paid directly to an employee and is calculated in addition to base salary and incentive pay (i.e., health/dental/vision insurance, vacation, retirement benefits, educational benefits, relocation expenses).

Individual incentive programs   Compensation paid to an employee for successfully completing tasks as assigned by the company.

Intrinsic rewards   A reward such as praise or the satisfaction of a job well done given to an employee for achievement of a particular goal, objective, or project.

Knowledge-based pay system   A salary differentiation system that bases compensation on an individual's education, experience, knowledge, skills, or specialized training, also referred to as skill-based pay.

Leveraged ESOP   The ESOP borrows money from a bank and uses these funds for capital use projects; the company repays the ESOP, which then repays the bank.

Mandatory benefits   Indirect financial compensation that must, by law, be offered to employees.

Medical insurance benefit   A monthly premium paid by the employer or employee to the insurance company for medical care (annual physical, x-rays, or more extensive care).

Meet the competitor   A company matches the prevailing market rate for employment (hourly or salary).

Merit pay system   A compensation system in which base pay increases are determined by individual performance.

Ordinary ESOP   A company contributes an annual amount into an employee's account to purchase stock. The employee receives the asset upon retirement.

Pay follower   A company pays less than the market average to an employee (hourly or salary) in hopes of generating cost savings.

Pay leader   A company pays more than the market average to an employee (hourly or salary) in hopes of recruiting better applicants, or retaining loyal employees.

Pay ranges   Associated with pay grades, the range sets the upper and lower compensation boundaries for jobs within that range.

Pension plans   An employer benefit plan funded through insurance, a trust, general assets, or other separately maintained funds designed to provide employees with a monthly income benefit upon retirement.

Perquisite   A form of incentives generally given to executive employees, granting them certain privileges or special consideration, such as memberships in clubs, physical fitness programs, or financial counseling.

Piecework wage system   A per-piece rate system that pays employees based on the number of pieces produced.

PPO   A preferred provider option usually has the insured employee pay a deductible up to a certain amount.

Prescription drug plans   A monthly premium paid by the employer or employee for drugs (prescription or generic).

Retirement benefits   A written qualified or nonqualified benefit plan funded by employer and employee contributions, which provides retirement income benefits for employees.

Service charge   An amount added to a guest's bill in exchange for services provided.

Skill-based pay system   A salary differentiation system that bases compensation on an individual's advanced skills, or specialized training.

Social security benefits   A federal program under the Social Security Act, which provides for retirement, disability, and other related benefits for workers and their eligible dependents.

Stock option plan   An organizational program that grants employees the option of purchasing a specific number of stocks in the company at a future date.

Time-off benefits   An employee is paid for time that is not actually worked; an example is paid holidays, vacation pay, sick days, or personal days.

Tip credit   The amount of tips employers are allowed to count (credit) toward the wage payments they make to employees.

Tip pool   An arrangement in which service providers share their tips with each other on a predetermined basis.

Unemployment compensation   A benefit paid to an employee who involuntarily loses his or her employment without just cause.

Vesting   An employee's right to receive present or future pension benefits, even if the employee does not remain in the service of the employer.

Vision care plans   A monthly premium paid by the employer or employee for vision care (eye examinations, x-rays, contact lenses, or glasses).

Voluntary benefits   Indirect financial compensation a company chooses on its own to offer its workers in an effort to attract and keep the best possible employees.

Workers' compensation   State laws enacted to provide workers with protection and income replacement benefits due to an illness or injury suffered on the job. Employers must carry appropriate workers' compensation insurance, as required by state law, or have a sufficient source of funding for claims incurred.

PART III

Skills Needed to Be a Strategic Partner

9

Individual Skills

KEY TERMS

Achievement orientation
Adaptability
Big five personality types
Brainstorming
Conscientiousness
Creativity
Critical thinking
Decision making
DiSC
Extrinsic work values
Hard skills
Interests
Initiative
Intrinsic work values

Myers-Briggs Type Indicator
Nominal group technique
Nonprogrammed decisions
Optimism
Problem solving
Programmed decisions
Self-assessment
Self-awareness
Self-confidence
Self-management (self-control)
Soft skills
Time management
Trustworthiness
Work values

OBJECTIVES

- Describe the differences between hard and soft skills
- Build self-awareness through self-assessment and self-management
- Define the personal abilities needed by hospitality managers
- Describe the problem-solving process and the role of decision making in the process
- Identify principles of creativity and critical thinking

> **Consider This**
>
> Sam considered himself to be a good assistant manager for his restaurant. The general manager had given him positive feedback on each of the technical skills that were identified as needed in his job. His strengths seemed to be in controlling costs, sanitation, and guest services. The weaknesses were what concerned Sam. These included time management and creative problem solving. What concerned Sam the most was that he was not aware of these weaknesses so he asked his general manager for some help in developing the weaknesses into strengths. Sam was referred to the human resources department and completed independent study modules that cover the material in this chapter.

INTRODUCTION

It is estimated that 85 percent of your effectiveness as a manager is based on your ability to use soft skills. Excellent managers should use the information they have about soft skills to help employees develop their soft skills. In this chapter, you will learn about the differences between hard and soft skills and the individual abilities that make up the soft skills needed to be a successful manager.

HARD AND SOFT SKILLS

There are many ways of thinking about the skills you need to be an effective manager. We are going to consider just two categories as they relate to working with human resources, which are **hard skills** and **soft skills**. Hard skills are routine technical types of skills required to do the job. Examples of these skills are labor scheduling, recipe costing, determining the amount to order, checking customers in, and checking customers out. Many organizations have developed extensive training programs for the technical or hard skills needed for their jobs. Previous chapters have covered all of the technical information and skills you will need to handle human resource issues at work.

Soft skills are those human relations skills that we use when interacting with others, making decisions, and thinking creatively. We will begin with individual skills because the more you know about yourself, the more successful you will be when working with others. Interpersonal skills will be covered in Chapter 10 and organizational skills will be covered in Chapter 11.

SELF-AWARENESS, SELF-ASSESSMENT, AND SELF-MANAGEMENT

The basis of all soft skills is **self-awareness** or the ability to recognize your own knowledge, skills, and abilities. You should be able to recognize how you react to cues in the environment and how these affect your performance. You should be aware of your own feelings, know why the feelings

Soft skills—communicating with others. *Credit:* Pressmaster / Shutterstock.

Factor	Definition
Extraversion	Tendency to be active, energetic, talkative, outgoing, and assertive
Agreeableness	Tendency to be forgiving, generous, kind, sympathetic, and trusting
Conscientiousness	Tendency to be efficient, organized, reliable, responsible, and thorough
Neuroticism	Tendency to be anxious, tense, self-conscious, moody, and impulsive
Openness	Tendency to be curious, imaginative, insightful, original, and introspective

FIGURE 9.1   **Big Five Personality Factors and Definitions.**

occur, and understand the implications of your own emotions. Self-awareness requires that you can accurately assess your skills, and abilities and develop a feeling of self-confidence.

Accurate **self-assessment** is about knowing your inner resources, abilities, and limits. It is being aware of your strengths and limitations. Another term for self-assessment is a personal SWOT analysis. Identifying strengths, weaknesses, opportunities, and threats for personal growth is possible through a variety of sources. Receiving feedback and new perspectives about one's self from others is used as a basis for continuous learning and self-development. It implies having the ability to target areas for personal change. You should have a sense of humor about yourself, be aware of your own strengths and limits, and be open to feedback.

Self-assessment includes determining your personality type, values, **interests**, skills, and abilities. Personality types indicate what motivates or what will drive you to perform, what influences your attitudes, and how you determine your needs. Since personality is one of the most important factors that influence hiring decisions and the ability to work as a team, it is important that managers understand their own personalities, which will assist them in understanding those of their employees.

There are many theories behind personality types. The **big five personality types**, **Myers-Briggs Type Indicator**, and **DiSC** are three of the most popular used in the hospitality industry. The big five personality types or the five factor model includes five basic factors that are used to classify personality types. The five factors are extraversion (E), agreeableness (A), conscientiousness (C), neuroticism (N), and openness (O).[1] Definitions of the five factors are presented in Figure 9.1. A personality is described as being low, medium, or high on each of the five factors.

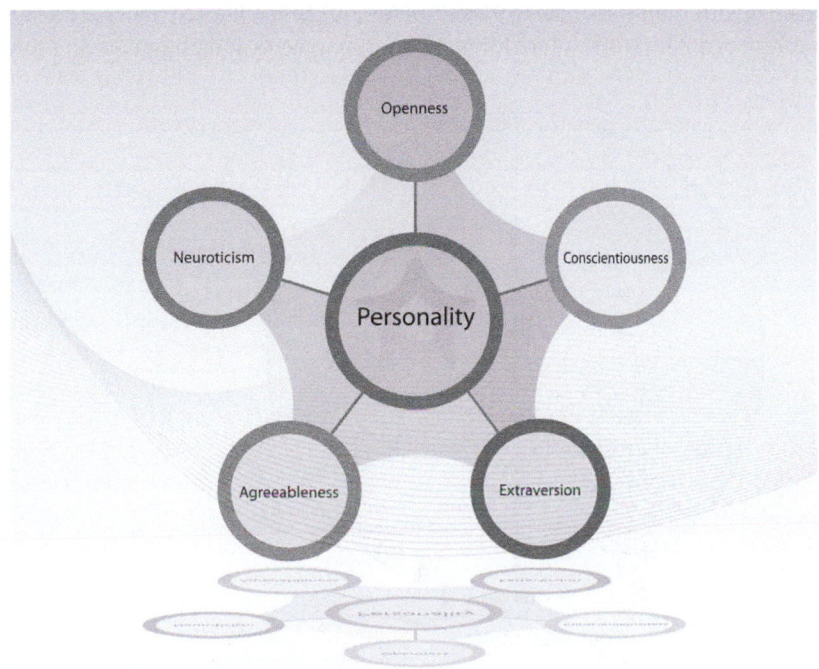

Big five.   *Credit*: John T Takai / Shutterstock.

Extroversion (E)—A need for socializing with others - being around others is energizing - 75% of the population	Introversion (I)—A need to be alone or in activities that involve a few people - energy is lost when around others and is re-charged through quiet and solitude - 25% of the population
Sensing (S)—A need for facts and experience for decision making - 75% of the population	Intuition (N)—Uses visions, intuitions, or hunches as a basis for operations - operates in the future and is imaginative - 25% of the population
Thinking (T)—A need for logic and objective principles for decision making - 50% of the population	Feeling (F)—A need for subjective, more personal, and emotionally based decision making - 50% of the population
Judging (J)—A preference for closure and settling things - may require deadlines that are followed - work comes before play - 50% of the population	Perceiving (P)—A preference for open and fluid options - more playful and believes work should be enjoyable - 50% of the population

FIGURE 9.2   Definitions of Myers-Briggs Scales.

The Myers-Briggs Type Indicator is a personality system based on four scales. The scales are similar to four of the Big 5 factors. The four scales are (a) extroversion (E) to introversion (I), (b) sensing (S) to intuition (N), (c) feeling (F) to thinking (T), and (d) judging (J) to perceiving (P).[2] Definitions of the scales are in Figure 9.2. The results are 16 combinations of letters that describe different personality types. Most hospitality jobs require extensive interactions with customers, which would indicate that high scores on extroversion (E) and feeling (F) are needed to be successful. Hospitality jobs have been classified using Myers-Briggs scales.[3] Restaurant workers often have ESFP or ENFP personality types.

There are four basic DiSC styles labeled dominance, influence, steadiness, and conscientiousness. Figure 9.3 presents the scales in the form of a circle.[4] The personality types that result from the DiSC evaluation are represented by each of the four letters D, I, S, C, and may be accompanied by a second letter from the section of the circle that is adjacent. For example, there are three D styles: D, DC, and DI.

Self-assessment includes evaluating the values that are important to you. **Work values** are feelings about work and your contributions to society through your work. Work values can be intrinsic or extrinsic. **Intrinsic work values** of work are due to an interest in the work itself or the contributions the job makes to society. **Extrinsic work values** are conditions that accompany the work such as earning potential and work setting. Work must have some intrinsic value for most people to be satisfied with their jobs. The work values for jobs in the United States are available from www.onetonline.org. The work values for restaurant managers, lodging managers, and

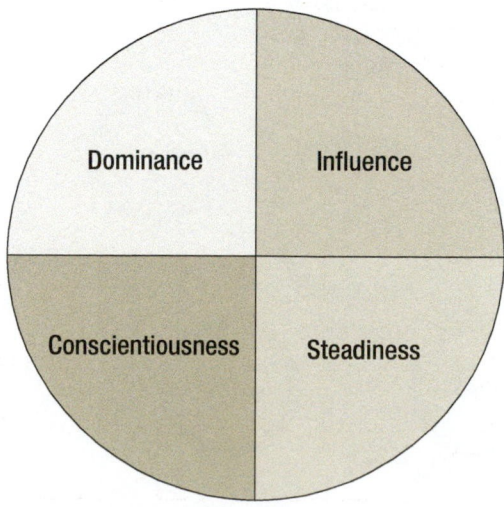

FIGURE 9.3   Four DiSC Styles.

Value	Restaurant Management	Lodging Management	Meeting Planners
Independence—Ability to work on one's own and make decisions	78	83	72
Relationships—Providing service to others and work with coworkers in a noncompetitive setting	61	100	89
Support—Management that is supportive and stands behind employees	61	50	39
Working Conditions—Job security and good working conditions are present	58	53	64
Achievement—Result-oriented jobs that give employees a feeling of accomplishment	56	67	67
Recognition—Opportunities exist for advancement and leadership	56	56	67

FIGURE 9.4 **Work Values for Three Hospitality Management Positions.**[5]

meeting planners are included in Figure 9.4. The values are rated on a scale that measures the extent the value exists in the position where 1 indicates it is not included and 100 indicates the value has a major presence in the job.

Another form of self-assessment is to determine your interests and how they are met through your work. John Holland has classified interests into six categories. The six categories form the basis of the strong interest inventory and have been used to classify jobs. The six types are realistic (R), investigative (I), artistic (A), social (S), enterprising (E), and conventional (C). The definitions of the six categories are included in Figure 9.5. The United States Department of Labor has identified the interest categories for jobs, which are included on the website www.onetonline.org. The top three interest codes for lodging management and meeting planner jobs are E, C, and S. The top four codes for restaurant management jobs are E, C, R, and S. The

Interest Category	Definition	Restaurant Managers	Lodging Managers	Meeting Planners
Realistic	A preference for concrete tasks and working alone or with other realistic people	56	50	11
Investigative	A thinker who likes to use abstract or analytical skills, often preferring to work alone	11	11	6
Artistic	A creative person who is very imaginative and usually extroverted	11	6	22
Social	A preference for interacting with people and helping others	56	50	56
Enterprising	Leaders who are willing to take on challenges	100	100	100
Conventional	A preference for structured tasks and handling details	72	72	67

FIGURE 9.5 **Interest Categories in Three Hospitality Management Jobs.**[6]

Strong Interest Inventory is available at the same website and can be taken to help you and your employees identify interests and determine if they are compatible with the current position.

The final type of self-assessment is to evaluate your skills and abilities. This type of information is often provided through periodic evaluations of work performance. The skills and abilities required for jobs are available at www.onetonline.org. It would be valuable information to identify those needed for your job and then to evaluate your effectiveness.

Self-confidence is the belief in your capability to accomplish a task and acknowledging that you are the best for the job. It is also about conveying your ideas and opinions in an assured manner and having a positive impact on others. You should present yourself in an assured and unhesitating manner, stand out in a group, and believe you are among the most capable for a job. Self-confidence requires that you have a "can do" attitude and view all obstacles as opportunities. Once you are confident about your abilities and have a job that helps you meet your needs, you self-confidence will follow.

Self-management or **self-control** is the ability to keep your impulsive feelings and emotions under control and direct your behaviors to reach goals. It is being able to restrain negative actions when provoked, when faced with opposition or hostility from others, or when working under pressure. You should be able to deal calmly with stress, display impulse control and restraint, and stay poised and positive, even in trying moments. In addition, **time management** or focusing your efforts on tasks that will help you meet your goals is an important component of self-control. There are many tools you can use to help manage your time. The steps for managing your time are as follows:

1. Set long-term goals or those goals you want to accomplish over the next five years.
2. Break long-term goals into those that can be accomplished within shorter periods of time (year, month, week, or day).
3. On a daily basis, establish goals that need to be accomplished and the tasks that are required, and then link these tasks to long-term goals.
4. Identify the best use of your time to accomplish tasks. When conflicting opportunities arise, select the task that will accomplish goals. You may use a ranking system and tackle those tasks that are most critical or directly related to your goals first, followed by less critical tasks as time permits. The time management matrix such as the one in Figure 9.6 can assist you in determining which tasks require your immediate attention.

Time management.   *Credit*: Oleksiy Mark / Shutterstock.

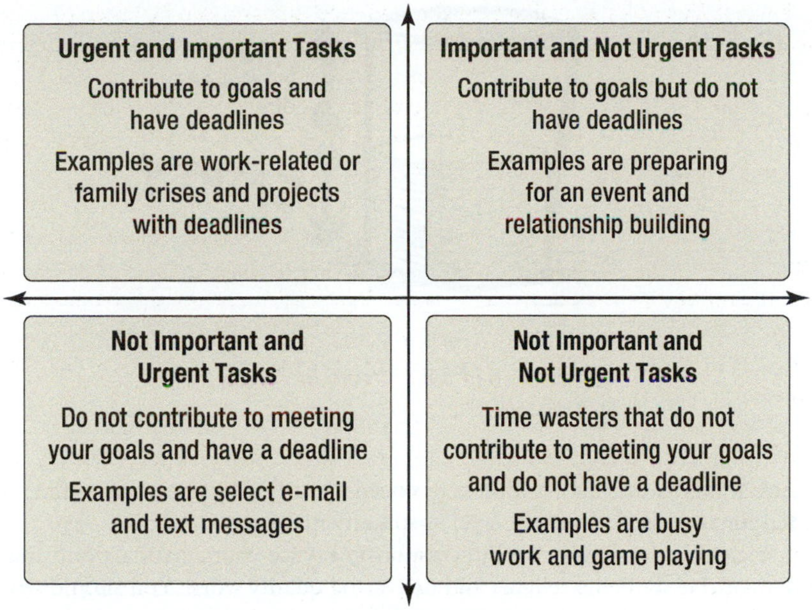

Urgent and Important Tasks Contribute to goals and have deadlines Examples are work-related or family crises and projects with deadlines	**Important and Not Urgent Tasks** Contribute to goals but do not have deadlines Examples are preparing for an event and relationship building
Not Important and Urgent Tasks Do not contribute to meeting your goals and have a deadline Examples are select e-mail and text messages	**Not Important and Not Urgent Tasks** Time wasters that do not contribute to meeting your goals and do not have a deadline Examples are busy work and game playing

FIGURE 9.6   Sample Time Management Matrix.

5. Watch for time wasters, such as e-mail, phone calls, and texting. Categorize these interruptions based on the same ranking system and use these as a way to accomplish your goals.
6. At the end of each day, identify goals that have been reached and those that need to be continued to the following day. Repeat steps 3 through 6.

PERSONAL ABILITIES

Personal abilities that are important when managing others include trustworthiness, conscientiousness, adaptability, optimism, achievement orientation, and initiative. These abilities serve as a basis for strong management skills and positive relationships with employees and customers.

Trustworthiness is taking action that is consistent with what you say and value. It includes openly communicating intentions, ideas, and feelings. Trustworthiness also includes welcoming openness and honesty in others. You should show integrity and take responsibility for your own behavior and performance. The ethical principles that you believe in should be used as a basis for all actions, which will be interpreted by others as integrity (see Figure 9.7). Trust is built by being reliable and authentic or "what you see is what you get." Trustworthiness is important to hospitality managers because it serves as the basis for developing a team and interacting with employees and customers. If you are not honest and trustworthy, others will view you as unreliable and

---

Honesty, truthfulness, not misleading, or misrepresenting

Integrity, doing what you know is right

Trustworthiness, candid in supplying information, does not try to dodge promises or commitments

Loyalty to company and colleagues, avoid conflict of interest, and maintain confidentiality

Fair and equitable in all dealings, do not abuse power

Concern, respect, and compassion for others

Commitment to excellence in their jobs

Leadership through accepting responsibility and setting a proper example

Build company reputation and morale of employees

Personally accountable for ethical quality of decisions

FIGURE 9.7   Ethical Principles for Hospitality Managers.[7]

Optimism—half full.   *Credit*: Joe Simmons / Shutterstock.

inconsistent. Integrity or trustworthiness has been identified by recruiters as the most important skill needed for success for an entry-level hospitality manager.

Conscientiousness involves taking responsibility for your personal performance. It reflects an underlying drive for being reliable and delivering quality work. You should work in a careful and organized manner, pay attention to detail, follow through on commitments/promises, and build trust through reliability. Following through on commitments is an important component of conscientiousness. Employees want to follow a leader or manager who sets high standards and helps others achieve those standards.

Adaptability is the ability to be flexible and work effectively within a variety of changing situations and with various individuals and groups. People with this competency are willing to change their own ideas or perceptions on the basis of new information or evidence. They are able to alter standard procedures when necessary, and juggle multiple demands as required. You should be able to juggle multiple demands, handle shifting priorities and rapid change, and change plans, behavior, or approaches to fit major changes in situations. Most management jobs in the hospitality industry require this skill. It is seldom that two days are the same when working in this industry. In addition, multitasking and making quick changes are required to be successful in hospitality management positions.

Optimism is about seeing the world as a glass that is "half-full" rather than "half empty." This is the ability to see good in others and in the situation at hand. Threats are viewed merely as opportunities that can be acted upon and taken advantage of to achieve optimal outcomes. You should be able to see opportunities rather than threats, have mainly positive expectations about others, and have hopes that the future will be better than the past. A manager who is optimistic can create a work environment that encourages employees to handle challenges and to be successful.

Achievement orientation shows a concern for working toward a standard of excellence. This standard may be a personal need to improve your performance over past accomplishments, to outperform others, or even to surpass the greatest accomplishment ever achieved. You should be able to anticipate obstacles to a goal, take calculated risks, and set measurable goals. This type of orientation leads others to work toward excellence.

Initiative is the ability to identify a problem, obstacle, or opportunity and take action on it. People who show initiative are consistently striving to do better, to experience new challenges and opportunities, and to be held accountable for their actions and ideas. Showing initiative means that you are able to act rather than wait for direction. Successful managers demonstrate the ability to take initiative and develop this strength in others.

PROBLEM SOLVING AND DECISION MAKING

Problem solving and decision making are interrelated skills. Figure 9.8 shows the relationship between problem solving and decision making.

Problem solving encompasses the broad range of activities that begin with identifying the problem and end with implementing the solution. The most critical part of problem solving is to correctly identify what is causing the problem. Managers often recognize symptoms

Problem-Solving Steps

1. Define the problem in terms of the cause of the problem
2. Identify alternative solutions for the problem
3. Select the best solution from the alternatives (**decision making**)
4. Implement the solution
5. Monitor and evaluate the effectiveness of the solution
6. Return to step 1 if the problem is not solved

FIGURE 9.8   Relationship between Problem Solving and Decision Making.

of problems while finding it more difficult to identify the cause of the problem. For example, a symptom of a problem is when an employee is consistently late to work. Lateness is being caused by something in the employee's life such as poor work ethic, unreliable transportation, poor organization or time management skills, or too many responsibilities outside the workplace. The solutions for each of these causes are different, so you can see how important it is to identify the cause for the problem.

Once the cause for the problem is identified, alternative solutions should be identified. Brainstorming is a creative exercise that can be used by a manager or with a group of employees. If the manager is solving the problem alone, many possible solutions would be generated before they are evaluated as possible solutions. One of the advantages of using a group for solving problems is that many ideas for solutions can be generated. Brainstorming is a method where everyone generates as many ideas as possible. When all of the ideas have been presented, each is then evaluated for effectiveness in solving the problem. A modification of brainstorming is the nominal group technique. The nominal group technique is appropriate when a group member dominates the group or when not all group members are participating. This method involves giving each member time to write down two to three solutions to the problem. The group leader then asks each member to share one solution as the speaking privilege moves from one group member to the next. The pros and cons of the solutions are not discussed until all solutions have been proposed. By allowing each member the opportunity to speak without criticism, the quality of the solutions is improved.

Brainstorming.   *Credit*: Peshkova / Shutterstock.

Decision making is the process of selecting a solution from the alternatives that have been generated. Criteria for selecting the best alternative are identified and then each alternative is evaluated using those criteria. For example, if the problem is high labor cost, then the alternative that generates the lowest labor cost will be selected. That means that cost for each alternative must be determined and the lowest cost alternative is selected. A list of pros and cons for each alternative may be used in other situations.

In some problems, multiple criteria may be used in selecting the best alternative. For example, the best solution to a problem may need to be cost-effective, easy to produce, and popular with customers. The multiattribute utility (MAU) model would be useful to evaluate the solutions. Chapter 5 included an application of the MAU model to the selection of applicants for a position. In the example in Chapter 5 where candidates were evaluated using the MAU model, each of the characteristics is a criterion that is given an amount of points out of 100 that are then assigned to evaluate each alternative. In this example low cost may be the most important so is given 50 points. Popularity with customers may be next in importance and is given 30 points. That leaves complications of production with the remaining 20 points. Each alternative is given points up to the maximum for each of the criteria. The points for each alternative are totaled and the alternative with the highest number of points is selected.

Once the alternative is selected, the final step is implementing and evaluating the effectiveness of the solution. The criteria used to evaluate the alternatives are used to determine if the solution solved the problem. If the problem still exists, the process is then repeated.

Managerial decisions can be programmed or nonprogrammed. **Programmed decisions** are those made by following policies and procedures that have been established. For example, if an employee does not show up for three days in a row, the manager will terminate the employee. This decision is programmed or based on the organization's policies. **Nonprogrammed decisions** are those decisions that are not routine and may not be repeated in the organization. For example, the decision to create a website for advertising and reservations is a nonprogrammed decision. This decision is a "one of a kind" decision. In general, managers at lower levels of the organization make more programmed decisions than nonprogrammed. At upper levels of management, more nonprogrammed decisions than programmed decisions are made.

CREATIVITY AND CRITICAL THINKING

Two interrelated skills that you must develop to be an effective manager are creativity and critical thinking. **Creativity** is the process used to develop new and useful ideas. Creativity requires that you look at a problem from many perspectives to identify as many unique alternatives as possible. There are many tools that can be used to encourage creativity. One method is to approach a problem from a variety of stakeholder views, such as from the customer, employee, and owner. Edward deBono has developed six thinking hats that are used to give six different perspectives to the issue.[8]

The six thinking hats method is used to look at a problem from six different perspectives. Each hat is a different color and represents a different style of thinking. White hat thinking requires that you evaluate the data that are available and identify additional data that are required to make a decision. A manager who is concerned about labor cost would gather data about employee hours, productivity, and sales before making a decision about methods to reduce costs.

Red hat thinking looks at a problem using intuition and emotion. A concern for the emotions of others may also influence a decision when thinking from the red hat perspective. Using this type of thinking may focus on the emotions involved with cutting employee work hours or the effect on customer satisfaction if staffing were to be reduced.

Black hat thinking requires a manager to look at the negative aspects of a decision. This will highlight the weak points of a plan before a decision is made. For example, focusing on costs alone may not give a true picture of the impact of downsizing of the workforce. Managers should look at all of the negative outcomes of a plan before implementing the plan.

Yellow hat thinking is the opposite of black hat thinking. Yellow hat thinking takes an optimistic viewpoint and looks at the best outcomes for a plan. Benefits of a plan are highlighted and valued using this type of thinking. For many managers, this is the only perspective that is evaluated when developing a plan because it is the easiest to identify.

Green hat thinking involves creativity. Many solutions to a problem are generated without evaluating the solutions by looking at the positive and negative outcomes. A manager may begin with this type of thinking when working on a problem and then move to the evaluation phase and use the previous thinking styles to evaluate the solutions.

Blue hat thinking involves process control. This type of thinking is used when chairing a meeting and when a change in thinking is needed. Blue hat thinking directs the decision process by identifying when other types of thinking would be used. A manager may use this type of thinking when working through a problem.[9]

While creativity involves generating new and different ideas, **critical thinking** is a method of analyzing an issue using facts and data. Components of critical thinking include the following:

1. Identifying the
   Purpose
   Point of view
   Assumptions
   Implications and consequences
   Data, facts, and experiences
2. To make inferences and judgments
3. Based on concepts and theories
4. To answer a question or solve a problem

Critical thinking requires managers to identify the purpose for the decision and be able to identify different points of view. Managers must also be able to identify assumptions that are unfounded beliefs about the issue. A manager will then make inferences about the accuracy or inaccuracy of data that have been collected. Deduction involves determining whether certain conclusions necessarily follow the information provided in the statements. Evidence is used to decide whether generalizations or conclusions are warranted. Finally, strong and relevant arguments are prepared to solve the problem or issue. This method of thinking is very powerful. A standardized test is available to evaluate critical thinking skills.[10]

THE BOTTOM LINE

Many hospitality recruiters state that they "hire for attitude." Part of the attitude that recruiters are looking for consists of the individual skills that we discussed in this chapter. As managers move up the levels of management, individual skills become more important. Self-confidence bolstered by self-awareness and self-management are important at upper levels of management. Personal abilities form the basis for motivation, drive, and behaviors that are needed for success. As managers move up the hierarchy, decision making and critical thinking are required more extensively. The types of decisions made at upper levels of management are less programmed and have a broader organizational impact than those made at lower levels of management. Successful hospitality managers practice each of these skills every day.

Discussion Questions

1. Define hard skills and soft skills and give five examples of each.
2. Describe self-awareness, self-assessment, and self-confidence. Give an example of how you have used these three concepts.
3. Describe the similarities and differences between the three personality theories.
4. Compare self-management to time management. Do you feel these are interrelated? Why or why not?
5. Define each of the following abilities. Give an example of how you have seen a manager demonstrate each of the abilities.
   A. Trustworthiness
   B. Conscientiousness
   C. Adaptability
   D. Optimism
   E. Achievement orientation
   F. Initiative
6. Give an example of a problem that was solved using the problem-solving steps. What were the methods for comparison used at the decision-making step?
7. What do you feel are some of the reasons why people don't encourage creativity at work?
8. Identify each of the components of critical thinking in a decision that you have made recently.

Application Exercise

1. Interview a manager that you feel is successful in the hospitality industry. Ask about the importance each of the skills that are discussed in this chapter. Also ask for examples of how the manager has applied the skills.

2. Complete the Strong Interest Inventory and compare your results to the job you wish to hold after graduation. Are there any inconsistencies? Your campus career planning services may be able to give you the Strong Interest Inventory for no charge. The Self Directed Search, which is based on the Strong Interest Inventory, is available for a small fee from the Internet.

3. Identify your goals/tasks that you want to accomplish for one day. As you proceed through your day, note the time wasters and amount of time each time waster takes. At the end of the day, note the amount of progress you have made for each goal/task. Identify those goals/tasks that have been completed and those that need to be moved to the next day. Repeat for five days and see what progress you have made.

Endnotes

1. For information on the big five factors, see: Barrick, M., & Mont, M. (1991). The big five personality dimensions and job performance: A meta-analysis. *Personnel Psychology*, 44(1), 1–26.

2. For more information on the Myers-Briggs Type Indicator, see http://www.myersbriggs.org/my-mbti-personality-type/mbti-basics/

3. For more information, see http://www.capt.org

4. For more information, see http://www.2020skills.com

5. For more information, see http://www.onetonline.org

6. McKay, D. R. The holland code. Accessed from http://career-planning.about.com/od/selfassessment/a/holland-code.htm

7. Jaszay, C., and Dunk, P. (2006). *Ethical Decision-Making in the Hospitality Industry*. Upper Saddle River, NJ: Pearson Prentice-Hall.

8. deBono, E.(1999). *Six Thinking Hats: An Essential Approach to Business Management*. Boston, MA: Little Brown and Company.

9. Ibid.

10. Watson-Glaser Critical Thinking Appraisal available at http://www.pearsonassessments.com/HAIWEB/Cultures/en-us/Productdetail.htm?Pid=015-8191-013

Key Terms

Achievement orientation   A concern for or focus on working toward a standard of excellence. Goal oriented is another term used for achievement orientation.

Adaptability   The ability to be flexible and work effectively within a variety of changing situations and with various individuals and groups.

Big five personality types   A personality typing theory that uses five factors to define personalities. The factors are (a) extraversion, (b) agreeableness, (c) conscientiousness, (d) neuroticism, and (e) openness

Brainstorming   A creative exercise where everyone generates as many ideas for solutions to a problem as possible.

Conscientiousness   Taking responsibility for your personal performance with an underlying drive for being reliable and delivering quality work.

Creativity   The process used to develop new and useful ideas.

Critical thinking   A method of making a decision by analyzing an issue using facts and data.

Decision making   The process of selecting a solution from the alternatives that have been generated.

DiSC   A personality typing theory that uses four basic styles. The styles are dominance, influence, steadiness, and conscientiousness.

Extrinsic work values   Feelings about the earning potential and work setting that are present in a job.

Hard skills   Routine technical types of skills required to do the job.

Interests   Components of a job that match preferences in work. Six interest categories are (a) realistic, (b) investigative, (c) artistic, (d) social, (e) enterprising, and (f) conventional.

Initiative   The ability to identify a problem, obstacle, or opportunity and take action without waiting for direction.

Intrinsic work values   Feelings about the interest in the work itself or the contributions the job makes to society.

Myers-Briggs Type Indicator   A personality typing theory that uses four scales to generate 16 personality types. The scales are extroversion/introversion, sensing/intuition, thinking/feeling, and judging/perceiving.

Nominal group technique   A brainstorming technique that gives each group member the opportunity to identify solutions to a problem and share them with the group one at a time.

Nonprogrammed decisions   Decisions that are not routine and may not be repeated in the organization.

Optimism   The ability to see good in others and in the situation at hand.

Problem solving   The broad range of activities that begin with identifying the problem and end with implementing the solution.

Programmed decisions   Decisions that are made following established policies and procedures.

Self-assessment   The ability to be aware of inner resources, abilities, and limits.

Self-awareness   The ability to recognize your own knowledge, skills, and abilities. Self-awareness includes accurate self-assessment and self-confidence.

Self-confidence   The belief in your capability to accomplish a task and acknowledging that you are the best for the job.

Self-management (self-control)   The ability to keep your impulsive feelings and emotions under control and direct your behaviors to reach goals.

Soft skills   Human relation skills that we use when interacting with others, making decisions, and thinking creatively.

Time management   An important component of self-control that requires focusing your efforts on tasks that will help you meet your goals.

Trustworthiness   Taking action that is consistent with what you say and value.

Work values   Aspects of a job that are important to a person's job satisfaction. Examples are working independently, job security, prestige, and service to others.

10
Interpersonal Skills

OUTLINE

KEY TERMS

Absentee member

Accommodating

Active listening

Assertiveness

Avoiding

Collaborating

Communication

Competing

Compromising

Conflict

Cooperativeness

Emotional intelligence

Empower

Followers

Formal communication

Forming

Group

Groupthink

Informal communication

Intimate space

Leaders

Managers

Message

Negotiation

Noise

Nonverbal communication

Norming

Performing

Personal space

Procrastinator

Public space

Receiver

Sender

Servant leadership

Social intelligence

Social loafer

Social space

Storming

Team

Transactional leadership

Transformational leadership

Verbal communication

Win–lose

Win–win

OBJECTIVES

- Describe the components of emotional intelligence and social intelligence
- Identify the components of the basic communication model
- Define nonverbal communication and listening skills
- Define the differences between managers and leaders
- Identify the needs of leaders and followers
- Identify the four phases of team development
- Define the characteristics of effective teams and problems in teambuilding
- Identify the stages of change and how to manage change
- Identify methods for empowering other
- Define the methods for handling conflict
- Identify the five-step process for negotiation

Consider This

Ellen, the front-desk manager at the Blue Dolphin Hotel, was discussing her frustration in supervising James, one of the front-desk representatives, to her general manager, Sue. Ellen gives directions to James, which he says he understands, but then never follows the directions. As an example, Ellen gave James written directions on how to close out the guest relations system. She finds she always has to redo the process after James closes his guest relations system. Ellen is asking Sue for advice. Is she following the communication model? Does she use the correct leadership style? Is it time for change? Has she properly empowered her employees?

INTRODUCTION

Managers in the hospitality industry must be able to develop a team of employees who can work together in a high-paced, high-stress environment to meet the needs of demanding customers. The skills covered in this chapter are the basic tools needed to develop such a team. In many cases, the manager sets the tone and develops employees to meet the demands of the hospitality industry. Interpersonal skills such as communication, leadership, teambuilding, and handling conflict are all required to be a successful hospitality manager.

EMOTIONAL AND SOCIAL INTELLIGENCE

Emotional intelligence is a concept that describes how people handle themselves and their relationships with others. The four components of emotional intelligence are as follows:

1. Self-awareness
2. Self-management
3. Social awareness
4. Relationship management.[1]

Self-awareness and self-management concepts were discussed in Chapter 9. Social awareness and relationship management skills have recently been identified as components of **social intelligence** and are covered in this chapter.[2] The skills a hospitality manager must develop to be socially aware and to be able to manage relationships include communication, leadership, teambuilding, change management, empowering others, conflict resolution, and negotiation.

COMMUNICATION

All of our interactions with others are based on communication. When we select, train, or develop employees, we are sending messages to others. Our effectiveness in working with others will be determined by our effectiveness as a communicator. Effective communications are a key requirement of every job in the hospitality industry. There are some differences in the type of communication needed in various jobs, but effectively using the basic model for communication is required for every job.

Basic Communication Model

Communication is the ability to send clear and convincing messages to others in an open and effective way. The basic communication model begins with a **sender** who prepares a message for a receiver. The sender determines the channel that will be used to deliver the message. The **message** is coded, packaged, and sent through the channel to the receiver. Once received, the **receiver** decodes the message, or interprets the meaning of the message. Based on the actions and reactions of the receiver, or feedback, the sender can determine if the correct message was received or if another message needs to be sent. At all stages of the communication, **noise** or interference may be present. Figure 10.1 shows a basic model for communication between the sender and the receiver.

There are decisions that must be made by both the sender and the receiver during the communication process. The sender must determine the channel that will be used to send the message. The model includes five channels that correspond to the five senses that a sender can use for the message. Figure 10.2 lists each of the five channels and an application for attracting customers to a restaurant. The most common channels used in working with human resources are sight and sound that are combined to form verbal and nonverbal communication. **Verbal communication** includes the visual components of a message in the form of printed words and pictures and a hearing component in the form of words and sounds. To be effective in communicating with another, the sender of the message must construct the message using words that have the same meaning when interpreted by the receiver. Many problems with communication exist because words have multiple meanings and cultural variations due to language differences between sender and receiver.

FIGURE 10.1 Basic Communication Model.

Channel	Restaurant Application
Sight	Clean, updated facilities
Sound	Appropriate music at an appropriate sound level
Smell	Pleasant aroma of food being prepared
Touch	Soft, comfortable seats and spatial table arrangements
Taste	Food that is acceptable to customers

FIGURE 10.2   **Examples of Five Communication Channels in Restaurants.**

Nonverbal communication includes the use of tone of voice, body, and facial movements, clothing, appearance, and use of space and the physical environment. The tone of voice that is used should be consistent with the words that make up the message. For example, a gruff voice usually indicates anger or threat, which would conflict with a message of praise for a job well done. Body and facial movements are also components of body language. Smiles, frowns, and scowls are often used to indicate happiness, disappointment, and anger, respectively. However, these may be misinterpreted due to cultural differences. Clothing and appearance of the sender may also be interpreted and impact the message that is received. Wearing clean appropriate clothing and having a neat and clean appearance will indicate that the message is important to the sender. The final component of nonverbal communication is the use of space and the physical environment. There are four basic zones of territorial space when interacting with others. **Intimate space** includes distances up to 1½ feet around a person. Crowding into a person's intimate space indicates dominance or force in most cultures. **Personal space** extends to 2½ feet around a person. This space is typically used when communicating among friends or close associates. **Social space** is about 4 to 7 feet around a person. This space is commonly used for interpersonal communications in social gatherings and offices. **Public space** is usually 10 feet or more around a person. This space is used with strangers or those people with whom you do not want interaction.

The arrangement of people around a meeting table or furniture in an office can also be used to communicate nonverbally with others. In most cases in a meeting, the person seated at the head of the table has the most power. Those seated close to the head of the table have the next most power while those at the opposite end of the table have the least amount of power. In some offices, the arrangement of desks and chairs for guests indicates who has the most power. For example, in an office where a desk divides the person with power on one side and guests on the other side is used to provide a barrier for those without power. In other offices, where a round table is used for meetings with guests, the power is less apparent.

Controversy exists on the importance of verbal communication over nonverbal, but what is known is that the message sent using these two forms must be consistent. The message sent by the sender is a package of verbal and nonverbal communication that will be interpreted by the receiver. Many of the problems we have when communicating with others in a written form are due to the lack of nonverbal signals that help with interpreting the message. Even with the insertion of happy faces and other symbols, it has been estimated that over 50 percent of e-mail and text messages are misinterpreted due to this lack of nonverbal signals.

Some of the things we can do when communicating with others to make sure they are receiving the message we intended are the following:

- Ask for feedback to make sure the receiver understands
- Use many channels, such as a written and oral message
- Use face-to-face communication as much as possible
- Use simple language that the receiver will understand
- Be aware of symbolic meanings of words and actions
- Reinforce words with appropriate actions
- Repeat the message multiple times
- Read the receiver for indications of understanding or questions
- Be careful to time your message to avoid sharing the attention of the receiver

Listening Skills

Carefully sending a message is an important component of the communication model; however, an equally important component is receiving the message, which is often accomplished by listening. The receiver of the message must make sure that there are few distractions that would interfere with receiving a clear message and might distort the message or meaning. Multitasking while listening requires the receiver to divide his or her attention, which leads to misinterpreted messages. The receiver should practice active listening or using ears, eyes, and minds to receive a message. **Active listening** includes concentrating on the sender's words and actions and interpreting them from the sender's point of view without judgment. An active listener summarizes and asks questions to make sure he or she understands the message. Nonverbal feedback through the use of eye contact and head movements is also a component of active listening.

Intercultural Communication

Managers in the hospitality industry must be aware of the differences in communication styles and values for each of the employees we manage. Often these differences are due to cultural differences in the workforce. Language differences are not the only concern as there are also differences in customs and behavior that will impact the effectiveness of communication. An awareness of the differences in the dimensions of culture is the first step in communicating across cultures. Hofstede developed five dimensions of culture that can be used to differentiate between countries. The five dimensions are (a) power/distance, (b) individualism, (c) masculinity, (d) uncertainty/avoidance, and (e) long-term orientation. Each of these dimensions ranges from high to low with countries given a score from 0 to 100 on each of the dimensions. This classification can be found at the Hofstede Center website. Figure 10.3 includes a description for each of the dimensions, example countries, and tips for working with employees from those countries.

There may be intercultural communication problems that come from differences within subcultures or subgroups. A good example of the variation in communication styles between U.S. subcultures can be found in the summary of normative communication styles and values at the Awesome Library website. The subcultures that are included are Asian American, African American, Anglo American, Native American, and Hispanic American. Some examples of differences in communication styles are as follows:

- African and Anglo Americans use direct questions and expect direct answers, which is the opposite for Native and Asian Americans.
- Gestures and animated emotional expressions are used by African Americans and seldom used by Asian and Native Americans.
- Direct eye contact is used by Anglo and African Americans and is avoided by Native and Asian Americans.
- Anglo American use handshaking while African and Hispanic Americans use other forms of touching. Native and Asian Americans use neither forms of touching.
- Hispanic Americans stand close to each other when communicating, which is the opposite for Native and Asian Americans.
- Hierarchical structures are recognized as important by Asian and Hispanic Americans and are less important to Native and African Americans.

Hospitality managers and human resource personnel can use this information to develop successful communication networks in the workplace. Most cultural conflicts come from a lack of understanding of the differences between cultures. To overcome this problem, managers will need to deliver cultural and diversity training that covers cultural differences, acceptance of differences, and effective communication procedures. Although this information is important, managers should also take the time to learn how to communicate with each employee and to avoid stereotyping that may be implied in the categories that have been provided. Policies and procedures that cover the importance of diversity and cross-cultural communication will need to be developed and consistently enforced.

Organizational Communication

In any organization, there are two forms of communication: formal and informal. **Formal communication** may be from the top down, from executives to employees, or bottom up from employees to executives. Examples of top down communication are policy and procedure

Dimension and Definition	High and Low Definitions	Characteristics	Example Country	Tips for Being Successful
Power/distance—The degree of inequality that is accepted	High indicates an unequal distribution of power is accepted	Centralized companies with strong hierarchies	Mexico	Acknowledge leader power Follow the organizational hierarchy
	Low means power is shared and members are viewed as equals	Supervisors and employees are considered as almost equals	New Zealand	Involve many people in decisions
Individualism—The strength of ties people have to others in the community	High indicates lack of interpersonal connection and little sharing of responsibility	Value people's time and need for freedom - Rewards are given for hard work	Canada	Acknowledge accomplishments - Respect need for privacy
	Low means strong group cohesion with loyalty and respect for members of the group	Emphasis is on harmony and intrinsic rewards	Panama	Respect age, wisdom, and traditions Suppress feelings to work in harmony
Masculinity—Belief in traditional roles for males and females	High indicates males are the provider, strong, and assertive	Well-defined work roles for males and females	Japan	Recognize male roles in leadership
	Low means roles are not based on gender	Men and women can perform any task and demonstrate same skills	Sweden	Treat men and women equally
Uncertainty/avoidance—Anxiety felt with uncertainty or the unknown	High means avoidance of uncertain situations by following rules	Very formal conduct with rules, policies, and structure	Belgium	Have detailed plans with clear expectations and parameters
	Low means a more informal atmosphere with few rules	New events and differences among people are valued	Australia	Do not impose rules or structure
Long-Term Orientation—Traditions and values are important	High means family structure is based on rule of parents	Strong work ethic with education and training highly valued	Japan	Respect traditions and reward perseverance, loyalty, and commitment
	Low indicates equality, creativity, and individualism	Self-actualization and treating others equally are important	United States	Be respectful of others and encourage creativity

FIGURE 10.3 Culture Dimensions, Examples, and Tips.

manuals, newsletters, and formal evaluations. Examples of bottom up communications are suggestion boxes and grievance procedures. Most of the formal communication in an organization is done through important documents, so they will consist of written and oral components. Informal communication in an organization is also called the grapevine. Many of us have played the game where a message is passed as a secret through a line of people until it is shared at the

"This was in the suggestion box with your name on it. The good news is the employees are starting to communicate."

Formal communication.   *Credit*: Cartoonresource / Shutterstock.

other end. The fun of the game was to see how different the final message was from the one that started the chain. That's the problem with informal communication in our organizations. The messages that spread through the grapevines in our organizations are often misinterpreted and become very different from the message that was intended. Good managers know how to tap into the grapevine to listen to the messages and to send the right messages through the system.

LEADERSHIP

Leadership skills are required to be an effective manager. There are many differences between managers and leaders. **Managers** integrate resources to accomplish the goals and objectives of an organization. The functions that managers perform are planning, organizing, controlling, staffing, and leading. This means that leadership is an important component of success as a manager. Managers have power over their subordinates because of the position they hold in the organization. Managers may not have the human relations abilities to inspire others. In contrast, leaders inspire others to get things done. **Leaders** are given their power over others through their expertise, personality, or rewards they bestow on their followers. It has been said that managers push and leaders pull followers to reach a goal.[3] Some of the differences between managers and leaders are presented in Figure 10.4

Leadership Styles

Over the years, there have been many attempts to determine what makes an effective leader. The initial research identified traits or characteristics of effective leaders. Traits such as intelligence,

Managers	Leaders
Have position power	Inspire others
Have formal positions	May be formal or informal
Plan and budget	Establish visions and strategies
Organize and staff	Convince and energize followers
Produce expected results	Generate positive change

FIGURE 10.4 **Differences between Managers and Leaders (adapted from Kotter[4]).**

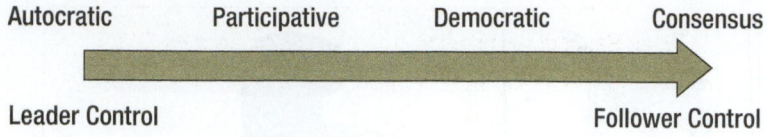

FIGURE 10.5   **Range of Leadership Styles.**

drive, motivation, integrity, self-confidence, expertise, and charisma were identified as important for leaders. The problem with this line of study was that not all effective leaders had all of the same traits.[5] Leadership styles were developed by Tannenbaum and Schmidt and were based on the involvement of the leader versus the involvement of the subordinate.[6] The styles ranged from total leader control or autocratic, to participative, to democratic, to control of the followers or consensus. Figure 10.5 shows the range of leadership styles from leader controlled to follower controlled.

Building on this line of study was the leadership (managerial) grid with leadership style based on two dimensions: concern for people and concern for production.[7] Figure 10.6 displays the managerial grid and the five managerial styles.

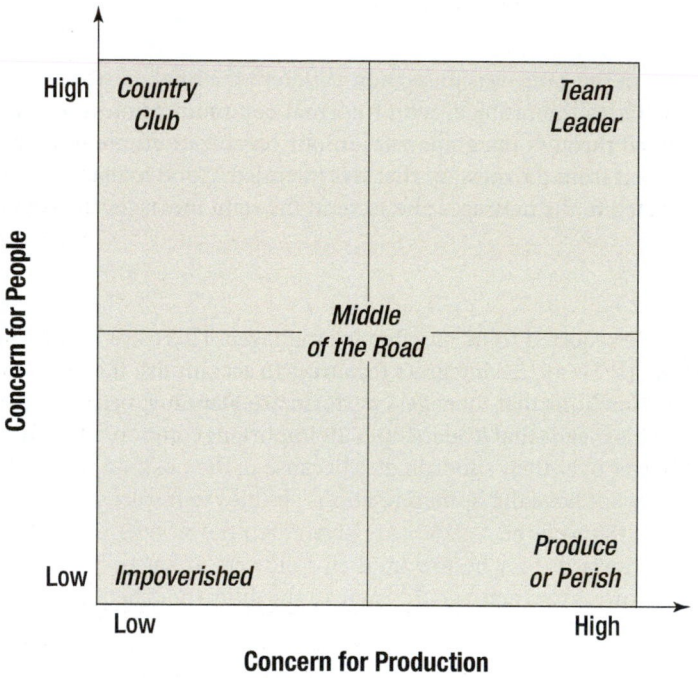

FIGURE 10.6   **Managerial Grid.**[8]

The situational approach to leadership considered the impact of three variables on leadership style. First, the characteristics of the task to be accomplished were to be considered. For example, when the task required immediate action by all parties, such as in an emergency, the leadership style would need to be autocratic. Next the characteristics of the leader were to be addressed. If the leader had a lot of experience and was respected by the followers, the followers may be more open to a more autocratic style. Finally the characteristics of employees were to be considered. If employees had more education and skills, the leader would not need to be as directing as with a less experienced group of employees.[9]

The interaction between leaders and followers has been used as a basis for **transformational**, **transactional**, and **servant leadership**.[10] Finally, there has been an application of emotional intelligence to leadership.[11] In all of the models for leadership, the leader works to bring people together to get a job done. Leaders are able to build a strong sense of belonging within the group, leading others to feel they are part of something larger than themselves. Leaders inspire others by articulating a vision or a mission, and motivate by arousing emotions.

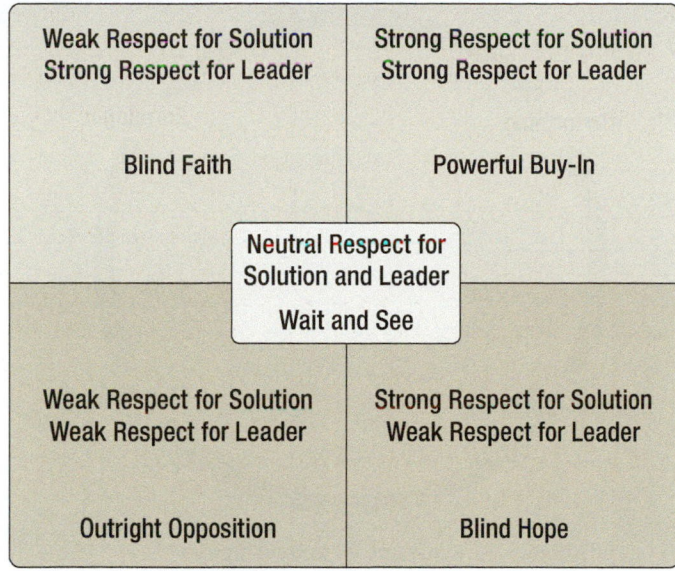

Weak Respect for Solution Strong Respect for Leader	Strong Respect for Solution Strong Respect for Leader
Blind Faith	Powerful Buy-In
Weak Respect for Solution Weak Respect for Leader	Strong Respect for Solution Weak Respect for Leader
Outright Opposition	Blind Hope

Neutral Respect for Solution and Leader
Wait and See

FIGURE 10.7   Why People Follow Leaders.

Followers

Leaders cannot be effective without **followers**. The reasons people follow leaders are due to a respect for the solution and a respect for the leader. Figure 10.7 shows how these two variables interact. When there is strong respect for the solution and strong respect for the leader, then the followers have a powerful buy-in and will work to reach the goal. When there is weak respect for the solution and weak respect for the leader, there is opposition by the followers. When the followers have a strong respect for the leader and a weak respect for the solution, the followers will follow the leader with blind faith in the leader. When the followers have a weak respect for the leader and a strong respect for the solution, they will follow the leader with blind hope that the leader can lead them toward the goal. A strong leader recognizes that followers need empowerment, support, trust, training, encouragement, a feeling of belonging, and sense of positive movement. In return, a leader needs support, trust, encouragement, realistic feedback, and open communication from the followers.

Teambuilding

A **team** exists when there is a leader and followers who are working to achieve the same goals. Team members work cooperatively with others as a part of a team, as opposed to working separately or competitively in a group. A **group** of people is not the same as a team. Groups of people who work separately and competitively may have a place in an organization, but do not work effectively in most customer-centered hospitality organizations. A group becomes a team when members demonstrate a commitment to each other and to the team's goals. The successful hospitality manager understands the need for teamwork and can develop a team from a group of people.

Leaders and followers.
Credit: Fotohunter / Shutterstock.

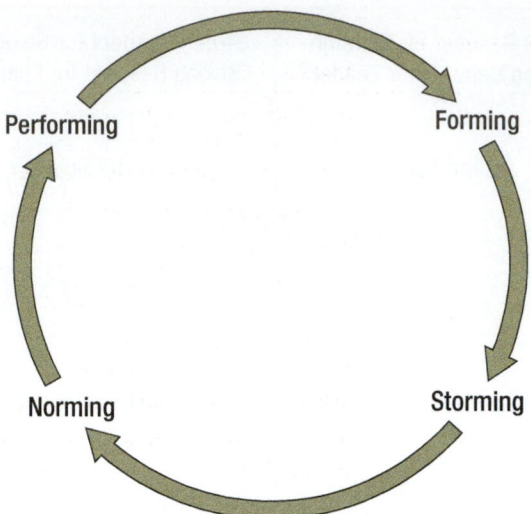

FIGURE 10.8   **Phases of Team Development.**

The four phases of development that most teams go through are: forming, storming, norming, and performing. Teams that come together to achieve a goal and then disband go through a fifth phase called adjourning. The hospitality manager may participate on one of those short-lived teams. However, the teambuilding process that most hospitality managers need involves the four phases. Figure 10.8 shows the relationships between these four phases of development. **Forming** is the first phase of team development. During this phase, members are beginning to see themselves as part of the team. The team comes together and everyone is very polite, reserved, and anxious. If a leader has been appointed for the team, now is the time to identify the purpose and goals for the team, acceptable team behaviors, and how the team will resolve conflicts. An informal leader may arise to lead the group to establish these three ground rules. This initial phase sets the climate and focus for the team.

Storming is the next phase of team development. During this phase of team development, factions form and personalities clash. This is a time of testing others and resistance to the opinions of others. Leadership of the team may be challenged and informal leaders may emerge. In some cases, there may be a movement to replace the appointed team leader. If the methods for handling conflict have been developed during the forming stage, then the amount of time the team spends in the storming stage can be minimized. The goal for this stage of development is to work through differences and move quickly to the next stage.

Norming is the phase of development when in-fighting diminishes and working together is recognized as the way to reach the team's goals. A formal or informal leader emerges to guide the group and a plan for completing tasks is developed. During the process of developing a plan of action, each group member is allowed to contribute and the opinions of others are respected. Respecting the opinions of others and developing a plan of action are outcomes achieved during this stage of development.

Performing is the goal of any team. This phase is when the group supports the plan of action and works toward achieving its goals. The performance of the group should be greater than the sum of the individual team member achievements. This is the reason for using a team rather than staff members with individual expertise. The goal for a leader during this stage of development is to keep team members motivated to achieve and to keep the team on target to reach goals.

The team will go back through the four phases when a new member is added to the team or when management makes a change in the goals or process for the team. A good team leader will help the team get through the first three phases of development so that the team spends most of its time in the performing phase. Figure 10.9 lists the some ideas for a leader who is working to develop the team through each phase of development.

Characteristics of Effective Teams

Patrick Lencioni, in *The Five Dysfunctions of a Team*, suggested that there are three characteristics of well-functioning teams.[12] These characteristics are (a) commitment of the team members

Phase of Development	Leader Behaviors
Forming	Help team members get to know one another Clearly define expectations, purpose, and task Move team through developing ground rules
Storming	Encourage open communication Reinforce ground rules Turn negative statements into positive statements Help team focus on the process that will be used
Norming	Remind the team about the goals to be achieved Encourage members to follow ground rules Develop an action plan for achieving results
Performing	Recognize and celebrate accomplishments Work with team members as problems are solved Make sure resources are available as needed Manage external relationships

FIGURE 10.9   Tips for Team Leaders.

to the work of the team, (b) competence of the team members or their ability to accomplish team goals, and (c) common goals that are shared by all team members.

Teams that work well together are usually comprised of six to ten members. An odd number of members will facilitate democratic decision making when a majority is required. Team members should be selected based on their knowledge, skills, and abilities. Effective team members contribute to the team's work to achieve the team goals. They should demonstrate strong communication, collaboration, decision-making, and self-management skills. Team members are required to be active listeners and able to influence others. Effective team members should handle conflict among the team members and work to build the team into an effective work unit. They should be able to analyze situations and provide new ideas to help solve problems or improve the way things are done. Effective team members should also help to create action plans and prioritize activities to reach team goals. They should use time effectively and build consensus among the team members.

Effective teams have clear and challenging goals with a structure that rewards achieving results. To encourage teamwork, support and recognition should be provided to the team and members when the goals or desired results are reached. A positive team culture where individuals place team goals ahead of their needs is required for the team to be effective. The team culture should also encourage the sharing of ideas and the valuing of opinions. Honesty, openness, and respect are characteristics of the team culture that will lead the team to achieve its goals. Effective teamwork requires frequent meetings and clear rules of conduct. The final characteristic of an effective team is a leader who can organize and direct the work that needs to be accomplished.

Problems in Teambuilding

Not all teams are effective. One of the problems that a team may face is lack of resources and support needed to complete the task that has been assigned. The team leader will need to make sure that resources are available for the team and make them available when and where they are needed. Another problem is that team members may not have the skills that are needed to accomplish the work that needs to be done. The team leader will need to assess the skills of team members and provide education and training to develop the skills that are needed. There may be a power struggle among the team members that will consume the time and resources that should be applied to achieving the team goals. In this type of situation, the team leader should try to focus the efforts of the team members on the task and control the efforts of members to complete the task. **Groupthink** is another problem that a team may face. This occurs when team members agree reluctantly to decisions made by the team. There are many reasons groupthink occurs in a team, such as agreeing to a solution to keep those in power happy or agreeing to a solution to avoid conflict. The team leader will need to encourage the sharing of ideas, allow time for the open discussion of alternatives, and give each member the opportunity to speak about the issue before a decision is made by the team to avoid groupthink.

Type of Member	Try This
Absentee member	Discuss situation with team member - Ask if time is available to contribute to the team - If time is not available, dismiss member if possible - If not, assign tasks that don't tie up the work of other team members
Social loafer	Divide responsibilities and set up checkpoints - Allocate work equally among the team members
Procrastinator	Set up interim checkpoints and set the final deadline earlier than required

FIGURE 10.10 **How to Handle Ineffective Team Members.**

The team may also include one of the three types of team members who interfere with team effectiveness.

1. **Absentee member**—A team member who is distracted by problems or conflicts and does not accomplish team assignments.
2. **Social loafer**—A team member who does not volunteer or contribute to the work of the team. Another team member usually steps in and assumes added responsibilities because of this type of member, thus allowing the member to be a social loafer.
3. **Procrastinator**—The team member who waits until the last minute to complete assignments.

Figure 10.10 includes some recommendations for handling each of these ineffective team members.

CHANGE MANAGEMENT

Change in an organization is viewed as necessary for survival. Changes in the hospitality industry are made typically while trying to maintain usual levels of business. Examples of common changes in the hospitality industry are improvements to products and services that we offer to our guests, revisions in staffing patterns due to changes in personnel or sales, and re-flagging or re-branding a property. Managers who manage change effectively recognize the importance in preparing employees for change and guiding the process through planning and open communications.

The reactions people have to change fall into three categories. About 20 percent of the employees will embrace change. These employees will assist in the change if they remain motivated and involved. About 50 percent of the employees are ambivalent toward change. A good manager will need to work with this group of employees to make sure they understand the need for the change and get assistance in accomplishing the change. The remaining 30 percent of the employees will resist the change. Some authors suggest that managers ignore this group and focus on the other 70 percent of the employees. Others suggest that these employees should be given training or assistance in making the change with the goal of transforming them into experts in the area of the change.

Stages of Change

Kurt Lewin described individual change as an ice cube that is changed from a cube shape to a crescent. The ice cube must unfreeze, change into water, and refreeze into the crescent shape. The same is true for individuals. They must unlearn behaviors and habits, learn new ways of doing things, and then practice those new behaviors until they become new habits. The manager who is successful in managing change understands this process and works with employees as they go through the stages of change. The stages of adjustment to change that all employees go through include the following:

- Awareness of the need for change
- Understanding the need for change
- Supporting the proposed changes
- Involvement in the change process
- Commitment to the new way of doing things

Factors for Change

The hospitality manager who is responsible for carrying out change in an organization needs to keep these stages in mind and to focus on three factors. The first factor is to engage employees in the change process. Employees who recognize the importance of the change and its impact on their jobs will be supportive of the needed changes. Involving employees in the decision-making stages and letting them plan their part of the change will assist employees in feeling a part of the change. Providing education and training opportunities for employees on new tasks that will be required after the change will assist them in making the change. Celebrating small milestones in the overall process of the change will help keep employees motivated and minimize the stress involved in the change.

Developing a project plan is the second factor that a manager will need to consider when implementing change. The change from the current state to the future state should be broken into small manageable steps. Employees should be assigned responsibilities for each step of the plan as appropriate. Feedback should be given on a regular basis through open communications with employees. Managers should make sure that the resources needed to accomplish the steps in the plan are available when and where they are needed.

The third factor involves leadership and support for the change process. Managers should provide a clear vision for the future and act as a role model for others. Support systems with appropriate rewards should be developed for employees. Leaders of change are also required to focus efforts of the team on areas where employees can be most effective. All of these factors will assist a manager in effective change management.

EMPOWERING OTHERS

Hospitality organizations depend on employees to deliver the goods and services that customers demand. Managers recognize that they cannot be present at every employee and customer point of interaction, so they need to develop employees to make quick decisions that maximize customer satisfaction. The organizational culture or work environment that allows employees to handle customers without constant supervision and feedback from managers serves to empower employees. In addition to a supportive work environment, the manager will need to train employees on appropriate procedures for handling customers and making decisions.

To empower employees means that employees feel in control of a situation and have the power and freedom to handle the situation as they see fit. As empowerment is something that is felt by employees, competence and the feeling of being able to do a good job are important. The hospitality manager can make sure that employees get feedback on their performance and provide training to keep their skills current. Employees need to feel that the job they perform is important to others and to themselves. Managers should provide a review of situations that were handled well and publicly recognize high-performing employees. Employees also need to feel

Conflict. *Credit*: Ljupco Smokovski / Shutterstock.

that they are able to influence the work they perform. To nurture the feeling of influence on the job, managers can develop a supportive work environment that allows well-trained employees to make independent decisions to deliver quality customer service.

CONFLICT RESOLUTION

Conflict occurs in an organization when there is a clash or disagreement between two people, a person and a group, or two groups of people. Conflict often begins with a triggering event that is caused by differences in attitudes or behavior. Most managers view conflict as negative. Negative conflict causes work delays, decreases work performance, and creates disorder among team members. Conflict is constructive if the situation results in new ideas, information, or ways of solving problems. Some common causes of conflict in the workplace include the following:

- Competition for limited resources
- Value and viewpoint differences
- Unclear lines of authority
- Miscommunication or misunderstandings
- Personality differences

Organizational approaches to handling conflict include the passive approach, dispute resolution policies, and mediation systems. In the passive approach to handling conflict, the parties involved are allowed to work out their differences. While it is important that the individuals closest to the problem solve the problem, there may need to be management intervention to assist with the process.

Dispute resolution policies are commonly called grievance procedures. Employees are trained to take problems to the manager or supervisor for solution. The formal grievance procedure may require multiple levels of management review until a solution to the conflict is found. Managers may need to provide mentoring to the employees involved in the conflict to assist in the resolution of the problem.

On the other end of the management intervention continuum is mandating a solution. Depending on the intensity of the interaction between parties, the manager may not be able to solve the problem without making and enforcing a decision. In other organizations and when time permits, there may be a formal process for handling differences between employees and other employees or customers. The use of a mediator or outside expert who hears both sides of the argument and then makes a binding judgment is another method companies use to handle formal conflicts.

When a manager experiences a conflict situation between two employees or an employee and customer, the goal for resolution should be a win–win situation for both parties. Depending on the intensity of the conflict situation, parties may need to be separated and interviewed individually, or may share openly in front of the other party. The focus of the interviews should be on clarifying the issues and determining solutions to address the problems. An acceptable solution to both parties should be determined and implemented.

Methods for Handling Conflict

Responses that individuals make to conflict have been classified by Thomas and Kilmann using the conflict mode instrument.[13] Figure 10.11 is a diagram that represents the five methods that individuals use when confronted with a conflict situation.

In this model, two dimensions, assertiveness and cooperativeness, are used as a basis for defining the five conflict handling methods. Assertiveness is defined as the extent an individual attempts to satisfy his or her concerns during the disagreement resolution process. Assertiveness ranges from unassertive (low) to assertive (high). Cooperativeness is defined as the extent an individual attempts to satisfy the other's concerns during the resolution process. Cooperativeness ranges from uncooperative (low) to cooperative (high). Using these two dimensions, there are five conflict handling methods:

Competing is assertive and uncooperative. A person using this method is concerned about winning in a situation at the expense of the other person. Collaborating is both assertive and cooperative. A person using this method works to find a solution that meets the needs of both parties involved in the dispute. Compromising is intermediate in both assertiveness

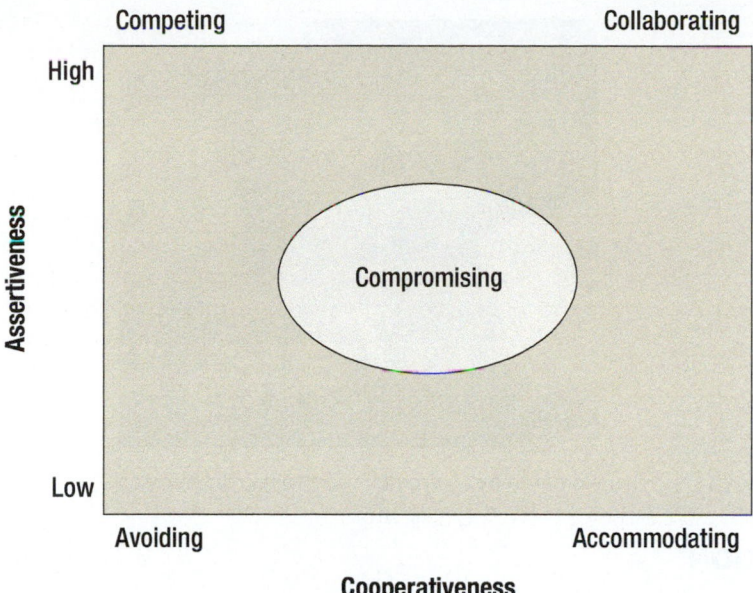

FIGURE 10.11   **Conflict Handling Modes.**

and cooperativeness. A person using this method is looking for a quick acceptable solution that partially meets the needs of both parties involved. **Avoiding** is unassertive and uncooperative. A person who uses this method does not address the conflict. **Accommodating** is unassertive and cooperative. The person using this method neglects his or her own views and to satisfy the other party in the dispute. Accommodating is the opposite of competing. Figure 10.12 includes appropriate uses for each method.

Conflict Method	Suggested Uses
Competing	During emergencies When standing up for your own rights Defending a position you believe is right When unpopular actions need implementing
Collaborating	Explore disagreement to learn from each other Trying to find a creative solution To merge different perspectives on a problem To work through hard feelings
Compromising	Exchange concessions that are not critical Achieve temporary settlements to complex issues When collaboration or competition fail Arrive at expedient solutions under time pressure
Avoiding	Postponing until a better time When issue is of little importance When you have little power to effect change Withdraw from a threatening situation
Accommodating	Demonstrate charity or generosity When the issue is more important to others When you are outmatched and losing To preserve harmony and avoid disruption

FIGURE 10.12   **Uses for Five Conflict Handling Methods.**

Compromise. *Credit*: Stuart Miles / Shutterstock.

NEGOTIATION

Negotiation is a process where two or more people or groups work through their differing opinions to achieve a resolution for a shared problem. Hospitality managers face these situations between employees in different work groups and employees and their customers. Examples of a negotiation process are when a customer asks to be upgraded when checking in or requesting a complimentary meal or beverage. The needs of the customer and the organization both must be considered when negotiating a settlement to the problems. The two strategies that can be used during the negotiating process are win–win and win–lose. The goal of the win–win strategy is an agreement that is acceptable to both parties and focuses on preserving a long-term relationship. This strategy requires that both parties collaborate and compromise through open communications. The win–lose strategy is used when limited resources are divided between two parties. The result is that one party receives resources at the other party's expense. This strategy is used when there is little importance for a continued relationship and is not recommended for most hospitality situations.

Issues that are negotiated typically follow a five-step process.

1. The first step involves preparation and planning. Determining the bottom line, or what you would be willing to accept, will be important during this step. A statement supporting your position should be written in terms the other party will understand. Information about the other party's position, strengths, and weaknesses should be gathered during this step.
2. The second step involves setting the ground rules. An agenda, location, and acceptable behaviors for the discussion should be established. Both parties should agree upon criteria that will be used for evaluating solutions. This step also includes determining what will happen if an agreement is not reached.
3. The third step is when both sides present their cases and discuss. During this step, each side should present its interests and share relevant information supporting its case. Open-ended questions should be used to clarify the position and support of both parties.
4. The fourth step is the bargaining and problem-solving step. During this step, alternatives are evaluated using the criteria that were established in step 2. The acceptability to each side and the benefits for each alternative should be evaluated. The focus of the discussions should remain on solving the problem and meeting the interests of both groups. A win–win solution should be the outcome of the discussions.
5. The fifth step is to close the discussions with a written documentation of the agreement. Both parties should sign the agreement so that there is clarity and commitment to the agreement.

THE BOTTOM LINE

The hospitality manager in today's industry must be able to work with a variety of tools to achieve the goals of the organization. Figure 10.13 provides a visual representation of the work a manager must perform. To achieve the task, the manager must develop individual employees and the team processes. Interpersonal skills are the basis for each of these components of the job.

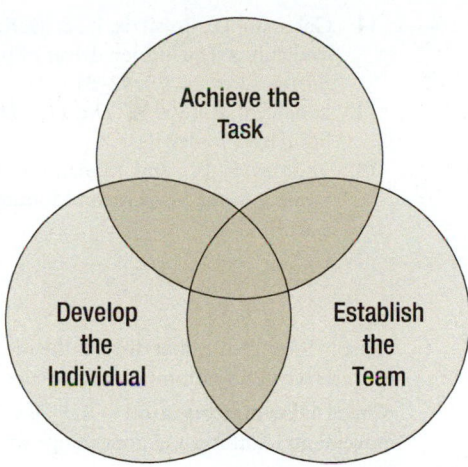

FIGURE 10.13   Model for Managers.

Getting the work done through others requires the use of all of the skills discussed in this chapter. Understanding the basics of communication is the cornerstone for working with employees, superiors, and customers. Leadership, teambuilding, and empowering others are skills used to develop a workforce that effectively meets the needs of our customers. Helping employees work through change happens when both major and daily changes occur. Handling conflict using effective negotiation skills can occur almost daily with customers and employees.

Discussion Questions

1. Use the basic communication model to diagram an interaction you had with someone at work. Are there any areas that could be improved? What recommendations would you make to improve communicating with that person in the future?

2. Describe the skills used by someone you would classify as an effective manager and those of someone you would classify as an effective leader. Are there any similarities? Are there differences?

3. Describe a team you have worked with in the past using the four phases of team development. Estimate the amount of time the team spent in each phase. Did the team move swiftly through the phases or did it spend too much time in one or more phase? How effective do you feel the team worked together?

4. Identify a change you have worked through in the past. Describe how you moved through each of the stages of change and the way the change process could have been improved.

5. Prepare a list of recommendations you would make for a manager who wanted to empower employees. Do you see any problems the manager may face during the empowerment process?

6. Describe your preferred method for handling conflict. Does your conflict style vary with the people involved and the issue that is the basis for the conflict?

7. Use the five-step negotiation process to describe an issue you have solved (or should have solved).

Application Exercise

1. Conduct an on-line search for the Thomas-Kilman conflict mode instrument. Complete the Thomas-Kilmann conflict mode instrument at one of the on-line websites you found. Describe your findings and evaluate how effective you are at handling conflict.

2. Develop a list of questions that you will use to interview a hospitality manager to get his or her opinions about each of the eight topics in this chapter. Determine which of these are the most used skills and those that are the most difficult for the manager. Write up the results of your interview and make recommendations to future hospitality managers based on your results.

Endnotes

1. Goleman, D. (2006). *Social Intelligence*. New York: Bantam Books.
2. Ibid.
3. Kotter, J. (1996). *Leading Change*. Boston, MA: Harvard Business Press.
4. Ibid.
5. Stodgill, R. M. (1974). *Handbook of Leadership: A Survey of the Literature*. New York: Free Press.
6. Tannenbaum, R., & Schmidt, W. H. (1958). How to choose a leadership pattern. *Harvard Business Review*, 36(2), 95–101.
7. Blake, R. R., & Mouton, J. S. (1985). *The Managerial Grid III*. Houston, TX: Gulf Publishing.
8. Ibid.
9. Fiedler, F. E. (1967). *Theory of Leadership Effectiveness*. New York: McGraw-Hill.

10. The following are samples:
Burns, J. M. (1978), *Leadership*, New York: Harper and Row.
Bass, B. M. (1985), *Leadership and Performance beyond Expectations*, New York: Free Press.
Greenleaf, R. (1977), *Servant Leadership: A Journey in the Nature of Legitimate Power and Greatness*, New York: Paulist Press.

11. Goleman, D., Boyatzis, R., & McKee, A. (2001), Primal leadership: The hidden driver of performance, *Harvard Business Review*, 79, 42–51.

12. Lencioni, P. (2002), *The Five Dysfunctions of a Team*, San Francisco: Jossey Bass.

13. Thomas, K. W., and Kilmann, R. H. (2009),. *Thomas-Kilmann Conflict Mode Instrument*, Mountain View, CA: CPP. Inc.

Key Terms

Absenteemember A team member who is distracted by problems or conflicts and does not accomplish team assignments.

Accommodating A method of handling conflict that is unassertive and cooperative.

Active listening Using ears, eyes, and mind to receive a message.

Assertiveness The extent an individual attempts to satisfy his or her concerns during the disagreement resolution process.

Avoiding A method of handling conflict that is unassertive and uncooperative.

Collaborating A method of handling conflict that is assertive and cooperative.

Communication The ability to send clear and convincing messages to others in an open and effective way.

Competing A method of handling conflict that is assertive and uncooperative.

Compromising A method of handling conflict that is intermediate in both assertiveness and cooperativeness.

Conflict A situation where there is a disagreement between two people, a person and a group, or two groups of people.

Cooperativeness The extent an individual attempts to satisfy the other's concerns during the resolution process.

Emotional intelligence Four components—self-awareness, self-management, social awareness, and relationship management—that describe how people handle themselves and their relationships with others.

Empower The ability of employees to maximize customer satisfaction without constant supervision and feedback from managers.

Followers People who are inspired by leaders.

Formal communication Official communication in an organization.

Forming First phase of team development. The team comes together and ground rules are established.

Group People who work separately and competitively in an organization.

Groupthink When group members agree to decisions made by the team to keep things moving or to minimize arguments.

Informal communication Commonly known as the grapevine. The social form of communication.

Intimate space Distances up to 1½ feet around a person.

Leaders People who inspire others to accomplish a task.

Managers People in positions of authority and responsibility in an organization who supervise the work of others.

Message The package in the communication model that is transferred from sender to receiver.

Negotiation A process where two or more people or groups work through their differing opinions to achieve resolution for a shared problem.

Noise Interference that distorts the message sent from the sender to the receiver in the communication process.

Nonverbal communication Tone of voice, body and facial movements, clothing and appearance, and use of space included in a message.

Norming The third phase of team development. Working together is recognized as the way to achieve the team goals.

Performing The final phase of team development. The team works together to reach the team goals.

Personal space Space between 1½ and 2½ feet around a person.

Procrastinator A team member who waits until the last minute to complete assignments.

Public space Space about 10 feet around a person.

Receiver The person in the communication model who receives and decodes the message that was sent by the sender.

Sender The person in the communication model who prepares the message for a receiver.

Servant leadership A leadership style where the leader shares power, puts the needs of others first, and helps people perform.

Social intelligence The components of emotional intelligence that include social awareness and relationship management that impact the way a person interacts with others.

Social loafer A team member who does not volunteer or contribute to the work of the team. Another team member usually steps in and assumes added responsibilities because of this type of member, thus allowing the member to be a social loafer.

Social space Space between 4 and 7 feet around a person. Commonly used for business communication.

Storming The second phase of team development. Differences are identified and personalities may clash.

Team Leader and followers who are working to achieve the same goals.

Transactional leadership A leadership style that focuses on power and position while working to achieve goals by following the policies and procedures that are in place.

Transformational leadership A leadership style that focuses on purposes, values, morals, and ethics through meaningful and challenging jobs.

Verbal communication Printed words, pictures, sounds, and spoken words combined to form a message.

Win–lose A negotiation strategy where limited resources are divided between two parties. One party receives resources at the other's expense.

Win–win A negotiation strategy where an agreement is found that is acceptable to both parties and focuses on preserving a long-term relationship.

Organizational Skills

OUTLINE

Introduction

Power and Politics

    Politics in an Organization

Building an Organizational Culture

The Bottom Line

KEY TERMS

Artifacts

Coercive power

Commitment

Compliance

Core assumptions

Expert power

Gatekeepers

Great Place to Work

High-performance organizations

Influence

Ingratiation

Legitimate power

Networking

Organizational awareness

Organizational culture

Organizational politics

Power

Professional networking

Referent power

Resistance

Reward power

Social astuteness

Social networking

Stakeholders

Values

OBJECTIVES

- Define five bases for power
- Identify the outcomes from power relationships
- Define the skills needed to be successful in organizational politics
- Identify professional and social networks
- Define the components of organizational culture
- Define the eight factors that make up culture in hospitality organizations
- List the components of high-performance organizations and great places to work

Consider This

Watching how employees were selected for promotions and training brought to light that it was not what you know, but who you know that led to a promotion. The question was how to use this to be an advantage.

INTRODUCTION

An understanding of personal and interpersonal skills is important for working with people in organizations. In addition to these skills, successful managers understand how to operate within an organization, which is also called playing the political game. **Organizational awareness** is the ability to understand the "power" relationship in one's own group or organization. This includes the ability to identify the real decision makers and who can influence them. It is also about recognizing the values and cultures of organizations and how those affect the way people act and behave. The person who possesses this understands the political forces at work in the organization, accurately reads key power relationships in groups or organizations, and understands values and the culture of groups or organizations.

POWER AND POLITICS

The basis for politics in an organization is the power held by a few and the influence the person who holds that power has over others. **Power** has been defined as source of influence over others. It is the ability Person A has to get Person B to do something that Person B would not normally do. **Influence** is a term used for the use of power by Person A. For the use of power or influence to be effective, Person B must accept the influence of Person A. There are five bases for power, which are legitimate, reward, coercive, expert, and referent.[1] Figure 11.1 shows the relationships between power and Persons A and B.

A manager has **legitimate power** because of the manager's position in an organization. The organization chart and its hierarchy outline the flow of legitimate power from the top down through an organization. The manager position gives the person filling that position the power to direct subordinates to perform a job and the authority to take action if the job is not performed correctly. Outside of work and the manager position, the same person will not have power over subordinates to get them to perform a task.

Reward power is based on the ability of Person A to provide incentives to Person B. The rewards must be viewed as valuable to Person B if they are to get him or her to perform a task or act in a prescribed way. A manager with reward power can provide incentives to employees to perform the tasks that need to be accomplished by the work group. Incentives or rewards must be tailored to each employee's wants and needs for this type of power to be effective.

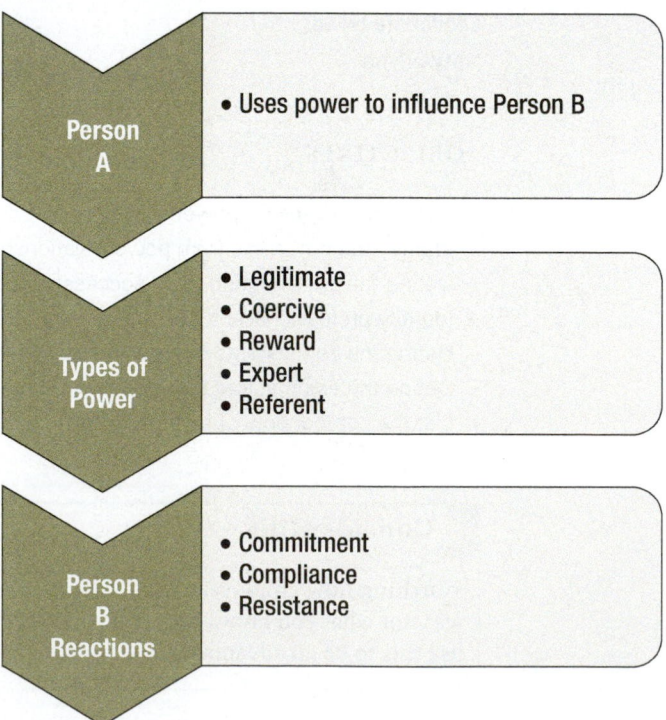

FIGURE 11.1 **How Power Works.**

Coercive power is the opposite of reward power. Coercive power involves punishing Person B for not performing the task or not acting as required by Person A. As with rewards, the punishment must be viewed as a punishment or deterrent for coercive power to be effective. Each employee will have differing views about actions that are punishments.

Expert power involves having knowledge, information, or experience that is viewed as valuable by Person B. The manager who has experienced the jobs employees are expected to perform is often viewed as more powerful than managers who have not experienced those jobs. Employees will follow managers who have valuable information or experience.

Referent power is also called charisma. This type of power allows Person A to have power over Person B because of A's charismatic personality. Person B wants to follow Person A because Person A has the feeling of belonging or identity with Person B. Managers who have charisma have a personality that is attractive to employees, which often combines expert and reward power.

Managers with legitimate power recognize the strength of combining all five types of power to lead employees. In addition, reward, coercive, expert, and referent power can exist outside a position in an organization. Employees who do not have legitimate power but have reward, coercive, expert, or referent power are called informal leaders.

The three outcomes that can occur in power relationships are **commitment**, **compliance**, and **resistance**. Commitment is the ideal outcome. With commitment, employees are enthusiastic and make maximum effort to perform. Compliance is a partially successful outcome. Compliant employees will go along with the manager, but will make minimal effort to perform the task. Resistance is the unsuccessful outcome. When employees resist, they will sabotage work or not perform the task.

Figure 11.2 shows the relationship between types of power and outcomes that can be expected. Using the combination of expert and referent power will produce a committed employee. Employees must respect a manager's knowledge of the policies and procedures required to perform their jobs. Committed employees will go to the manager for advice and

Employee commitment.   *Credit:* Andrey_Popov/ Shutterstock.

Base of Power	Commitment	Compliance	Resistance
Legitimate	Possible	Likely	Possible
Reward	Possible	Likely	Possible
Coercive	Unlikely	Possible	Likely
Expert	Likely	Possible	Possible
Referent	Likely	Possible	Possible

FIGURE 11.2   **Relationships between Types of Power and Relationship Outcomes.**

suggestions instead of going to an informal leader. A manager with referent power uses his or her personality or charisma to establish a vision for the work group that entices employees to contribute to achieving the vision. Employees always want to do their best work for a charismatic manager and will be committed to helping achieve the vision of the charismatic manager.

Using legitimate and reward power will lead to a compliant employee. While this is an acceptable outcome, it is not optimal. Managers relying on the position and ability to reward employees as a base of power over employees will get just the amount of work required for a reward. If there is a need for employees to volunteer to help with an unusual event, the manager relying on the power from his or her position or the ability to reward employees will get minimal response from the work group.

Coercive power will generally not lead to commitment; instead, it will lead to resistance in employees. The threat of punishment does not encourage employees to do their best work. Instead of feeling part of a work group, employees feel that their work is not recognized, so they will sabotage or resist the manager who uses coercive power. The last type of power managers should use is coercive power.

Politics in an Organization

Political games exist in most organizations. To be successful in playing the game of politics requires knowledge of the situations that lead to politics in an organization and tactics and specialized skills needed to work within the political structure. Some individuals may see organizational politics as a negative force in the organization while others may see it as a positive force. No matter what you believe about politics, politics exist in most organizations; so it is necessary to understand the rules of the political game and develop the skills needed to be successful.

Organizational politics can be defined as the ability to promote or protect oneself (or group) by influencing those with resources. When organizational politics are used to reach the goals of the organization, it is considered to be a positive force in the organization. When politics

Stakeholders.   *Credit*:
Blackdaliya/Shutterstock.

are used to achieve individual goals at the expense of organizational goals, it is considered to be a negative force. Organizations that foster politics typically have rewards for political behavior, encourage competition for limited resources, and have unclear decision-making procedures. You can see examples of this in your organization when promotions are given to employees. Are the promotions based on the acquisition of new skills and abilities? Are the promotions viewed as a reward for good performance? If the answers to these questions are yes, then scarce resources are not being given based on politics, but are given based on performance. If the answer to one of these questions is no, then politics may be a source for the promotion. If the answers to both are no, then politics are definitely present in the organization.

An organization that fosters a political climate includes stakeholders, that is, those who have control of information and resources. Those who control access to the stakeholders are called gatekeepers. In most organizations, the formal organizational chart reflects the stakeholders as those in the upper levels of the organization. In some organizations, there is an informal structure that can be identified outside the formal chart and these stakeholders are more difficult to identify.

To be successful, the manager must maintain a positive impression on and be viewed as an ally by both the stakeholders and their gatekeepers. Rather than going to a supervisor (stakeholder) with a problem, the successful manager brings both the problem and the solution to the attention of the supervisor. In addition, the stakeholder should view the manager as a positive supporter. Some people refer to this as being a "yes-man." However, one must be able to read the stakeholder, because some superiors want to be told the truth, while other leaders must be treated as if they were right even if you know they're wrong. You will need to be able to identify which of these best represents the stakeholder you are trying to influence.

The successful manager must align himself or herself with others who are more powerful by gaining the support of those with power. Establishing a network of friends who owe the manager favors accomplishes this. The key to playing the political game is to be friends with those in power and to have them owe you favors. These favors can be used for individual gain or to protect a work group and its resource base. For more guidance on office politics see *Organizational Politics* by Bacharach and Lawler.[2]

The skills required to win the game of politics include social astuteness, interpersonal influence, apparent sincerity, networking, and positioning ability.[3] The successful manager has the social skills to interpret the actions of others and the ability to understand the social network that exists outside the official organizational structure. Interpersonal influence includes ingratiation (establishing oneself in good favor of others or looking good to others), self-promotion, and assertiveness. A person who demonstrates apparent sincerity appears to have self-control and confidence.

Networking and positioning are required to be successful at the game of politics. Both professional networking and social networking are required to build coalitions within the

Networking. *Credit*: Andresr/ Shutterstock.

organization and outside the organization. Linkages in networks or the ties between people can be strong (us-versus-them attitude) or weak (acquaintances). In addition, there are those people in a network who are connectors or those who link with many other people. Professional networking includes developing coalitions within the organization. These relationships should be developed upward with those higher in the organizational structure, laterally with peers, and downward with subordinates. Networking outside the organization can occur in professional or social settings with the strongest networks developed by combining professional and social alliances.

Developing a network of influential people occurred in face-to-face meetings in the past. Now, through social networking sites, such as Facebook, Twitter, and LinkedIn, global networks can be developed for both social and professional purposes. Over half of the current workforce uses social networking sites, and that number is expected to increase in the future. These sites are easy-to-use ways of keeping social networks up to date and viable. However, social networking sites should be used with caution. A majority of human resources recruiters are using these sites to determine the professionalism of applicants for positions. In some cases, applicants have not been invited for an interview or offered a position because of the unprofessional postings on their social networking site. In other cases, employees have been fired or not considered for promotions because their supervisors have found postings on their social networking site that were not what they would want for their employees to be sharing with the public.

Personal networks provide a variety of benefits to a manager. Six benefits that can be gained from a network are as follows:

1. Information
2. Political support and influence
3. Personal development
4. Personal support and energy
5. Sense of purpose or worth
6. Work–life balance

A personal network should be established by identifying people within and outside of the organization who can help in each of these areas.

A review of professional and social networks can be helpful in achieving personal goals. A graph such as the one in Figure 11.3 can identify current relationships and the need to develop

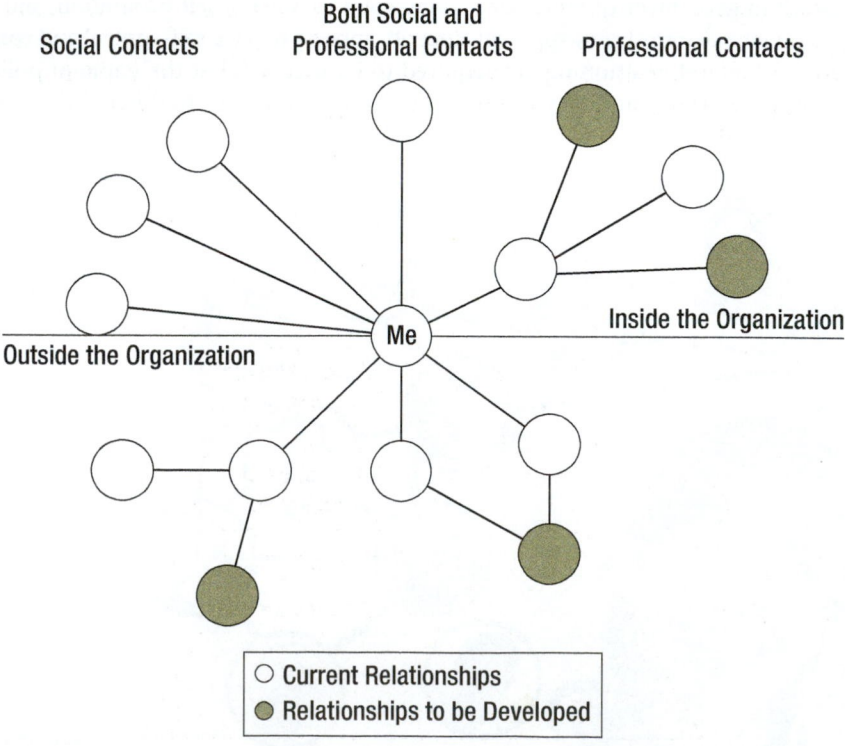

FIGURE 11.3   **Diagram of Professional and Social Networks.**

future contacts to reach a targeted goal. To be effective at networking, the manager should build mutual understandings with others and act in ways that benefit all parties involved in the network. Determining how to increase professional and social networks is important to managers who are politically astute.[4]

BUILDING AN ORGANIZATIONAL CULTURE

A work culture or **organizational culture** has been called the personality of the organization. Culture is comprised of the assumptions, values, norms, and tangible signs (**artifacts**) of organization members and their behaviors. The relationship between assumptions, values, and tangibles is presented in Figure 11.4.

At the deepest level of the organization are the **core assumptions**. These are the beliefs that drive all activities in the organizations. An example of an assumption is the belief that if you take care of your employees they will take care of your customers. **Values** are based on assumptions and are used as norms to direct behavior and as a basis for decision making in the organization. Examples of values are hard work, creativity, relationships, and honesty. The tangible signs of these assumptions and values are the artifacts that can be seen in an organization. Signs of culture in an organization include artifacts such as offices, uniforms, and visible rewards. Other visible signs of culture include stories, rituals, and language.

Employees are socialized into the organizational culture at the point of selection and through orientation, training, and assimilation into the organization. Selection criteria used to differentiate among applications for a position often reflect the culture of the organization. Emphasis on creativity for one organization may be important when selecting new employees. For another organization, the ability to follow policies and procedures may be more important. Orientation and training sessions often include personal anecdotes about the organization that will give new employees an introduction to the organizational culture. The sharing of items with company logos such as pens or shirts will give employees a feeling of commitment and identity with the company. Learning the terms that are used in the organization will allow a new employee to be effective and feel more secure in the work unit.

Organizational culture is present at the organization level, at the subunit level, and at the work group level. New employees soon learn about the similarities and differences between these levels of culture as they are socialized into the work group. At the organizational orientation session, policies and procedures for work time and personal time may be covered as they exist in the employee handbook. When the employee is oriented at the work group level, those same procedures may be implemented in a different manner by the supervisor or the informal leader, who may tell the employee "This is how we really do it."

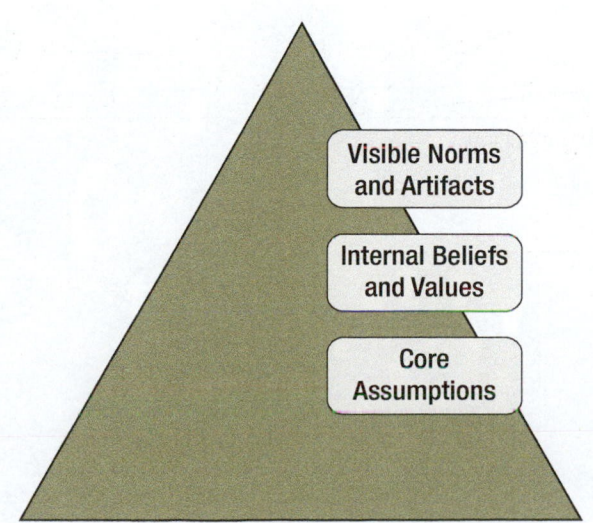

FIGURE 11.4   Layers of Organizational Culture.

Organizational culture can be classified according to seven dimensions.[5] These dimensions and their ranges in characteristics are as follows:

1. Innovation and risk taking, ranging from encouraging creativity and entrepreneurship to following established rules and processes
2. Attention to detail, ranging from precision to lack of precision
3. Outcome orientation, ranging from results oriented to process oriented
4. People orientation, ranging from low to high respect and value of people
5. Team orientation, ranging from and emphasis on team to individual efforts
6. Aggressiveness, ranging from competing to easy going
7. Stability, ranging from status quo to high growth

Research investigating the perceived organizational culture of hospitality organizations includes eight factors that can be identified in the industry.[6] These factors are characteristic of cultures in most service and customer-oriented organizations. While this may not be descriptive of the organizational culture in a specific hospitality business, this information is applicable to the industry as a whole. The eight factors are as follows:

1. Team and people-oriented factor that includes an emphasis on cooperation, collaboration, teamwork, and respect for individuals. Hospitality organizations recognize the importance of individuals and teamwork that are required to accomplish organizational goals.
2. Innovation, which also includes creativity and a willingness to experiment. Hospitality organizations encourage employees to make independent decisions and take risks as needed.
3. Fair compensation that is based on good performance. Growing hospitality organizations provide good financial rewards and equitable pay for employees who are high performers.
4. Attention to detail, which includes precision and accuracy. Hospitality organizations are characterized as detail oriented when producing goods and services for customers.
5. Valuing customers and developing strong relationships with customers. Hospitality organizations recognize the importance of meeting customer expectations and emphasize the quality of service provided to customers.
6. Employee development, which includes promotion from within and opportunities for career development in hospitality organizations.
7. Honesty and ethics, which include keeping promises. The organizational culture in hospitality organizations is based on honesty and carrying through with promises made to customers and employees.
8. Results orientation or the focus on getting results done through the hard work of employees.

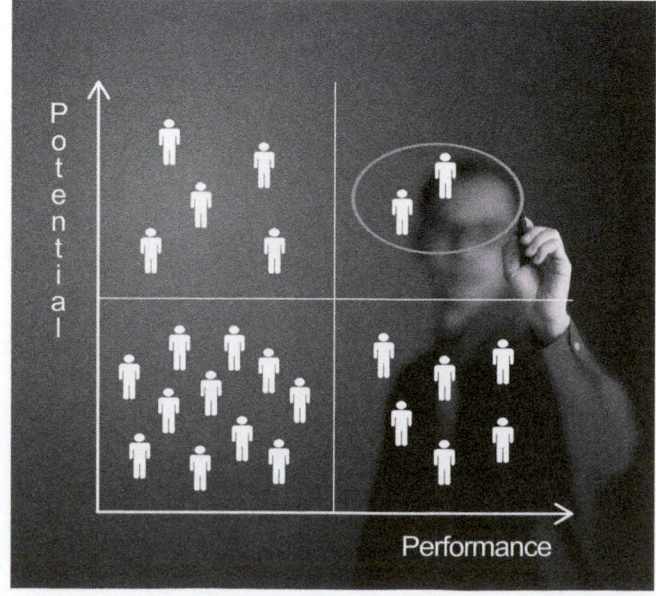

High-Performance Organizations.   *Credit*: Dusit/Shutterstock.

In some organizations, there may be a need to change the culture. Changing the culture of an organization is a difficult process and requires commitment from leadership. Toxic workplaces have been described in the literature as contributing to employee stress and stress-related diseases. When working to change the culture, hospitality managers should incorporate the principles of **high-performance organizations.**[7] These principles are specific actions that are based on the generic hospitality organizational culture that was just described. High-performance managers selectively hire new employees to ensure that there is a match between employee skills and the jobs that need to be performed. Empowering employees and decision making at the source of the problem are other principles that are used. Being a pay leader and rewards based on performance are also incorporated into the culture of high-performance organizations. Extensive training of employees and employee development are needed for high performance of employees. Job security will allow employees to focus on doing their best work rather than on whether their job will exist in the near future. High-performance organizations have fewer status distinctions such as different uniforms for managers and employees and reserved parking for managers. The final characteristic is the extensive sharing of information throughout the organization.

Another model for effective organizational culture is **Great Place to Work,** developed by the Great Place to Work Institute.[8] Organizations are self-nominated for this recognition. In an application process, these organizations demonstrate that they have met the criteria in the Great Place to Work model. Four hospitality corporations were listed on the top 100 companies in 2013 in the United States by this organization. Marriott, Four Seasons, Darden, and Kimpton Hotels and Restaurants were listed in the top 100 for 2013. These four companies plus IHG were listed in the top 100 for 2012. Marriott and Four Seasons have been included in the top 100 since 1998. Kimpton has been in the top 100 since 2009 and Darden has been in the top 100 since 2011. In 2012, McDonald's was ranked 20th on the best multinational workplaces.[9]

The basis for the Great Place to Work model is trust, which is made up of credibility, respect, fairness, pride, and camaraderie. The model is included in Figure 11.5. A trust index and culture audit are used to measure the effectiveness of the organization in meeting the requirements of a Great Place to Work. Qualifying as a Great Place to Work recognizes a commitment to developing a highly effective work culture.

THE BOTTOM LINE

Politics and organizational culture exist in every hospitality organization. It is important for hospitality managers to recognize the role of these concepts in working with employees because the

Dimension	Evidence in Workplace
Credibility	Open communication Human and material resources are coordinated Vision carried out with integrity and consistency
Respect	Professional development supported and rewarded Employees are included in relevant decisions Employees are viewed as individuals with personal lives
Fairness	Rewards are distributed equally Favoritism not considered in hiring and promotions No evidence of discrimination and appeals process in place
Pride	Individual contributions appreciated Team or work group recognized Products and community standing of the organization
Camaraderie	Ability to be oneself Friendly and welcoming atmosphere Family or team feeling

FIGURE 11.5   Great Place to Work Model.[10]

culture that is developed in a work group can override a negative culture at the organizational level. Some of the things a hospitality manager can do include the following:

- Communicate a vision or goal for the group and make sure all members of the group are working to achieve the same goal.
- Make sure each employee knows what you expect from him or her in terms of performance and attitudes.
- Provide enough time and the right tools for employees to perform their jobs.
- Recognize positive work performance of employees each day.
- Demonstrate a caring attitude and interest in developing each employee.
- Provide opportunities for employees to grow professionally.
- Make each employee feel that his or her work is important in achieving the goal you have shared with him or her.
- Allow employees to make decisions within their realm of influence.
- Make sure all employees in the work group are committed to working as a team and to excellence.

Successful managers make sure they practice each of these on a regular basis to develop a positive work culture.

Discussion Questions

1. Give an example of the use of each of the five types of power you have seen in your workplace.
2. Describe and give an example of the three outcomes of power. Identify the type of power that was used.
3. Identify a situation at work where political skills were used to positively influence a stakeholder.

4. Identify the stakeholders and gatekeepers in your place of work.
5. Give an example of artifacts, stories, rituals, and language at your place of work.
6. Use the seven dimensions of organizational culture to describe the culture in your workplace.

Application Exercise

1. Use the diagram in Figure 11.3 to identify your current social and professional networks. Write a professional goal for yourself and add the networks you will need to develop to reach that goal.

2. Complete the following exercise to determine your ability to play the political game.
   How Political Are You?[11]
   Circle the number that most describes your ability in each area.

Total the numbers you circled. If your score is less than 30, then you have a natural ability to be political in organizations.

	Agree		Neither		Disagree
Articulate	1	2	3	4	5
Sensitive	1	2	3	4	5
Competent	1	2	3	4	5
Extroverted	1	2	3	4	5
Self-confident	1	2	3	4	5
Assertive	1	2	3	4	5
Collaborative	1	2	3	4	5
Intelligent	1	2	3	4	5
Logical	1	2	3	4	5
Socially adept	1	2	3	4	5

Endnotes

1. Carson, P. P., Carson, K. D., & Roe, C. W. (1993). Social power bases: A meta-analytic examination of interrelationships and outcomes. *Journal of Applied Social Psychology*, 23(14), 1150–1169.
2. Bacharach, S. B. & Lawler, E. J. (2000). *Organizational Politics*. Stamford, CT: JAI Press.
3. Ferris, G. R., Treadway, D. C., Perrewe, P. L., Brouer, R. L., Douglas, C., & Lux, S. (2007). Political skill in organizations. *Journal of Management*, 33, 290.
4. Allen, R. W., Madison, D. L., Porter, L. W., Renwick, P.A., & Mayes, B. T.(1979). Organizational politics: Tactics and characteristics of its actors. *California Management Review*, Fall, 77–83.
5. O'Reilly, C., Chatman, J., & Coldwekk, D. (1991). People and organizational culture: A profile comparison approach to assessing person-organization fit. *Academy of Management Journal*, 34, 487–516.
6. Tepeci, M., & Bartlett, A. L. (2002). The hospitality industry culture profile: A measure of individual values, organizational culture, and person-organization fit as predictors of job satisfaction and behavioral intentions. *International Journal of Hospitality Management*, 21(2),151–170.
7. Combs, J., Liu, Y., Hall, A., & Ketchen, D. (2006). How much do high-performance work practices matter? A meta-analysis of their effects on organizational performance. *Personnel Psychology*, 59, 501–528.
8. See http://www.greatplacetowork.com
9. See http://www.greatplacetowork.com/best-companies/100-best-companies-to-work-for
10. http://www.greatplacetowork.com
11. http://www.greatplacetowork.com

Key Terms

Artifacts   Tangible signs of the organizational culture seen through stories, rituals, language, and rewards.

Coercive power   Influence over others because of the ability to punish.

Commitment   Characteristic of employees who are enthusiastic and make a maximum effort to perform.

Compliance   Characteristic of employees who go along but with minimal effort.

Core assumptions   Beliefs that drive all activities in the organization.

Expert power   Influence over others that results from knowledge, information, or experience.

Gatekeepers   Those in the political structure who control access to stakeholders.

Great Place to Work   A model of effective organizational culture developed by the Great Place to Work Institute.

High performance organizations   A model of effective organizational culture that focuses on developing and supporting employees and rewards for performance.

Influence   The use of power over others.

Ingratiation   Establishing oneself in good favor of others.

Legitimate power   Influence through authority that comes with a position.

Networking   Developing coalitions with others both inside and outside of your job.

Organizational awareness   Ability to recognize the power structures and politics in a workplace.

Organizational culture   The personality of the organization that is experienced through values, norms, and artifacts.

Organizational politics   The ability to promote or protect oneself or group by influencing those with resources.

Power   The ability of Person A to get Person B to do something Person B would not normally do.

Professional networking   Developing coalitions with others in the realm of your job.

Referent power   Personality characteristics that attract others to follow.

Resistance   Characteristic of employees who refuse to follow or sabotage work.

Reward power   Influence that is based on the ability to provide valuable resources.

Social astuteness   The ability to interpret the actions of others and the social networks that exist.

Social networking   Developing coalitions with others outside your job.

Stakeholders   Those in the political structure who control information and resources.

Values   Beliefs that guide decisions in organizations.

Continuous Renewal

KEY TERMS

Advice network

Autonomy career anchor

Career anchor

Career development

Challenge career anchor

Coach

Communication network

Deep acting

Emotional labor

Entrepreneurial career anchor

Establishment/advancement stage

Late-career stage

Lifestyle career anchor

Maintenance stage

Managerial career anchor

Mentor

Mid-career crisis stage

Security career anchor

Self-assessment process

Service career anchor

Sponsor

Stress

Surface acting

Technical/functional career anchor

Trial stage

Trust network

Work–life balance

OBJECTIVES

- Identify the characteristics of the stages in a career
- Evaluate the career anchors that motivate you at work
- Describe the components of career development
- Describe the effects of stress, emotional labor, and work–life balance

Consider This

Almost one-third of graduates from a four-year hospitality management degree program have left the industry within five years of graduation.[1] The most frequently cited reasons for leaving the industry are long hours, low compensation, and lack of time for family. The reasons graduates stay in their positions are because of the opportunity to work with and serve people, the excitement of the job, and job flexibility. Understanding the changes one faces during the stages in career development, the career anchors that are important to each individual, and the programs for developing professional skills and abilities are important to each hospitality management manager.

INTRODUCTION

Continuous renewal is a process that each of us go through as we reach critical times during our careers. Taking a look at our place in the career lifecycle and developing a plan for growth and development are important to every manager in the hospitality industry. Tools we can use to manage stress and maintain a healthy work–life balance will be covered in this chapter.

CAREER STAGES

A cycle begins when each of us enters the workforce. Figure 12.1 presents the five stages we move through during our work life.

The first stage is called the **trial stage**. Individuals enter the workforce and try many careers/jobs before they decide on an occupation or a career. This stage is characterized by job hopping and changing jobs between many organizations. The trial stage will end when a career or occupation is selected, typically around the age of 25. Many entry-level employees in the hospitality industry are at this stage, which contributes to high turnover rates in the industry. The estimate was that 75 percent of the workforce has worked in the hospitality industry at one time during their careers.

The second stage is the **establishment/advancement stage**. A career choice has been made, and this stage is one of achievement, performance, and advancement. Individuals are motivated to succeed and accept challenges as a form of growth. During this stage, individuals are working for financial gain and are not concerned about how much time they spend on the job. This stage occurs during the ages of 25 and 44 and continues until a mid-career crisis stage or the maintenance stage is reached.

Not everyone goes through a **mid-career crisis stage**. During this stage, people make a major reassessment of their choice of career and the progress they are making. Choosing a different career or pursuing a different educational program may be the outcome of this stage. When

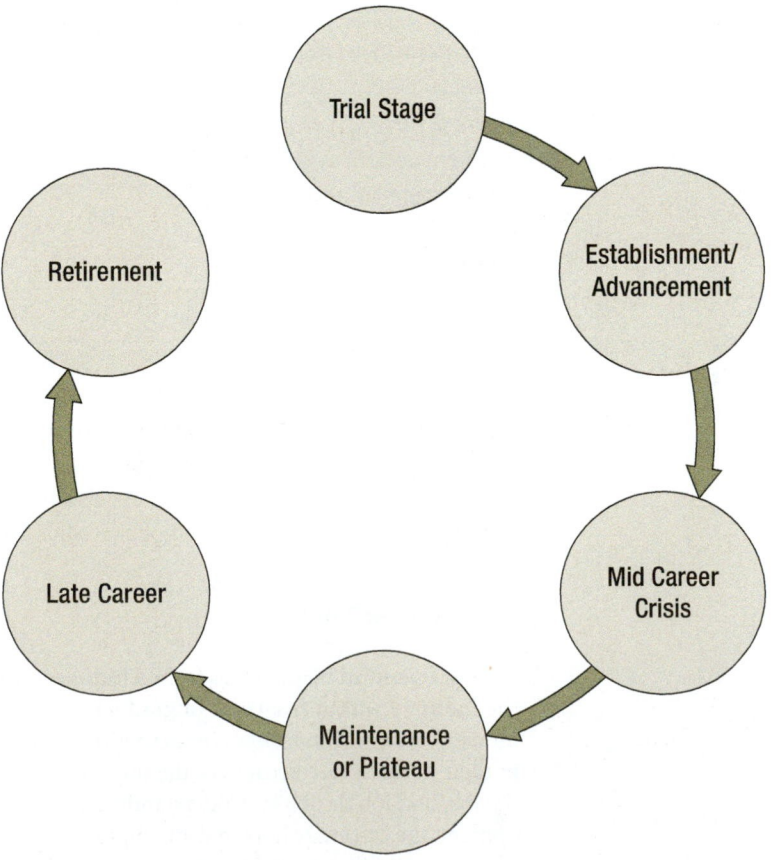

FIGURE 12.1 Career Stages.

Establishment and advancement.
Credit: Ollyy / Shutterstock.

that occurs, the establishment/advancement stage begins again with the goal to progress to the maintenance stage without another crisis. Future predictions are that everyone will complete this stage and change careers at least once during their work lifetime.

The mid-career or **maintenance stage** is also considered a plateau. The goal of this stage is to maintain the current position and avoid stagnation and decline. Updating skills and knowledge in the field will assist the person in this stage to avoid decline in productivity.

The final stage is the **late-career stage**. During this stage, the individual plans for retirement and develops a life outside of work. Time outside of work becomes more important than increasing the amount of money that is earned. Using employees in this stage as mentors for newer employees may be a way to pass on their knowledge and skills without losing those resources.

Mid-career crisis stage.
Credit: Alphaspirit / Shutterstock.

CAREER ANCHORS

The concept of career anchors was developed and revised by Schein.[2] A **career anchor** describes the values that a person holds as important and will not be given up when making a job change. Figure 12.2 includes the eight career anchors and the characteristics that drive career decisions for individuals.

A manager who is motivated by the **technical/functional career anchor** likes to be recognized as an expert in his or her field. This type of manager enjoys doing a job properly and better than anyone else. The manager who is motivated by the **managerial career anchor** enjoys positions that involve problem solving and dealing with others. These managers thrive on responsibility. The **autonomy career anchor** is characteristic of people who prefer to work alone using their own standards or rules. The manager who is motivated by the **security career anchor** will avoid risk taking and seek stability as a primary factor in his or her life. He or she is committed to a company or location when making career decisions. A manager who is motivated by the **entrepreneurial career anchor** is very creative and likes to generate new ideas. Entrepreneurs are very likely to run their own businesses and become easily bored. Those managers who are motivated by the **service career anchor** seek jobs that allow them to help other people. Managers who are motivated by the **challenge career anchor** seek constant stimulation through difficult problems. These managers will change jobs when their current job becomes boring. Managers who are motivated by the **lifestyle career anchor** are interested in work and life balance. They may search for a position that allows them to combine work and life outside of work through travel or other interest.

Research indicates that individuals may make a career decision using more than one career anchor and that as society changes, so does the application of the career anchors. For example, in the past the security career anchor has meant that a person considering a job change would make the decision based on the desire to stay with a current employer or in a certain geographic area. With changes in the economy, security now may be interpreted as the need to keep a job and not the desire to stay with a certain company.

Career Anchor	Characteristics	Hospitality Example
Technical/functional	Career decisions based on the opportunity to apply and develop technical competencies	Director of sales and marketing staying in position rather than move to general manager
Managerial	Career decisions that lead to positions with responsibility for total organizational output	General manager positions
Autonomy	Career decisions that involve the ability to define a job and how it is carried out with a preference for working alone	Owner of a bed and breakfast
Security	Career decisions based on desire to stay with current employer or in geographic area	Lateral transfer from food and beverage to rooms division
Entrepreneurial	Career decisions that involve creativity and working with others	Opening a new restaurant concept
Service/dedication to a cause	Career decisions based on helping other people.	Human resource positions
Challenge	Career decisions based on stimulating work and difficult problems	Chef or food and beverage director
Lifestyle	Career decisions that attempt to integrate work and life outside of work	Regional or district managers

FIGURE 12.2 **Characteristics of Career Anchors.**

Service career anchor. *Credit*: Dennis Owusu-Ansah / Shutterstock.

Research by Beck and LaLopa found that food and beverage and rooms managers make career decisions based on the managerial career anchor while sales and marketing managers made decisions based on the technical career anchor.[3] Their findings indicated that food and beverage and rooms division managers are interested in career moves that move them up through the levels of management in a hotel. On the other hand, sales and marketing managers were found to be motivated to make a career move based on developing more expertise that related directly to their jobs. Individuals should be aware of the career anchor or anchors that drive their decisions about changing jobs or careers. The motivation for a job change may be related to one of these needs and should be considered when planning for career development.

CAREER DEVELOPMENT

Career development and training for employees are covered in Chapter 6. In this chapter, we will focus on your own career development. **Career development** involves managing your career either within or between organizations. It also includes learning new skills and making improvements to help you in your career. Career development is an ongoing process to help you learn and achieve more in your career. The career development cycle begins with a self-assessment of current values, skills, and abilities. Research into the possible career opportunities and the required skills and abilities is the next step in the process. The third step involves identifying a goal position or profession and developing a career development plan. The fourth step includes implementing the plan by gaining the education and experience along with networking and mentoring. The final step is to perform successfully in the new position. Figure 12.3 introduces the career development cycle.

Self-Assessment

The **self-assessment process** is the first and most critical step in the career development cycle. An analysis of what you value related to work and your strengths and weaknesses will serve as a basis for your career development plan. The first assessment that needs to be completed is the career anchor inventory or similar instrument. It is important to identify the factors that you are looking for in a job and how those factors are met in your current position. If they are not met in your current position, you will need to develop a plan that places you in a position that does meet your needs. For example, if security is important to you and you want to stay with your current employer, you will need to look closely at the organization and the opportunities available to you as you move in your career.

Assessments of your strengths and weaknesses can come from a variety of sources. To assess your strengths and weaknesses, you can use standardized instruments, feedback from

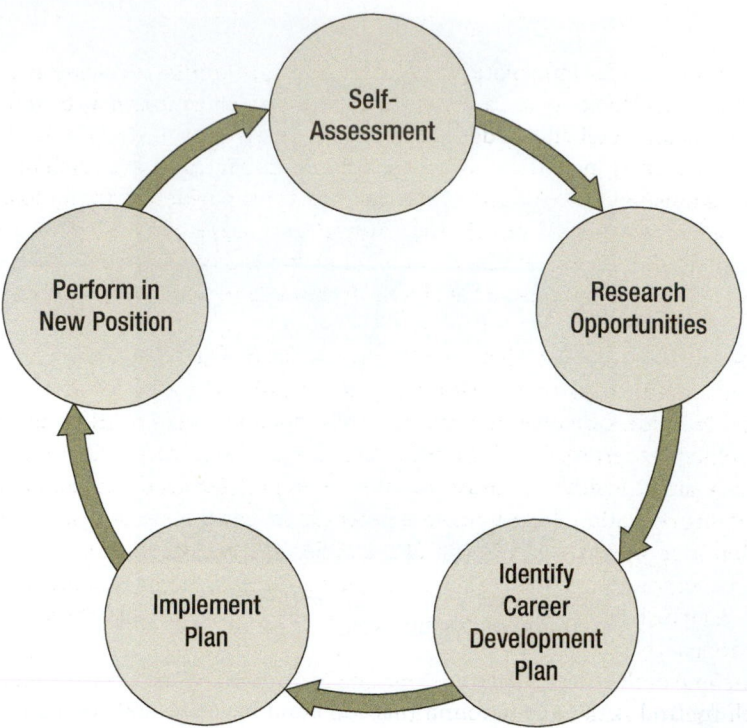

FIGURE 12.3 **Career Development Cycle.**

supervisors, and feedback from those you supervise. Since the types of skills required for management positions will change with the level of management (entry level, mid-level, and upper level), you can complete instruments that evaluate specific generic skills such as the leadership profile inventory for leadership or technical skills such as those required for certification programs in the lodging and restaurant industries. Skills that have been identified as important for hospitality managers include generating profit, service quality management, self-confidence, communication, leadership, team building, project planning, and problem solving.

The assessments found at the CareerLeader website and Career OneStop will help you identify your interests, motivators, and skills. Your results are compared to those in their database of business careers and recommendations for career development are the outcome. Once your values, strengths, and weaknesses are identified, the next step is to research to opportunities that are available to you.

Self-assessment. *Credit*: iQoncept / Shutterstock.

Research Opportunities

There are many sources for information about career opportunities. Professional organizations are a good place to start looking for career options. These organizations may be industry oriented such as the American Hotel and Lodging Association, the National Restaurant Association, or function oriented such as the Society for Human Resource Management. Each organization will provide information about careers and the requirements for positions within those career paths. Career information is available on the web from the websites of hCareers, Career OneStop, CareerBuilder, and the Bureau of Labor Statistics of the U.S. government. Each of these websites gives a variety of job options and includes the education and skills requirements for those positions.

Many businesses have established career paths (also called career ladders or career networks) for movement from one position in the organization to another. As presented in Chapter 4, career ladders involve movement up the organizational chart through promotions due to management expertise. Career lattice refers to movements across the organization to differing functional areas. Figure 12.4 illustrates the differences between a career ladder and career lattice in a lodging operation. Identifying the potential for promotion or skill development with an organization is appropriate at this step of the cycle. In other organizations, you may need to look to other properties or operations for career advancement. In larger companies and organizations, there may be opportunities for training, mentoring, and job enrichment programs that lead to promotions.

The outcome of this step is to have identified ideal jobs and the opportunities for developing the knowledge and skills required for those jobs.

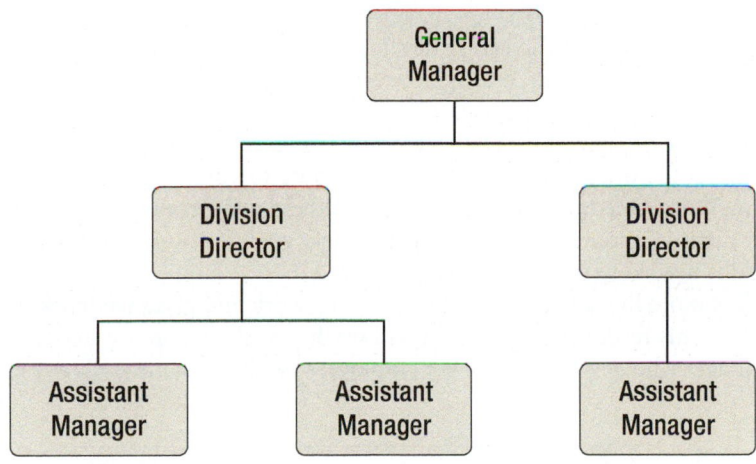

Career Ladder moves up through the chain of command.

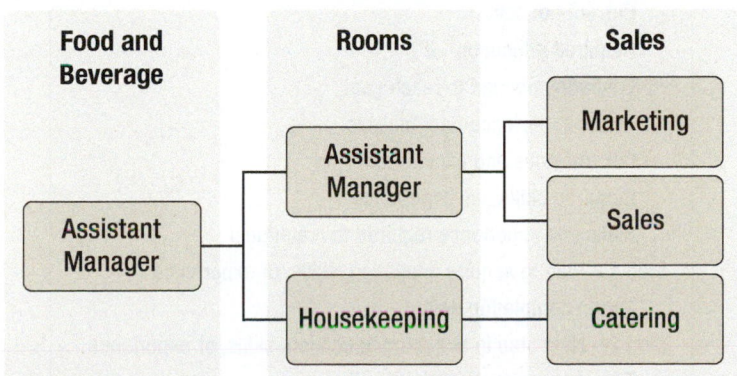

Career Lattice moves horizontally across the organization chart.

FIGURE 12.4 **Career Ladders and Career Lattices.**

Career Development Plan

The next step in the career development cycle is to prepare a career development plan. This plan begins with a career goal. The career goal should include a target position in an organization and should be focused. The next section includes your current education and the education required to reach your goal. A gap analysis should be conducted to determine the difference between the education you need and the education you have. The result is the type and amount of education that you will need to complete to achieve your goal.

The next component of the career development plan is a listing of your current skills and experiences that are related to your career goal. Next, the skills and experiences that are required by your career goal are listed. A gap analysis of the differences should result in a listing of the skills and experiences you will need to reach your career goal.

The final component of the career development plan is a series of steps and completion dates that will be needed to reach your goal. This plan may change as you proceed through your career, and the steps may change. Some identify a series of steps and then revise the plan as each step is accomplished. An example form for a career development plan is included in Figure 12.5.

Research indicates that a combination of education and experience is required for management positions in the hospitality industry. Most hotel managers spend time in food and beverage, rooms, and sales and marketing before becoming a general manager. The typical manager moves about five times in his or her career to reach the general manager position. Keeping up to date on management issues through lifelong learning, developing a clear career path with a mentor, and a willingness to relocate have been identified as strategies for growth in the hotel industry.[4]

Implement Career Development Plan

The next step is to implement the career development plan. There are a variety of methods to achieve the education, experience, and skills needed. A mentor, coach, or sponsor is often used to help guide the process. A mentor acts as a counselor and is typically in a management position above you in the organization. Your mentor will give advice on development opportunities and placements in the organization that will contribute to you reaching your goal. There are two types of mentors. One is a skill mentor who will help you develop expertise in a functional area. A career mentor is someone who is in your career goal position. This mentor will help you develop the skills needed to be in your goal position.

A coach is more like a tutor who observes your work and gives feedback on your performance. Based on this feedback, your coach will teach you skills that are needed for success. A successful manager who develops his or her employees needs the same skills as a coach.

> Goal: Specific career goal
> Education Gap Analysis
>   Current education
>   Required education
>   Education needed to reach goal
> Skills and Experience Gap Analysis
>   Current skills and experience
>   Required skills and experience
>   Skills and experience required to reach goal
> Step 1—Plan to acquire education, skills, or experience
>   Target completion date
> Step 2—Next step in acquiring education, skills, or experience
>   Target completion date

FIGURE 12.5   Sample Career Development Plan.

Career development plan. *Credit*: ALMAGAMI/
Shutterstock.

A **sponsor** is a senior manager in an organization who gives you exposure to other executives who will help your career. Your sponsor will protect you from negative situations and will make sure you are considered for promotions. As you move higher in an organization, you may need to identify a sponsor to assist you in your development.

Networking as discussed in Chapter 11 is another tool that can assist with career development. To apply social and professional networking to career development, one must understand the informal networks in an organization. The three informal networks in an organization include the advice network, the trust network, and the communication network. The **advice network** consists of the people who are looked to for technical information and for solving problems. People in this network are considered to be experts in the field and as such are good sources of technical information. The **trust network** includes people who share delicate information

Informal networking. *Credit*:
Luba V Nel/Shutterstock.

and back each other up in a crisis. People in this network are good sources of insider information, which may be needed as you move through an organization. The **communication network** includes employees who talk about work-related issues on a regular basis. People in this network will be good sources for information about issues that might impact promotions and changes in the organization. Recognizing each of these networks in an organization and building relationships that tap into each of these networks is an important way to grow in an organization.

As you go through each of the steps in the career development plan, revisions may need to be made. For example, as changes are made in certification programs, those changes need to be reflected in your plan. As new training programs are added by your company or profession, you may want to add those to your career development plan. Keep in mind that there may be a variety of workshops, meetings, and other educational opportunities that will help you achieve your goal.

Perform in New Position

The goal of your career development is to develop the knowledge, skills, and abilities required for a new position. In addition to developing these, securing a new position may require acting on feedback from your current supervisor and working through networks both within and outside of your organization. As you work in your new position, you should evaluate how well the job meets your needs and the success of your move. Watch for signs that a career move is needed. Some examples are presented in Figure 12.6.

CONTINUOUS RENEWAL

One of the cautions in taking on a new position is controlling the amount of stress you are feeling. It has been found that **stress** leading to burnout is a common problem among managers in hospitality organizations. Sources of stress include interpersonal relationships, work conditions, personal issues, and time conflicts. Daily hassles, or the annoying events that occur during the workday, are the most frequent cause of stress for managers. Some managers have less than six minutes a day of uninterrupted time to do their jobs. Some of the organizational factors that contribute to stress in our industry are mistrust among employees, close control over employees, and a lack of encouragement for teamwork. Time management skills, daily goal setting, and prioritization of tasks that need to be accomplished may assist with handling the stress of a new position.

Customer service positions in our industry require **emotional labor** to be successful. Emotional labor is the act of expressing socially desirable emotions through feelings and behavior during service transactions.[5] There are two responses that employees can use when an emotional event occurs. These responses are deep acting or surface acting. In **deep acting**, an employee modifies feelings by pulling those feelings up from within themselves. Using deep acting requires an employee to feel the hurt and inconvenience in negative situations, or feel the happiness in positive situations, and demonstrate those feelings to the customer. An example of deep acting would be hiding feelings of concern while singing happy birthday and acting happy. **Surface acting** allows an employee to display expressions that reflect an appropriate feeling. An example is showing a smile on the outside while feeling anger inside. Management positions may require a lot of deep acting, which will lead to burnout and dissatisfaction with a job.

> 1. Your job lacks challenge and excitement for you.
> 2. You are feeling unappreciated.
> 3. Your promotional and/or development opportunities are limited.
> 4. You are no longer having fun.
> 5. Learning is replaced with routine.
> 6. You sense that your skills and talents are being wasted.
> 7. You are suffering from stress or depression.
>
> Adapted from the Mindtools website.

FIGURE 12.6   **Signs a Career Move May Be Needed.**

In addition to the individual skills presented in Chapter 9, taking a look at work–life balance may help cope with the emotional labor required in our jobs. One definition of **work–life balance** is equalizing the levels of achievement and enjoyment on a daily basis.[6] Achievement and enjoyment can be accomplished at work, with family and friends, or by yourself. Some of the recommendations for building in time for minimizing stress and increasing enjoyment include scheduling activities that help you recharge, drop activities that sap your time or energy, outsource errands and jobs to others, exercise regularly, and relax 10 to 15 minutes when stress levels are high. These recommendations should lead to a feeling of renewal, which will improve your outlook. In this state of mind, negative issues will be perceived as positive and work will seem less formidable.

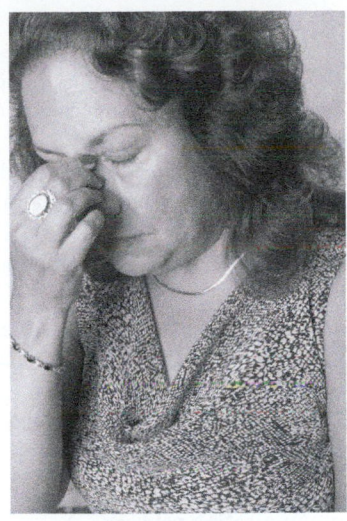

Monitor stress.   *Credit*: Palmer Kane LLC/Shutterstock.

THE BOTTOM LINE

Making career choices and concentrating on achieving personal goals may be difficult during downturns in the economy. The hospitality industry is one that recognizes the importance of work experience in a variety of positions before becoming a manager in the field. It is important that you identify all work experience you have in terms of the skills needed by hospitality managers. The categories of knowledge and skill needed include technical skills, human skills, and conceptual skills. Technical skills are those skills that are routinely performed while producing goods and services. Some examples of technical skills are those involved with food preparation; calculations for costs, sales, and profit; and equipment operation and maintenance. Human skills are those used when interacting with employees and customers. Examples of human skills are communication, motivation, leadership, and conflict management. Conceptual skills are those skills used in forecasting and planning. Examples of conceptual skills are scheduling, production planning, strategic planning, and creative thinking. Using these three categories for skills is a unique way to present your work experiences to future employers.

Discussion Questions

1. Describe each of the five career stages. Identify one person who is in each stage and describe the characteristics of the job they have.
2. Define the eight career anchors and identify the two career anchors that motivate you to work.
3. Identify three assessment tools you can use to determine your career preferences and strengths and weaknesses.
4. Give an example of a career ladder and a career lattice at an organization where you have worked.
5. Describe the components of a career development plan.
6. Define *mentor*, *coach*, and *sponsor*, giving an example of each.
7. Describe the three types of informal networks with an example of how you could use each in your career development plan.
8. Identify the sources of stress that most affect you.
9. Give an example when you have used deep acting and surface acting at work or at school.
10. Identify sources of achievement and enjoyment at work, with family, with friends, and by yourself.

Application Exercise

1. Complete the career anchor inventory online and identify the career anchors that will motivate you to work. Interview a manager in a position that you would like to have and ask about the career anchors that motivate him or her. Determine how well his or her position meets those needs and how well the position would meet your needs. Determine if a different position would better meet your needs.

Endnotes

1. Brown, E. A. (2011). Hospitality management graduates' perceptions of career factor importance and career factor experience and the relation with turnover intentions. Ames, Iowa, PhD dissertation.
2. Schein, E. H. (1990). *Career Anchors*. San Diego: Pfeiffer, Inc.
3. Beck, J., & LaLopa, L. M. (2001). An exploratory application of Schein's career anchors inventory to hotel executive operating committee members. *International Journal of Hospitality Management, 20,* 15–28.
4. Kim, S. S., Chun, J., & Petrick, J. F. (2009). Career path profiles of general managers of Korean super deluxe hotels and factors influencing their career development: Vocational insights for HTM students and hotel employees. *Journal of Hospitality, Leisure, Sport & Tourism Education, 8*(2), 97–116.
5. Grandey, A. A. (2000). Emotion regulation in the workplace: A new way to conceptualize emotional labor. *Journal of Occupational Health Psychology, 5*(1), 95–110.
6. See Worklifebalance.com

Key Terms

Advice network An informal grouping of employees who are looked to as the source for technical information and for solving problems.

Autonomy career anchor Career decisions that are based on the ability to define a job and how it is carried out with a preference for working alone.

Career anchor Values that are important to individuals when making a job change decision.

Career development Process of assessing where you are in your work life, deciding where you want to be, and making the changes to get there.

Challenge career anchor Career decisions that are based on stimulating work and difficult problems.

Coach A tutor who observes your work and helps you develop skills that are needed.

Communication network An informal grouping of employees who talk about work issues on a regular basis.

Deep acting A response to a work situation that requires pulling up and displaying emotions such as crying or anger as needed.

Emotional labor The act of expressing socially desirable emotions through feelings and behavior during service transactions.

Entrepreneurial career anchor Career decisions that are made based on the need to be creative and the need for ownership of the business.

Establishment/advancement stage The second career stage that occurs when a career choice is made and personal goals include growth, achievement, and advancement.

Late-career stage The final career stage when plans are made for retirement.

Lifestyle career anchor Career decisions that attempt to integrate work and life outside of work.

Maintenance stage A plateau where the goal is to maintain the current position and avoid stagnation and decline.

Managerial career anchor Career decisions that lead to positions with responsibility for total organizational output.

Mentor A counselor who will help you develop expertise in a functional area or skills needed for a career goal position.

Mid-career crisis stage A point in a person's career where a major reassessment of career choice is made. This stage may result in choosing a different career or educational program. Not everyone goes through this stage.

Security career anchor Career decisions that are based on a desire to stay with a current employer or within a geographical area.

Self-assessment process The first step in a career development cycle. Values, strengths, and weaknesses are determined during this step.

Service career anchor Career decisions that are based on the need to help other people.

Sponsor A senior manager who gives you exposure to other executives who will help your career.

Stress A condition or feeling experienced when a person perceives that demands exceed the personal and social resources the individual is able to mobilize.

Surface acting A response to a service situation that requires an employee to demonstrate appropriate feelings.

Technical/functional career anchor Career decisions that are based on the opportunity to apply and develop technical competencies.

Trial stage The first stage in a career where jobs and careers are experienced on a trial basis. This stage ends when a career or occupation is selected.

Trust network An informal work group who share delicate information and back each other up in a crisis.

Work–life balance Equalizing the levels of achievement and enjoyment at work, with family and friends, or by yourself.

INDEX